Ready, Set... Go Alef Bet!

TEACHER'S EDITION

BY DINA MAIBEN

Techniques for Students With Special Learning Needs:
Lisa Friedman

Book and Cover Design: Itzhack Shelomi
Project Editor: Terry S. Kaye

Springfield, New Jersey
www.behrmanhouse.com
ISBN: 978-0-87441-859-0
Manufactured in the United States of America

CONTENTS

PURPOSE OF READY, *SET...GO ALEF BET!*

Welcome to *Ready, Set...Go Alef Bet!*—a multimedia Hebrew letter recognition experience!

Introducing children to reading and setting the tone for their journey into literacy is an essential task in any language or culture. The first steps are critical. As a teacher who introduces the process of Hebrew reading, you play a crucial role—one that profoundly influences your students' success. *Ready, Set...Go Alef Bet!* will assist you in this important and challenging work.

Ready, Set...Go Alef Bet! facilitates the learner's acquisition of Hebrew pre-reading skills—including sound-symbol association, letter recognition, and directionality—using the instructional sequences and approaches that researchers in Israel have found to be most effective.

The lessons in *Ready, Set...Go Alef Bet!* all follow these nine steps, with the exception of Lesson 1, which has no review:

1. Reviewing recently learned key words, consonants, and vowels
2. Introducing new key words, consonants, and vowels
3. Making sound-symbol associations of new letters and vowels through a multisensory presentation
4. Reading practice of letter-vowel combinations ("Word Building" and "I Can Read Hebrew!")
5. Completing book activities
6. Presenting an oral language lesson
7. Completing the "Game On" activity
8. Completing online activities
9. Assessment

The oral language lesson is an important step because research shows a strong link between spoken language and the acquisition of reading skills. No matter the type of learner or teacher, no matter how many hours of instruction are available, or the nature of the learning environment, a knowledge of the language has been shown consistently to improve reading. For this reason, a Hebrew language activity has been incorporated into each lesson of *Ready, Set...Go Alef Bet!* You will find techniques for presenting this material in each lesson of this guide.

HOW IS *READY, SET...GO ALEF BET!* DIFFERENT FROM OTHER PRE-PRIMERS?

Ready, Set...Go Alef Bet! is the pre-primer for *Alef Bet Quest*. It is the first Hebrew pre-primer to combine the best practices of Hebrew reading readiness instruction with the best of today's technology, integrating print letter mastery with computerized learning. It is designed to teach young students to recognize Hebrew letters accurately and fluently; the cutting-edge technology brings the language to life in animated computer activities and games.

Ready, Set...Go Alef Bet!:

1. **Stands on a solid foundation of research on Hebrew reading instruction and second language acquisition.** All elements of instruction and drill—from the presentation of key words to the sequence of letter introduction—follow the methods of Hebrew reading instruction developed in Israel. For example, when more than one symbol represents a single sound (such as ת/תּ and ט—"*t*" sound), they are taught together. Researchers have found that when such symbols are introduced separately, students tend to remember one symbol but not the other. In contrast, researchers have found that the introduction of visually similar symbols (like ד and ר) should be widely separated, allowing the learner to become completely at ease with one before having to make the fine visual distinction required to recognize the other. Researchers have found, too, that the introduction of symbols that represent *similar*, but not identical, sounds, (like ס, ז, and צ), should also be widely separated. Introducing items that are similar together or one right after the other actually *increases* the likelihood that students will confuse them. These types of letters are introduced far apart to decrease this likelihood.

   In addition, *Ready, Set...Go Alef Bet!* introduces five basic vowel sounds. The purpose here is to give students practice in oral blending of syllables. *Ready, Set...Go Alef Bet!* does not include vowels that serve multiple purposes, such as the *sh'va* (◌ְ); those that pose the greatest difficulty for young learners to acquire, such as וּי or ◌ַי; and those for which there is no consensus regarding pronunciation (◌ֵ). The five vowels taught are introduced in an order

that resembles the sequence in which they are acquired by children as they learn to speak their native language—a sequence that has been shown effective when introducing young learners to the vowels in alphabetic languages. Here, there are a few exceptions. While "ah" is both the first vowel sound young children acquire and the first vowel sound presented in *Ready, Set...Go Alef Bet!*, it is often followed by "ee," then "oo," "eh," "oh," and finally "ay."

However, the visual complexities of Hebrew reading require a slightly different approach in this learning tool. For example, וֹ and וּ not only represent similar sounds, but are very similar visually and are a frequent source of confusion for those learning to read Hebrew. As a result, *Ready, Set...Go Alef Bet!* reverses the presentation order of "ee" and "oo," providing a greater separation between the confusing items וֹ and וּ. At the same time, because "eh" tends to be a particularly difficult vowel sound for new Hebrew readers, it is the last vowel presented in *Ready, Set...Go Alef Bet!* Finally, just as letters that represent the same sound are introduced together, the same approach is used with the introduction of the vowels. To best facilitate sound-symbol associations, Hebrew letters that represent two sounds are treated as separate phonetic items. For example, בּ and ב (a single letter that represents two sounds in English—*b* as in ball and *v* as in video) are visually similar—the only difference being a tiny dot. Despite the fact that these symbols actually represent a single letter, they are both visually similar and represent two similar sounds. They are therefore treated as two phonetic items and are introduced far apart (בּ in Lesson 4 and ב in Lesson 12).

2. **Introduces all new Hebrew letters through Hebrew "key words."** Each lesson in *Ready, Set...Go Alef Bet!* opens with between one and three key words. These words often reflect the child's direct experience, providing young learners with Hebrew vocabulary that is immediately accessible (כֶּלֶב, בַּיִת, עִפָּרוֹן, גְלִידָה). Some key words represent basic Jewish concepts that are connected to Jewish holidays or rituals (תּוֹרָה, שׁוֹפָר, מְזוּזָה).

   Key words provide the learner with a simple means of verifying the sound of each letter. If students are unsure about a particular letter, you can review the key word that contains that letter in order to remind them of the sound it represents. Whenever possible, the new letter can be found in the initial position of the key word because it is easiest to identify the first sound in a word.

3. **Uses a multisensory approach to introducing letters, appealing to the widest range of learners.** Students learn in different ways. The three primary modalities (or sensory pathways) of learning are visual, auditory, and kinesthetic or tactile. By employing a multisensory approach to letter recognition—in other words, students see, hear/say, and use their hands or bodies to integrate new letters—more students in the class are able to master the material. A variety of kinesthetic and tactile activities are recommended for introducing and reinforcing each letter shape. A complete description of this procedure can be found in the "Multisensory Approach to Sound-Symbol Associations in Hebrew" on page 12.

4. **Is the first Hebrew pre-primer with a fully integrated digital companion.** Students will delight in using their new skills when completing activities or playing games online. Students practice their new decoding skills with computer-based activities and online video games. The digital companion is fully integrated with the textbook. An activity or puzzle at the end of each lesson in the book ("Game On") provides students with clues for scoring bonus points in a computer game. They can even personalize their own avatar! Students are motivated to use the website at home—creating additional practice time and opportunities. Students can e-mail their online lesson summaries directly to you or you can assess their progress in the Behrman House Online Learning Center. For more about the digital companion, see "Using the Digital Companion" on page 15.

5. **Focuses on individual vowels and vowel patterns through decoding drills.** As vowels are introduced, students are presented with "Word Building" activities. These decoding drills encourage learners to use their newly acquired letter- and vowel-recognition skills with a variety of practice syllables. In the early stages, the "Word Building" activities are composed entirely of Consonant-Vowel (C-V) syllables. Gradually Consonant-Vowel-Consonant (C-V-C) syllables are added. All of these syllable-

reading drills focus on individual vowels and vowel patterns. They are also tightly structured to follow patterns of rhyme and rhythm that assist beginning readers in recognizing the patterns of Hebrew words. Finally, in the last three lessons, students are asked to apply their syllable-decoding skills to reading some of the real Hebrew words they have already learned ("I Can Read Hebrew!").

6. **Provides mnemonic hints for every letter and vowel taught.** The ability to associate symbols with the sounds they represent is the most basic and most important skill that pre-readers must master. Many learners find mnemonic devices helpful for that purpose.

   While many pre-primers incorporate mnemonics for some letters and vowels, *Ready, Set...Go Alef Bet!* is the first pre-primer to provide mnemonics for *every* letter (including final forms) and every vowel sound. These mnemonics are all reinforced visually through a cute drawing that incorporates both the letter shape and the association ("Letter Hints"). For example, *kaf* "looks like someone with a Cough drop." These illustrations are animated in the digital companion. Even the chapter titles reinforce the sound of the letters introduced in that chapter, generally through alliteration ("Ship Shape" for שׁ or "Hip Hip Hooray!" for ה).

7. **Builds a bridge between symbol recognition and syllable decoding, and from decoding to reading real Hebrew words.** Beginning in Lesson 4, students are introduced to their first vowels and practice blending the vowels with all of the letters that they have learned up to that point. From Lesson 4 to Lesson 6, students practice blending C-V syllables only. From Lesson 7 on, students also practice C-V-C syllables as they occur in isolation (such as the word שֵׁם) or at the end of a word. No closed syllables that occur within a word are presented, because the *sh'va* (ְ) is not taught in *Ready, Set...Go Alef Bet!* From Lesson 13 on, students decode and blend two-syllable words. Finally, in the last three lessons, students read real Hebrew words (טַלִּית, עִפָּרוֹן, רֹאשׁ).

8. **Provides direct instruction for difficult reading rules**. Students learning to read Hebrew will encounter rules and exceptions that are foreign to native English readers. For example, beginning Hebrew readers often have difficulty with directionality. They forget that Hebrew is read from right-to-left. An activity early in Lesson 1 assists students in determining where Hebrew words begin. The right-to-left directionality of Hebrew is reinforced by every "Word Building" activity and the sentences in "I Can Understand Hebrew!" sections, which both have the line numbers placed on the right-hand side. In addition, "Word Building" activities provide the visual cue of a "start arrow" on the top right corner of the section.

STRUCTURE OF THE PUPIL EDITION

Each of the twenty lessons in *Ready, Set...Go Alef Bet!* contains the following features:

Key Words Each lesson opens with between one and three key words. Because children learn second-language vocabulary best through a direct association between a word and the item it represents, every key word is accompanied by a picture that illustrates its meaning.

"What's New?" Immediately under the key words, "What's New?" presents the lesson's new letter or letters. The names of new letters are included in English. It is important to note that the names of the letters are far less important for reading than the sounds that they represent. The names are provided to assist with identification but should not be overly emphasized with the student.

"Letter Hints" and **"Color the Letter"** Mnemonics for every letter and letter form are provided in sections called "Letter Hints." These, along with opportunities to color in each letter shape, are provided early in each lesson. The coloring activities provide a kinesthetic reinforcement, giving students the opportunity to explore the parameters of the new letter's shape.

"Now I Know My Alef-Bet!" In this section students practice writing the new Hebrew letters. For beginning readers, the act of writing the letter in block print provides excellent kinesthetic reinforcement.

"I Can Understand Hebrew!" Every lesson contains a page devoted to oral Hebrew language instruction. New vocabulary words are introduced by the teacher, and, like the key words, these vocabulary words are accompanied by pictures that illustrate their meanings. These sections also contain activities that demonstrate the learner's

comprehension of the Hebrew language, including key words, with built-in review of previous lessons as well.

"Word Building" Beginning in lesson 4, after the first vowel sound is introduced, students practice blending individual syllables. Initially, only Consonant-Vowel (C-V) syllables are presented. Later, Consonant-Vowel-Consonant (C-V-C) syllables are included with C-V syllables. Finally, students practice two-syllable words that begin with a C-V syllable and end with a C-V-C syllable.

"Game On" Each lesson ends with a puzzle whose answer allows students to earn bonus points in a game in the digital companion. The integrated computer application allows you to extend classroom learning into the home with homework students like to do!

Ready, Set...Go Alef Bet! also contains several features that enhance student mastery of phonological awareness and other Hebrew pre-reading skills:

- **"Take a Close Look"** Research conducted in Israel indicates that a good visual memory is the single greatest predictor of success in learning to read Hebrew, and the researchers highly recommend that Hebrew reading readiness programs include activities that help students develop their visual skills right from the beginning. The activities called "Take a Closer Look!" teach students how to focus on the visual images of the Hebrew letters.

  An important pre-reading skill in Hebrew, and by far the most difficult for many students to master, is fine visual discrimination. The reason for this lies mostly in the significant number of letters that are visually similar. While vocalized Hebrew has fewer than 35 letter shapes, there are some thirty pairs of letters that are visually similar. There are three types of visually similar letters. The largest category by far consists of those letters that are identical except for one tiny difference. This includes such pairs as בּ/ב, ד/ר, and ו/ן.

  The second category consists of letters that share an overall shape. While these letters do not appear as similar as those in the first category, they pose a significant challenge if students try to recognize them at a glance. These include such pairs as מ/ט and ע/צ. The final group consists of letters that are similar when rotated. These include ט/פ and ב/ת. Students who have difficulty with spacial orientation will find these pairs particularly challenging.

  As students progress through the program, greater and greater demands are placed on their ability to make fine visual distinctions and recall which letter represents a given sound. It is worth noting that this approach applies to initial exposure only. In order to become proficient in Hebrew decoding, students will need to be able to recognize each letter correctly no matter what it may be near. To help facilitate this skill, beginning in lesson 7, all of the "Take a Closer Look!" activities provide discrete practice in making fine visual distinctions. Some of these activities ask students to discriminate between visually similar letters and associate the correct letter that begins a key word. Others ask students to circle the letters that match a boxed example or to eliminate those that are different from the example in a box.

- **"Sound Check"** These activities use cognates (objects whose names sound similar in Hebrew and English), such as טֶלֶוִיזְיָה, to provide students with practice in fine auditory discrimination, an important precursor to the most important pre-reading skill—proper sound-symbol associations.

- **"Letter by Letter"** and **"In the Beginning"** These activities ask students to segment the initial sound of a word or words and identify the letter that makes this sound.

- **"End Game," "Sound Advice,"** and **"Beginning, Middle, or End"** It is easiest for pre-readers and beginning readers to identify which sound begins a word. It is more difficult to identify the sound that ends a word, and most difficult of all is identifying a sound that is embedded in the middle of a word. These activities provide students with practice segmenting sounds in various positions within a word.

STRUCTURE OF THE TEACHER'S EDITION

This Teacher's Edition contains the entire text of *Ready, Set...Go Alef Bet!* in a reduced format. The pages are annotated with instructional techniques and suggestions for activities that correspond to features in the student book. The information and suggestions included here

will assist you in developing your lesson plan. You need not follow every suggestion presented; rather, the guide provides you with several options from which you may choose. You know best what will work with your group of students and your teaching style.

Each chapter in the section beginning on page 20 of this guide contains the following information:

Pages in Student Text

Key Words

New Letters Whenever letters represent a single sound, they are taught together (ט תּ ת).

Vocabulary Words (if applicable): *Ready, Set...Go Alef Bet!* employs a naturalistic approach in teaching the Hebrew language component. This means that students are asked to deduce the meaning of the words from pictures, by handling real objects, and through gestures, mime, and acting. Translation into English is used only when there is no clear way to teach the Hebrew directly. Research supports using such an approach to second-language acquisition for children. To make sure that the meaning of these items is clear, any new Hebrew vocabulary introduced in the lesson is identified at the beginning of this guide along with an English translation.

Cognates (if applicable): Cognates are words that one language borrows from another. English has many words that are borrowed from Hebrew, including "camel" and "cinnamon." These ancient Hebrew words entered the English language when the Bible was translated into English. In much the same way, modern Hebrew borrowed many words from the international vocabulary, and many of these words are from English. Because the Hebrew pronunciation of the words differs from the English, the Hebrew version has been provided to afford every teacher the ability to teach the Hebrew pronunciation to their students. Students are often charmed by the fact that Hebrew and English share so many words, and are quite amused by the Hebrew pronunciation of words they already know.

Recommended Materials A list of Phonics Flash Cards (numbered flash cards that contain the individual letters and vowels taught in each lesson); Word Picture Cards (numbered Word Picture Cards that contain pictures of the key words, most of the vocabulary words, and some of the cognates taught in each lesson); and other materials and props suggested for teaching the lesson.

For a complete list of Phonics Flash Cards and Word Picture Cards, see page 14 in this guide. You can also find black-line masters for the cards in Appendices A and B on pages 120 and 125.

Review (except Lesson 1) This section describes a game or other activity that reviews material students have previously learned.

Oral Language Lesson Each chapter of the guide includes a short, modern Hebrew language lesson. This oral Hebrew language instruction is central to the program and should be included with every class.

Set Induction An activity that introduces and helps students relate to the central concepts that will be presented in the new lesson, such as the idea that multiple symbols can represent a single sound.

Introducing the Key Words and Deducing Their Sound-Symbol Relationships *Ready, Set...Go Alef Bet!* promotes a multisensory approach to Hebrew pre-reading skills. This approach integrates auditory, visual, and kinesthetic or tactile information and uses all of these modalities (or sensory pathways) to help all learners master the requisite skills necessary for Hebrew reading. You can find a full explanation of how to use this multisensory approach on page 12 of this guide.

Techniques for Individual Activities For every activity in the student text, you will find directions and, in many cases, the theoretical basis for its inclusion in the book. For example, some activities focus on training students to hear the component sounds of Hebrew words. Others are designed to help students develop the ability to distinguish between letters that look similar. As the teacher, you may find it helpful to know what skill students are practicing in order to assess students' progress and remediate when necessary.

Game On In addition to providing guidance about the final activity in each lesson, this section includes challenge questions to help heighten student interest and motivation for using the digital companion at home. It will also help you follow up on students' use of the digital companion.

Assessment Periodic assessment of student progress is an important procedure. Assessments can be informal, such as making notes during class activities, or they can be formal using standardized assessments. Formal assessments can be written or can test oral decoding. In this type of assessment the teacher listens to each student's syllable reading, noting errors and the level of fluency. Appendix C on page 137 in this guide contains three formal assessment tools. First, there is a page that contains five brief oral assessments that must be administered individually. Each set consists of ten syllables and should be accompanied with error analysis, so that you can track each student's progress. The first assessment can be used after Lesson 4, followed by those that can be administered after Lessons 8, 12, 16, and 20. Since you probably will not be able to complete an oral assessment of every student in a single class session, you can test a few students over several sessions. Appendix C also contains a set of written quizzes that can be administered after Lessons 5, 10, and 15, as well as a three-part final assessment to be administered at the end of the year. The final assessment is written and can be administered in conjunction with the last of the oral assessments.

In addition to classroom assessments, there are three ways to assess students' progress in the digital companion:

1. Log on to www.behrmanhouse.com with your teacher account, click "My Account" then "Online Learning Center," then select your class and click the green "View Assessment" button on the top of the left menu options. Review your students' results. See "Using the Digital Companion" on page 15.
2. Students can print out and bring into class the lesson summary that automatically appears on their computer screens when they have completed all the activities in a lesson.
3. Students can e-mail the lesson summary directly to you. You may wish to set up a separate e-mail account to receive this information.

Inform your students how often you intend to assess their progress online. It is best to check their progress each time they complete a chapter in the book.

PACING

Many variables contribute to the pace at which a class completes a Hebrew program. Students have different levels of ability, teachers have different styles, and schools vary in the number of instructional hours devoted to Hebrew. Ultimately, you will have to decide how slowly or quickly you want your class to move through the text. However, you should plan to complete *Ready, Set...Go Alef Bet!* within one school year.

The twenty lessons in *Ready, Set...Go Alef Bet!* consist of four to six pages each. Certain Hebrew letters and phonemes (sounds contained in the language) are more difficult than others for native English speakers and may require more time for mastery, for example, ח, כ, and ך, and צ and ץ.

Learning time is the scarcest and most precious resource in Hebrew education. Deciding how you will spend your time is critical when planning lessons. Ideally, every lesson should include the following five components:

1. An activity that reviews material students have previously learned
2. An activity that introduces the new concepts or sets the tone for the lesson
3. Presentation of new material
4. Reinforcement of new material
5. A closing activity that summarizes or reinforces the lesson's content and prepares students for the next session

The amount of time you spend on each component will depend on the overall amount of time available to you for Hebrew instruction and on your goals for the lesson. Preparing your lessons in advance will help you manage your time so that you and your students can successfully meet your goals. Remember that the digital companion provides you with an exceptional tool for extending class time with fun, online learning that can be completed at home.

Your lesson plans should include your goals for the lesson, the instructional materials you will need, specific activities you plan to use with time estimates for each, homework assignments, and any other relevant notes.

If your class meets one to one-and-a-half hours per week for twenty-four to twenty-six weeks, you should aim to complete one lesson per week on average.

Lessons 4, 11, and 16 may each require two class sessions, as the material covered in these lessons is complex. Similarly, Lessons 18, 19, and 20 include actual word reading, which may require extra time for student mastery.

THE HOME-SCHOOL CONNECTION

A partnership between home and school can help your students reach their greatest potential. Make every effort to facilitate this partnership. A significant number of parents cannot read Hebrew and are therefore unable to assist their children with Hebrew reading homework. *Ready, Set...Go Alef Bet!* uses an innovative approach to solving this problem: the digital companion. Students will enjoy playing the interactive games, which review and practice the pre-reading skills students have learned in class. The digital activities are self-correcting, and the results are easily accessible to you, the teacher. Parents can also join in the fun. They may even learn to recognize the Hebrew letters themselves!

You may wish to e-mail or send home a letter after the first day of class telling parents about *Ready, Set...Go Alef Bet!* and introducing them to the digital companion. Explain that you will be able to assess their child's progress online. (See "Using the Digital Companion," page 15, and "Assessment," page 10.) You can find a sample letter to parents at www.behrmanhouse.com (go to the *Ready, Set...Go Alef Bet!* product page).

THE FIRST DAY OF SCHOOL

Setting the Stage

Oral Language Lesson

In the first class session introduce the following words without translation.

שָׁלוֹם. שְׁמִי ________ פֹּה. לֹא פֹּה.

For example, wave to the class and say: שָׁלוֹם. Ask students to repeat the word. Point to yourself and say שְׁמִי, followed by your name. When students understand, they should introduce themselves in Hebrew. Spread your arms and step firmly forward, saying פֹּה. Introduce לֹא by shaking your head while you say the word and by pointing to the ground in front of you while you say the word. This word is not as easy to illustrate directly, and you may end up needing to translate it. If that is the case, translate the word once with the accompanying hand gesture, and rely on the gesture thereafter. Once you feel that students understand the words, take attendance, asking students to respond in Hebrew when you call their names. If a student is absent, the class can respond:

________ לֹא פֹּה

Introducing the Book and the Digital Companion

Distribute the books and allow students a few minutes to examine them. Show students the cover and ask what they think the book is about. (*Hebrew, learning the alef bet*) Explain that by the end of the year they will be able to recognize every Hebrew letter and will even begin learning to read Hebrew words.

Explain that Hebrew is read from right to left, so the book opens the opposite way from English books. Direct students to open their books to page 4. Ask what they see on this page. (*Hebrew letter outlines*). Explain that there is a digital companion that they will use at home. As they complete a lesson in the digital companion they will color in the new letters on this chart. Next, direct students to turn to "Game On" on page 8 and explain that at the end of each lesson they will solve a puzzle that will help them earn bonus points in online video games.

With the approval of your education director, distribute candies, *alef-bet* sugar cookies, or some other sweet treat (you may want to have pretzels, fruit, or a sugar-free treat for students with dietary concerns). Tell students that there is a custom of eating a sweet treat on the first day of school, and especially on the first day of learning to read Hebrew. Ask students what they think the purpose of this custom is. (*study is sweet, learning to read Hebrew is a treat*) Together recite the Shehecheyanu, the blessing we say when we begin something new:

בָּרוּךְ אַתָּה, יְיָ אֱלֹהֵינוּ, מֶלֶךְ הָעוֹלָם,
שֶׁהֶחֱיָנוּ וְקִיְּמָנוּ וְהִגִּיעָנוּ לַזְּמַן הַזֶּה.

Blessed are You, Adonai our God, Ruler of the universe, who has kept us alive, sustained us, and enabled us to reach this season.

WORK AT HOME

Review and practice at home will help students hone their Hebrew decoding skills and the vocabulary they acquire in school. The digital companion provides the

ideal method for at-home practice. It extends Hebrew learning time and allows parents to participate in their child's Hebrew studies. Students are likely to be captivated by the Hebrew computer games. They can personalize their own avatar. In addition, eight of the online games offer students the opportunity to collect inventory. Those games appear at the end of Lessons 1, 3, 6, 9, 12, 14, 15, and 20. It's homework they will want to do!

ASSESSMENT

Ongoing assessment will help you track student mastery of the material and plan remediation as necessary. It can also reveal areas that the class should review as a whole. If you see that several students are having difficulty with the same item—for example, confusion of look-alike or sound-alike letters—a classroom or small group review will help. Assessments can be oral or written. In Appendix C, pages 137–143, you will find three sets of formal assessments: an oral assessment, three short written assessments, and a three-part final assessment.

The oral assessment consists of a single page that contains five sets of ten syllables each. The first can be administered after students complete Lesson 4, the second after Lesson 8, and so on. It may not be possible to test every student in a single class session, but you can listen to a few students each day until everyone has completed each oral assessment.

Use the following procedure for oral assessments:

- Provide students with a master copy of the assessment sheet. On separate copies, one for each student, make notes about student errors. Ask each individual to identify all ten letters or to read all ten syllables without stopping. Put a check next to each item that the student completes correctly.
- Mark a slash (/) through any item on which the student makes an error and write a phonetic equivalent of the mispronunciation above the slash; for example, *mal* instead of *tal*.
- If the student skips an item, put a slash (/) through it, but without a phonetic note.
- If the student adds a sound, such as an extra vowel at the end of a C-V-C syllable, draw a circle and write the addition inside it, for example: אֶתָ
- Do not let students see what you are writing. Accept self-corrections, but do not give feedback until the student has completed the evaluation. Remain encouraging, warm, and supportive.
- If the student makes mistakes on the first three items, or on five items total, stop the assessment and remediate. For example, allow the student to practice these items with a classroom aide or the resource room tutor. For syllable blending, you can also review the material in the appropriate "Word Building" selections in the book.

Appendix C also contains three short written assessments for use after Lessons 5, 10, and 15. These assessments will give you feedback on how students are mastering specific skills, such as sound-symbol association and visual discrimination. Students can complete these independently while you test individuals orally or work with students who have fallen behind.

Finally, Appendix C also contains a three-part diagnostic test to be used at the end of the year. It should be administered after students have completed the entire program in order to assess each individual's skills. It can also be completed by the class as you complete the fifth oral assessment. Information culled from these year-end assessments will enable the faculty and administration to develop an educational plan for individual students for the coming year.

See also "Tracking Students' Digital Activities" on page 15 for information on assessing each student's progress with the digital component.

SCOPE AND SEQUENCE

PAGE IN STUDENT BOOK	VOWELS	LETTERS	VOCABULARY WORDS	KEY WORDS	LESSON
5		תּ ת ט	עַל	תּוֹרָה טַלִּית	1
9		שׁ	שַׁבָּת שָׁלוֹם!	שַׁבָּת שָׁלוֹם	2
13		י	שֻׁלְחָן	יָד	3
17	◌ָ ◌ַ ◌ֲ	בּ	בַּ־	בַּיִת	4
22		א ע		אַבָּא אִמָּא עִפָּרוֹן	5
26		מ ם		מְזוּזָה שָׁלוֹם	6
31		ג	גֶּשֶׁם	גְּלִידָה	7
36	◌ֻ וּ	ד	דָּג מַיִם	דֶּגֶל	8
41		כּ ק	מוֹרָה כִּתָּה	כִּפָּה קִדּוּשׁ	9
45		ה	הַ־ יֶלֶד יַלְדָּה	הַבְדָּלָה	10
49		צ ץ		צְדָקָה מִיץ	11
53		ו ב	שֶׁל	וָו כֶּלֶב	12
57	◌ִ ◌ִי	ל	וְ־	לוּלָב	13
62		ס שׂ	סֻכָּה	סֻכּוֹת שִׂמְחַת תּוֹרָה	14
66		נ ן		נֵר עִפָּרוֹן	15
70		ח כ ך	חָתוּל	חַלָּה בְּרָכָה מֶלֶךְ	16
75	◌ֹ וֹ	פּ	אוֹכֵל אוֹכֶלֶת סָלָט	פּוּרִים פֶּסַח	17
80		ר		רֹאשׁ רֶגֶל	18
85	◌ֶ ◌ֱ	ז		זֶבְּרָה	19
90		פ ף		שׁוֹפָר אָלֶף	20

MULTISENSORY APPROACH TO HEBREW SOUND-SYMBOL ASSOCIATIONS

Students learn in different ways. The three primary modalities for learning are visual, auditory, and kinesthetic or tactile. The most effective way for the greatest number of students to master Hebrew phonetic decoding is for you to use a multisensory approach, in which students see, hear, and physically form the letters and vowels.

Use the following approach to introduce all new Hebrew letters and vowels in *Ready, Set...Go Alef Bet!*

Example: Lesson 1

Key Words: תּוֹרָה טַלִית

New Letters: תּ/ת ט

Introducing the Key Words and Deducing Their Sound-Symbol Associations

1. Hold up Word Picture Card #1 and say the Hebrew word טַלִית. Ask "What is the first sound that you hear in this word?" (*t*) Hold up Phonics Flash Card #1 and say "t." Ask students to repeat the sound with you.
2. Create a kinesthetic link between the letter shape and its sound by snapping your finger while you say "t." Ask the class to repeat the movement. You can also ask students to create the letter shapes through yoga poses. Students can create a ט by lying on their backs with their legs up straight in the air, feet parallel to the ground, and with arms raised on a diagonal toward, but not touching, the legs. Post Phonics Flash Card #1 on the board with Fun-Tak or magnetized tape. No matter which kinesthetic association you use, ask the students to repeat the letter sound (t) while they do so.
3. Ask students to draw the new letter in the air with their index fingers while repeating the letter's sound. Model this action for them first, with your back to the class, so they follow the correct directionality. Then ask the class to draw the letter as they say the sound.

Repeating the sound is crucial, as this reinforces the connections between the auditory, visual, and kinesthetic pathways. Make sure that students are also "writing" in the proper direction.

4. Hold up Word Picture Card #2 and say the Hebrew word תּוֹרָה. Ask "What is the first sound that you hear in this word?" (*t*) Hold up Phonics Flash Card #2 and say "t." Ask students to repeat the sound with you.
5. Create a kinesthetic link between the letter shape and its sound by snapping your finger while you say "t", or miming the tapping of a snare drum and repeating the sound each time you "tap" the drum. Ask the class to repeat the movement. Post Phonics Flash Card #2 on the board with Fun-Tak or magnetized tape.
6. Ask students to draw the new letter in the air with their index fingers while repeating the letter's sound. Repeat the steps in #3 above.
6. Hold up Word Picture Card #1 again, and say the Hebrew word טַלִית. "What sound do you hear at the end of this word?" (*t*) Hold up Phonics Flash Card #3 and say "t." Ask students to repeat the sound with you.
8. Create a kinesthetic link between the letter shape and its sound using either of the suggestions above. As an alternative, students can create the letter ת in a yoga pose by getting on the floor on their hands and knees with their legs flat on the floor and their heads tucked in between their arms. Post Phonics Flash Card #3 on the board with Fun-Tak or magnetized tape.
9. Repeat the steps in #3 above.
10. Practice drilling the new letters by asking students to make the letter's sound when you point to it.
11. Ask students what they notice about the letters on cards 2 and 3. (*they look the same except one has a dot in the middle*)
12. Ask students if they sound the same or different. (*the same*) If a student answers incorrectly, ask the class to say each sound again while the student listens. Repeat the question to make sure that the student can hear the sound correctly.
13. Ask students if all three letters make the same sound or a different one. (*the same sound*)
14. Practice drilling the new letters by asking individual students to make the letter sounds when you point to the letters. Tell the class that, if an individual is correct, they should repeat the sound. But if the

individual is incorrect, they should remain silent.

15. If the class is silent, ask the individual to try again. If a student in the class repeats an incorrect sound, ask that student to go next.
16. Repeat this procedure until you feel confident that every student knows the sound of all three letters.

The following is a brief outline of the steps above:

1. Display the Word Picture Card that illustrates a key word. Ask students to repeat the key word and to identify the new sound in it.
2. Hold up the Phonics Flash Card that represents that sound.
3. Ask students to repeat the sound with you.
4. Create a kinesthetic link with the sound. Ask the class to repeat the sound with an associated motion.
5. Have students draw the new letter in the air with their index fingers as they say the sound.
6. Drill the sound-symbol relationships by pointing to the letters and asking individual students to make their sounds. If the student is correct, the class should repeat the sound. If the student is incorrect, the class should remain silent. Repeat this until you are confident that all of the students have mastered the sound associated with each new letter.

Note: You may wish to mark this page with a paper clip or bookmark so that you always have quick and easy access to these steps.

Hebrew vowels are particularly difficult for beginning readers. This is mostly due to the fact that they are much smaller than the letters and, with one exception, they tend to be placed above or below the line of print. To help facilitate student mastery add an extra step when introducing the vowels. Use props that reinforce the mnemonics in the student text to assist you in introducing each vowel. For example, bring in an art stick or tongue depressor to help introduce the *"ah"* vowel or a bead on a string to help introduce the *"ee"* vowel. Pass these items around the class, allowing students to manipulate them. Then, write a few sample letters on the board, and allow each student to place the prop in the correct place for the vowel.

Here is a list of props for the vowels introduced in *Ready, Set...Go Alef Bet!*

"ah": an art stick or tongue depressor
"oo": three Tinker Toy spools evenly spaced and connected in a straight line with medium rods
"ee": a bead on a string
"oh": a small ball that students can hold over their heads
"eh": five ping pong balls and a basket

Kinesthetic and Tactile Activities

All students benefit from learning new materials through tactile (touch) and kinesthetic (movement) activities. This is especially crucial for any student who has weak visual and auditory processing skills. Incorporating some of the activities below will enhance learning and enliven your classroom at the same time.

1. Cut large letters out of sandpaper and paste them on sheets of construction paper. Ask students to close their eyes and feel the letters with their fingers. Based only on touch, ask students to name their letters.
2. Place foam or plastic Hebrew letters in a bag. Students take turns selecting a letter, and, without looking, determine the letter/sound.
3. Give students some clay or Playdough. Tell them the sound and ask them to create the letter or letters that represent the sound.
4. Ask students to create letter shapes using their bodies. The book *Alef-Bet Yoga for Kids* by Ruth Goldeen (Kar-Ben Publishing, 2009) is an excellent source of ideas for this activity.
5. As students master a variety of letters and the yoga poses that reinforce them, you can play letter charades. Write the letters that the students have learned on index cards. Select a student to begin. The student selects a letter and creates the correct yoga pose while the class attempts to guess the letter. The first student who calls out the correct answer gets the next turn.
6. When the weather is good, take the class outside. Give each student a cup of water and a paint brush and ask them to paint Hebrew letters on the sidewalk. Either say a key word and ask them to write the letter with which it begins, or ask them to say the sound each letter makes as they paint it.
7. The sense of taste is powerfully connected to memory. Bake cookies in the shape of Hebrew letters or make *alef-bet* chocolates using a plastic mold. In order to eat the treat, students must identify the sound each letter represents.

Word Picture Cards Master List

1. טַלִית
2. תּוֹרָה
3. עַל
4. שַׁבָּת
5. שָׁלוֹם
6. יָד
7. שֻׁלְחָן
8. בַּיִת
9. בַּ־
10. אַבָּא
11. אִמָּא
12. עִפָּרוֹן
13. מְזוּזָה
14. גְלִידָה
15. גּוֹרִילָה
16. גֶשֶׁם
17. דֶגֶל
18. מַיִם
19. דָג
20. כִּפָּה
21. קִדּוּשׁ
22. מוֹרָה
23. כִּתָּה
24. הַבְדָלָה
25. יֶלֶד
26. יַלְדָה
27. צְדָקָה
28. מִיץ
29. פִּיצָה
30. וָו
31. כֶּלֶב
32. שֶׁל
33. לוּלָב
34. סֻכּוֹת
35. שִׂמְחַת תּוֹרָה
36. סֻכָּה
37. דוֹלְפִין
38. נֵר
39. חַלָּה
40. בְּרָכָה
41. מֶלֶךְ
42. חָתוּל
43. קַנְגָרוּ
44. פּוּרִים
45. פֶּסַח
46. אוֹכֵל
47. אוֹכֶלֶת
48. סָלָט
49. קוֹלָה
50. בָּנָנָה
51. יוֹגוּרְט
52. תֵּה
53. הַמְבּוּרְגֶר
54. לִימוֹן
55. פּוֹפְּקוֹרְן
56. רֹאשׁ
57. רֶגֶל
58. זֶבְּרָה
59. שׁוֹפָר
60. אָלֶף

Phonics Flash Cards Master List

1. ט
2. תּ
3. ת
4. שׁ
5. י
6. בּ
7. ◌ָ
8. ◌ַ
9. ◌ֲ
10. א
11. ע
12. מ
13. ם
14. ג
15. ד
16. וּ
17. ◌ְ
18. כּ
19. ק
20. ה
21. צ
22. ץ
23. ו
24. ב
25. ל
26. ◌ִ
27. ◌ִי
28. ס
29. שׂ
30. נ
31. ן
32. ח
33. כ
34. ך
35. פּ
36. ◌ֹ
37. וֹ
38. ר
39. ז
40. ◌ֶ
41. ◌ֱ
42. פ
43. ף

USING THE DIGITAL COMPANION

Students will love playing the online games in the digital companion. The activities reinforce the pre-reading skills and vocabulary introduced in the book. The digital companion also expands the amount of Hebrew instruction time and extends learning into the home. The computer becomes your teaching assistant! With the digital companion, parents can help their children even if they cannot read Hebrew themselves.

When presenting the digital companion to the students focus on the fun that they will have playing the computer games, and remind them that they will be able to score even more points by using the Hebrew they learn in class. Tell students they can personalize their own avatar (boy or girl, hat, shirt, pants, and shoes). They will also be able to collect inventory in eight of the games. Inventory items are: *shofar, mezuzah, neir, yad, kippah, Torah, lulav, tallit.*

When introducing the digital companion to parents, emphasize the ways it can help their children, such as seeing the Hebrew letters brought to life through animation, hearing Hebrew syllables and words read aloud in American and Israeli accents, and practicing their new letter recognition skills in online games. Tell parents their children can even e-mail their online scores directly to you, the teacher!

Introducing the Digital Companion

Ask students if they enjoy playing computer games and which ones they most like to play. Discuss what makes this activity fun. Tell students that after they complete a lesson in the book, they will play games on their computer to practice what they have learned in class.

Before you assign activities in the *Ready, Set...Go Alef Bet!* digital companion for the first time, your education director must create an account at www.behrmanhouse.com, then register for the Behrman House Online Learning Center by contacting customersupport@behrmanhouse.com or calling 1-800-221-2755. Your education director will then e-mail an invitation with a link to you and other teachers asking you to join the "online synagogue." Your education director can add classes to the online synagogue and make you the teacher of a class. Once you have been assigned a class, with *Ready, Set...Go Alef Bet!* as the digital application in that class, you will easily be able to e-mail a link to your students, inviting them to join your class online. When students click on the link, they become part of the class and will see a "Play" button for *Ready, Set ...Go Alef Bet!* in the upper left corner of the classroom wall. The database will automatically begin to track and store their results.

Tracking Students' Digital Activities

There are three ways to assess students' progress in the digital companion:

1. Log on to www.behrmanhouse.com with your teacher account, click "My Account" then "Online Learning Center," then select your class and click the green "View Assessment" button on the top of the left menu options. Review your students' results.
2. If you prefer, students can print out a lesson summary when they have completed all the activities in a lesson and bring it in to class. Or students can e-mail the lesson summary directly to you.
3. Inform your students how often you intend to assess their progress online and check their progress after they complete a lesson in the Online Learning Center (OLC).

GAMES AND REVIEW ACTIVITIES

Games can add variety and energy to your classroom. They reinforce learning and capture students' attention through a fun, lively medium. Consider the following when playing classroom games:

1. Choose games that contribute to improving specific Hebrew pre-reading skills—games that have pedagogic value.
2. Use games that move quickly. Don't spend more time on a game than it deserves.
3. Stop when students' interest begins to wane.
4. Choose age-appropriate games.
5. Use games that are easy to follow and organize. Explain rules clearly. Avoid complicated directions. You want students' attention focused on the skills being reinforced, not on rules.
6. Maintain control of the class.
7. When playing a game with the entire class, make sure that all students are actively involved and can experience success.

The games below have been listed according to the pre-reading skills that they reinforce. Where applicable, games that can be used to reinforce key words or vocabulary items have been noted.

Games That Reinforce Sound-Symbol Associations

Around the World

In this review game students sit in a circle facing inward. Choose one student to stand behind a seated student. Hold up a letter or vowel. Both students try to make the sound of the symbol on the card. The first one to do so correctly continues "around the world" by standing behind the next student. The object of the game is for students to move, place by place, completely around the circle. You can also use this game to review vocabulary by showing a picture of a key word and asking students to provide the correct Hebrew word.

Sound Toss

For this game you need a muffin tray and two sets of chips, each in a different color. Write the letters or vowels you wish to review on slips of paper and place one paper in each cup of the muffin tin. Line up the teams. The first student from one team tosses his or her chip into one of the cups. If the student can identify the sound represented by the symbol written in the cup, his or her chip is allowed to remain. If the student does not remember the sound, you say it, then remove the chip from the cup, leaving the paper. The teams take turns tossing their chips. The team that gets the most chips in the cups wins. You can easily vary the game by changing the papers as students learn more letters. As students become more adept at the game, you can increase its difficulty by requiring that teams get multiple chips in each cup in order to win.

Tic-Tac-Toe

Divide the class into two teams, X and O. Draw a tic-tac-toe grid on the chalkboard or whiteboard. Depending on what you wish to review, in each square, write a Hebrew letter, vowel, or syllable. In order to place an X or an O in a square, a student must read the item in the square correctly. You can create a permanent tic-tac-toe grid on a piece of oak tag and use Fun-Tak to post printed flash cards in the spaces, or you can use magnetic tape on a set of cards and post them on the board if it is magnetized.

Hint: Place the most difficult combinations, such as C-V-C syllables, in the four corners and the center of the game.

This game can also be used to review vocabulary by placing pictures in the squares and asking students to provide the Hebrew word.

Musical Sounds/Musical Syllables

Create a deck of ten or more cards. For Musical Sounds, each card should depict a single letter or vowel, and for Musical Syllables each card should contain a single C-V or C-V-C syllable. Students sit or stand in a circle and pass the deck around while you play Jewish or Israeli music. (Suggested music includes *Z'man LaShir* and *Shiru Shalom Ivrit*, music for *Shalom Ivrit 1*, both from Behrman House.) When the music stops, the student holding the deck must say the Hebrew sound for the letter, vowel, or syllable printed on the top card. If that student cannot do so, it goes to the next student. Once a student has correctly identified what is on the card, he or she puts the card at the bottom of the deck and play continues.

You can also play a Musical Words version to review key words or vocabulary. In this version each card should contain a picture of a key word or vocabulary item. When the music stops, the student holding the deck must provide the Hebrew word for the item pictured on the top card.

Letter Contest/Sound Contest

In this game students focus on one letter at a time as they hunt for a specific letter or sound inside a paragraph or other text passage.

Give each student a copy of a short text passage and a highlighter pen. Select a letter, especially one that can be confused with other letters that look similar; for example, ר and ד or מ and ט. Ask students to search for that letter and highlight as many examples as they can in one minute. When you call time, ask the students to write down the number of examples they found. In order to "win," each student must point out all the letters to you and the class. You can play multiple rounds of this game using different letters. Ask students to swap markers so that they use a different color for each round. You can also use this game to review Hebrew homophones (multiple symbols that represent the same sound). Ask students to find all the examples of letters that make a certain sound, such as *m* (מ and ם) or *s* (ס and שׂ).

Bingo

For this game you will need to prepare a paper Bingo card for each student, divided into nine squares of three rows and three columns, or twenty-five squares of five rows and five columns. The center square is free—חָפְשִׁי (pronounced *ḥofshi*). The other squares contain letters or syllables that students have learned. Be sure to write neatly and clearly or print out large letters to paste in the squares. These symbols should also be written or printed and taped on index cards that you will read aloud to the students. Each student will need a small pile of beans, tokens, buttons, or squares of colored paper to use as Bingo markers.

Distribute Bingo cards and markers to the class. Select an index card and say the sound of the symbol written on it. Students should locate the letter on their cards and place a marker on it. The first student who covers three or five squares in a row—either vertically, horizontally, or diagonally—calls out "Bingo." He or she must then produce the sounds of each letter covered. If the student is correct, he or she wins. (*Note*: Allow classmates to help the student, if he or she gives an incorrect sound.) You can also use this game to review blending by using C-V and C-V-C syllables, or to review vocabulary using pictures in the squares on the Bingo cards.

Games That Reinforce Visual Skills

Concentration

Researchers in Israel have pointed to visual memory as the pre-reading skill that best predicts success in learning to read Hebrew. "Concentration" is a terrific way to help students develop this crucial skill. Prepare six to twelve pairs of cards. Pairs consist of two items that match, such as a Hebrew letter or vowel and its English sound equivalent or pairs of Hebrew letters and vowels that represent the same sounds. Make sure that all of the cards are the same size and color, and that students will not be able to see through them.

Place the cards facedown in neat rows on the table. The first player turns two cards over. If the cards match, the player collects the set and takes another turn. If the cards do not match, the player turns them back over in the same spot, and the next player turns two cards over. Play continues until all the cards have been matched. The winner is the player who has collected the most matches.

Same or Different?

For this game you will need a pile of cards (or paper strips), each with a line drawn down the middle. Write two letters on a card, one on each side of the line. Some cards can have two of the same letter.

שׂ	שׂ

Other cards can have two different though similar-looking letters.

שׁ	שׂ

Divide the class into two teams. Each team chooses their first player. Hold up a card. The players call out "Same!" or "Different!" The student who calls out the correct answer first collects the card. At the end of play, the team with the most cards wins.

Begin with single letters, then move to two-letter and three-letter words:

שׁם	שׂם
גיר	גור

Note: Since the words contain no vowels, students are simply distinguishing visually between similar letters. They are not decoding the words.

Games That Reinforce Auditory Skills

Beginning, Middle, or End?

A paper-and-pencil version of this game can be found on pages 61 and 79 of the student book. The version here provides additional, and active, practice with a group. In this game students identify the location of specific sounds within a word. This skill is known as auditory segmentation. Researchers have found that there is a strong correlation between a child's awareness of the sounds in words and later reading achievement.

Take three paper cups. Label one "Beginning," one "Middle," and one "End." Place the "Beginning" cup on the *right*, and so on. Divide the class into two teams. You will also need tokens or plastic chips in two different colors, one for each team. One at a time, alternating teams, students come up. Tell the team what sound they should listen for when you read a Hebrew word. The player must determine if the sound is at the beginning, in the middle, or at the end of the word. Read the word. The student has five or ten seconds to

determine where the sound occurs and to place a token or chip in the correct cup. Feel free to repeat the word. If the student is correct, the chip remains in the cup. If the student is incorrect, remove the chip. Repeat until each member of the team has had a turn, then tally up their accumulated tokens or chips. The team with the highest score at the end of play wins.

Note: Begin with sounds that occur at the beginning of a word, then progress to those that fall at the end of a word, and only then ask students to determine sounds in the middle of the word. This is especially important the first time you play this game.

Games for Individuals Who Need Additional Practice

Many of the games described above can also be used with students who need one-on-one review. The following games are designed for use by you, a teaching assistant, or a resource room teacher to help individuals practice the specific skills in which they are weak.

Phonics Checkers

For students who have difficulty with fine visual discrimination or who do not remember the sounds that specific letters represent, phonics checkers uses a familiar board game to practice this essential skill. Create an 8 by 8 grid of squares (you can do this by inserting a table in a computer word processing document). Color every other square in a bright color. In the white squares, write a Hebrew letter. If you are working on fine visual discrimination, use pairs or sets of letters that students commonly confuse (such as בּ and כּ). If you are reviewing sound-symbol associations, write the specific letters with which the student is struggling. Allow the student to sit facing the grid so that the letters are right-side-up. Place the checkers on the squares that contain letters. To capture a square, the player needs to make the sound that the letter represents.

If the player misidentifies the letter or cannot recall what sound it makes, say the sound and ask the student to repeat it, then he or she must select another square.

Mazes

Many beginning readers have difficulty mastering directionality, even in their native language. For our students—English readers who are learning Hebrew—directionality can be especially problematic. Mazes are often used to teach young readers the visual perception needed to trace the shapes of letters and follow a line of print. Because mazes for young English readers most often begin in the top left-hand corner and end in the lower right-hand corner, they train the learner's eyes to scan from left to right, mimicking the manner in which one reads a page of printed English. Conversely, mazes used to train young Hebrew readers should begin in the upper right-hand corner and end in the lower left-hand corner to reinforce the right-to-left directionality used by Hebrew.

You can create mazes of your own, or adapt those that reinforce English reading by turning them clockwise by 90 degrees and exchanging the start and finish spaces. You can find a variety of printable mazes for children on the Internet. You can also add Judaic themes (such as "Help the Children Find the Afikoman" or "Take a Trip to Israel") to many of these basic mazes.

TECHNIQUES FOR STUDENTS WITH SPECIAL LEARNING NEEDS

Children learn and develop differently; no two students will acquire Hebrew decoding skills in exactly the same way. Although students with special learning needs can bring additional challenges to the classroom, you can serve your students best by recognizing each child's individual strengths. Consult with your religious school director to learn about each student's specific learning needs.

Ready, Set...Go Alef Bet! provides a wide variety of learning activities, such as drawing, coloring, writing, and puzzles and games, as well as animated online activities and video games, that are ideal for all students, including those with learning challenges.

The techniques and modifications listed below, while designed to benefit students with specific learning needs, will be useful for all students:

- Form a bond with your students. Reach out to students before the school year starts by sending home a letter or e-mail or by calling to introduce yourself. Begin the first class with a "get-to-know-you" game. Throughout the year, show a personal interest in students and their lives. Students will learn best in a setting where they feel safe, valued, and respected.
- Complete the review activity at the start of each chapter in *Ready, Set...Go Alef Bet!* This will help you determine if a student is having difficulty with the material from previous lessons. You will be able to catch problems such as students confusing look-alike letters or mispronouncing sounds, and remediate appropriately through repetition and review.
- Model the correct pronunciation for letters, vowels, and words. Repeat several times, and do not assume that all of your students will be able to read the same items fluently and accurately when they see them again later. Repetition is essential for students with special learning needs.
- Use the "Multisensory Approach to Hebrew Phonics" (see page 12) when introducing key words, letters, vowels, and their sounds. Activities that incorporate visual, auditory, and kinesthetic or tactile modes of learning give *all* students a pathway to success using the approach that is most comfortable and effective for them.
- Encourage students to consistently use the *Ready, Set...Go Alef Bet!* digital application. These appealing activities provide essential review and practice at students' own pace. By assessing students' progress online, you will be able to see where they are having specific difficulties, enabling you to review the corresponding lesson in class. See "Using the Digital Companion" on page 15 for more information.

For students with:

- **Attention problems:** Seat the student close to you. Repeat directions. Privately establish a refocusing system with the student, such as a gentle tap on the shoulder or moving closer to the student's desk. Assist students organizationally, for example, by sending home a sheet with the questions students should answer after completing a lesson in the digital application.
- **Auditory processing issues:** Minimize noise and classroom distractions. Have the student repeat sounds and words back to you to ensure correct pronunciation.
- **Visual processing difficulty:** Read written directions aloud. For individual work, allow the student to work with an aide, a *madrich* or *madrichah,* or a classmate who can read directions or listen to the student read aloud. Have the student use an index card to track the line being read or cover the portion of the page not being worked on.
- **Emotional concerns, such as shyness or lack of self-esteem:** Allow the student to participate in choral reading so he or she does not feel singled out. Assess the student individually to strengthen his or her confidence. Provide matter-of-fact and low-key positive reinforcement regularly to boost self-esteem.
- **Behavioral problems:** Set firm but reasonable expectations. Minimize transitions from one activity to another, and inform students of schedule changes. Maintain a positive relationship with parents through regular contact and open communication. Find out what types of behavior strategies work at home and in secular school and replicate wherever possible.

By providing your students with opportunities to succeed in a nurturing, safe environment, fostering tolerance, and creating a supportive atmosphere, you will help all of them reach their highest learning potential.

in a natural manner without having to provide extensive explanations in English.

Introducing the Key Words and Deducing Their Sound-Symbol Associations

Introduce the new letter using the "Multisensory Approach to Hebrew Sound-Symbol Associations" described on page 12. You can create a kinesthetic link between the shape of the letter ט and its sound by snapping your finger while you say "t," or miming the tapping of a snare drum and repeating the sound each time you "tap" the drum. Ask the class to repeat the movement. As an alternative, ask students to create the letter shapes using their bodies. They can make the shape of the letter with their hands (see page 14 in the student edition) or use their whole bodies to form the letter. Similarly, introduce the ת through the key words טַלִית and תּוֹרָה.

Off to the "Right" Start

Tell the students to look at the two lines of words and to find the number 1. Read the first line aloud asking students to draw an arrow above every letter that makes the "t" sound. Circulate to make sure that students are completing the task

TEACHING TECHNIQUES FOR EACH LESSON

1 Tip Top

Pages: 5–8

Key Words: תּוֹרָה טַלִית

New Letters: תּ ת ט

Vocabulary Word: (on) עַל

Cognates: טֶלֶוִיזְיָה, טֶלֶפוֹן, תֵּה, דוֹלְפִין, דִינוֹסָאוּרוּס

Recommended Materials: Phonics Flash Cards #1–3, Word Picture Cards #1, 2, and 3, tallit and miniature Torah, crayons or colored pencils.

Oral Language Lesson

Begin the first class with the following oral Hebrew language lesson. If you are completing this lesson during the second class session and have already taught this material, review it. Begin each subsequent class by taking attendance in this manner. Teach students the following words:

שָׁלוֹם שְׁמִי ________ פֹּה לֹא פֹּה

Then, take attendance, asking students to respond in Hebrew when you call their names.

If a student is absent, the class can respond:

________ לֹא פֹּה

Set Induction

Allow a volunteer to read the chapter title. Ask the class what sound they think they will learn in this lesson. (*t*) Next, ask students what items that begin with the sound *t* they might see at services. When a student says either "Torah" or "tallit," hold up the object. Pass it around so that students can handle it. You may have to give them hints like, "Some people wear this around their shoulders when they are at services" or "We read from this special scroll.")

Once students have identified both objects, repeat the terms with the adjective גְּדוֹלָה/קְטַנָּה after the noun. Use your arms to indicate "big" and "small." This step will teach students the gender (feminine) of the new nouns

correctly. Write words #1–3 on the board. Ask volunteers to circle the letters on the board that they circled in their books. Repeat this procedure with the second line. Ask students on which side Hebrew words and sentences begin. (*the right*)

Letter Hint & Color the Letter

Distribute crayons, colored pencils, or markers. Ask a volunteer to read the sentence in the first Letter Hint. Write the תּ on the board and invite a volunteer to circle the toe. Give students time to color in the first letter. Repeat the procedure for the ט, this time asking a volunteer to draw an arrow to show where the letter is open.

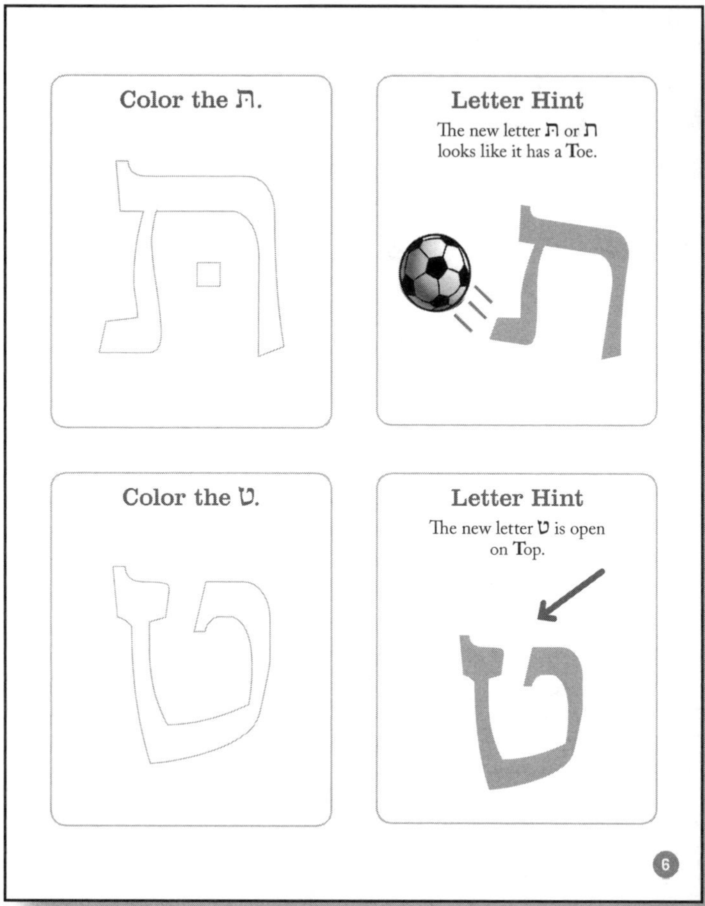

I Can Understand Hebrew!

Your teacher will read this word to you:

עַל

Your teacher will read this sentence to you.
Circle the picture that matches the sentence.

טַלִּית עַל תּוֹרָה.

7

I Can Understand Hebrew!

Tell students to look at the the new vocabulary word and the picture that illustrates it. Read the word to them, and ask them to repeat it. Act out the meaning of the word by placing a tallit on something while you say עַל with the class repeating after you. Place the Torah on the tallit and say תּוֹרָה עַל טַלִּית with the class repeating. Place the tallit on the Torah and say טַלִּית עַל תּוֹרָה with the class repeating. Next, ask volunteers to place the items correctly after you say a sentence. The volunteer should say the sentence after completing the task. If the student is correct, the class should repeat the Hebrew sentence. If the student is not correct, the class should remain silent. Give the volunteer a chance to correct what is wrong. You may need to repeat the sentence a few times to allow students to verify the sentence and its meaning for themselves. This is especially true in the early rounds, when students are unfamiliar with the process as well as the Hebrew material. Continue this activity until every student has had a turn.

Then, ask students to look at the two pictures on page 7. Read the sentence, and ask them to circle the correct picture. Circulate to assist students as needed.

Now I Know My Alef-Bet!

Ask students to trace the letter on the first line with their fingers, then to trace it in pencil while repeating the sound that the letter represents. (*t*) Next, ask them to write two examples of the letter in pencil while repeating the letter's sound. Repeating the letter's sound provides an auditory reinforcement for the visual and kinesthetic activity. Students use the same process with the letter on the second line.

Sound Check

The ability to separate words into their component speech sounds (or phonemes) is known as phonemic segmentation. Reading researchers have found that there is a strong correlation between a child's awareness of the sounds in words and later reading achievement.

This activity provides students with practice in segmenting the initial phoneme of several words using cognates (words that sound similar in both Hebrew and English). Since it is easiest to isolate the initial sound of a word, the early "Sound Check" activities focus on initial phonemes. At the same time, this activity provides students with practice in making fine auditory distinctions. The sounds *t* and *d* are very similar, and some students confuse them. If a student struggles with this activity, it may indicate that he or she has difficulty with auditory distinctions and may need additional practice in this area.

Give the Hebrew pronunciation of each item in the activity. (See "Cognates" on page 20.) Ask students to point to each item as you say its Hebrew name. Circulate to make sure that everyone can complete this crucial first step. Ask volunteers to identify the item on the right side of the top line. Encourage them to use the Hebrew pronunciation. Tell the class to listen for the first sound in the word then ask a volunteer to say it clearly. Ask the class what sound they heard at the beginning. (*t*) Ask them to look at the two Hebrew letters in the instructions, and ask them, "Do these letters make the same sound as the first sound in תֵּה?" If any students have difficulty with this, ask them to isolate the sound using the mnemonics taught earlier in the lesson.

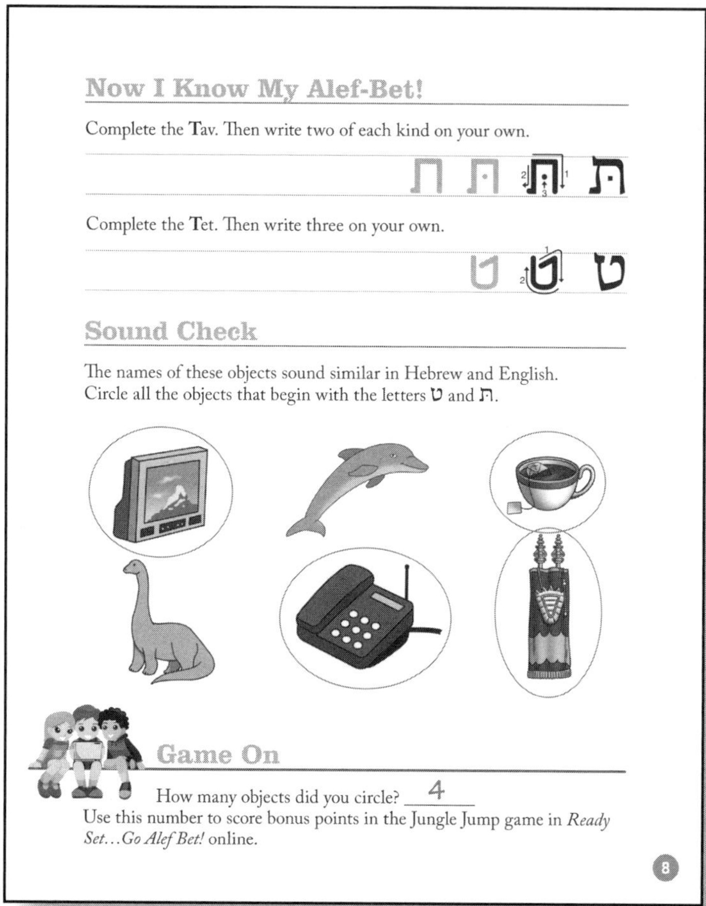
Now I Know My Alef-Bet!

Complete the Tav. Then write two of each kind on your own.

Complete the Tet. Then write three on your own.

Sound Check

The names of these objects sound similar in Hebrew and English. Circle all the objects that begin with the letters ט and ת.

Game On

How many objects did you circle? 4

Use this number to score bonus points in the Jungle Jump game in *Ready Set...Go Alef Bet!* online.

8

Repeat using the middle item on line one. If students have difficulty distinguishing this sound (*d*) from the first sound in טַלִּית, ask them to isolate the two initial phonemes. (*t* and *d*) Once students can distinguish the two sounds have them complete the activity individually. They should say each Hebrew word out loud as they work. Circulate to provide assistance as needed.

Game On

If you have not already done so, send students an e-mail invitation with a link to join your *Ready, Set...Go Alef Bet!* class in the Behrman House Online Learning Center. Encourage students to personalize their avatar (boy or girl, hat, shirt, pants, and shoes). They will see their avatar before they start playing every computer game.

"Game On" provides a mechanism for checking the students' answers to "Sound Check." Ask students how many words they circled. (4) Ask students to complete Lesson 1 in *Ready, Set...Go Alef Bet!* online at home. Remind them to play the Jungle Jump game when they have completed the lesson. You might ask students to print out or e-mail their lesson summaries to you when they have completed all the activities

in the lesson. Or you can assess their progress in the Online Learning Center.

Challenge students to come to the next class with answers to the questions below. They will find the answers in Lesson 1 of the digital companion. Consider sending home a sheet with these questions, or e-mail them to parents, when you assign the lesson in the digital companion. Ask students to write the answers on the sheet and return it, with a parent's signature, at the next class.

1. What does the תּ do in the Letter Hint? (*it kicks the soccer ball*)
2. How many objects did you circle in the Sound Check activity? (*4*)
3. What inventory item did you collect in the Jungle Jump game? (*Torah*)

When students complete this lesson in the digital companion, and you have checked that they have done so, allow them to color in the ט, the תּ and the ת on the Alef-Bet Chart on page 4 of their book.

Assessment

Make notes about students who had difficulty with any of the material in this lesson.

Next, address the female puppet and and ask: ?מִי אַתְּ Use the puppet to respond:

אֲנִי __________ or שְׁמִי __________

Repeat this action several times, then ask each of the girls, ?מִי אַתְּ and solicit the response:

אֲנִי __________ or שְׁמִי __________

Finally, go back and forth between the boys and the girls asking the question ?מִי אַתָּה or ?מִי אַתְּ, according to the correct gender and allowing each to introduce himself or herself.

Set Induction

Ask a volunteer to read the chapter title. Ask the class what sound they think they will learn in this lesson (*sh*). Next, ask students what Hebrew words they know that begin with the "sh" sound. If they have trouble, ask them what word they use as a greeting. (שָׁלוֹם) Ask them what they think this word might mean (*peace, hello, good-bye*), and explain that the Hebrew word for "perfect" is related to the word שָׁלוֹם. Ask, have you ever had a "perfect day," a day when everything goes right? Allow a volunteer to describe their "perfect day." Tell

2 Ship Shape

Pages: 9–12

Key Words: שַׁבָּת שָׁלוֹם

New Letter: שׁ

Vocabulary Words: (Special greeting for Shabbat) !שַׁבָּת שָׁלוֹם

Cognates: סִירוֹפּ, סָלָט, שַׁמְפּוֹ, שֵׁרִיף

Recommended Materials: Phonics Flash Cards #1–4 and Word Picture Cards #1–5; two candles, a challah, juice, and a Kiddush cup (or a large picture of these items); a photo or drawing of a dove and an olive branch; two hand puppets or dolls, one of which is clearly male and one which is clearly female; crayons or colored pencils.

Review Activity: Play "Around the World" (see page 16 for instructions) using Phonics Flash Cards 1–3 and Word Picture Cards 1 and 2. After you have used each card, insert it randomly back into the pile. Play continues until at least one student wins. Ask students to answer the questions you posed at the end of Lesson 1 (see page 24).

Oral Language Lesson

Begin class by greeting each student with שָׁלוֹם then take attendance in the manner described on page 9. Introduce students to the question word ?מִי and the pronouns אַתְּ, אַתָּה, and אֲנִי. This is best accomplished by using hand puppets (or dolls). Begin by introducing yourself by saying, אֲנִי __________ Allow students to introduce themselves the same way.

Then, place a male puppet on one hand and a female puppet on the other. Address the male puppet and ask: ?מִי אַתָּה Use the puppet to respond:

אֲנִי __________ or שְׁמִי __________

Repeat this action several times, until you feel that some of the students understand, then ask each of the boys, ?מִי אַתָּה and solicit the response:

אֲנִי __________ or שְׁמִי __________

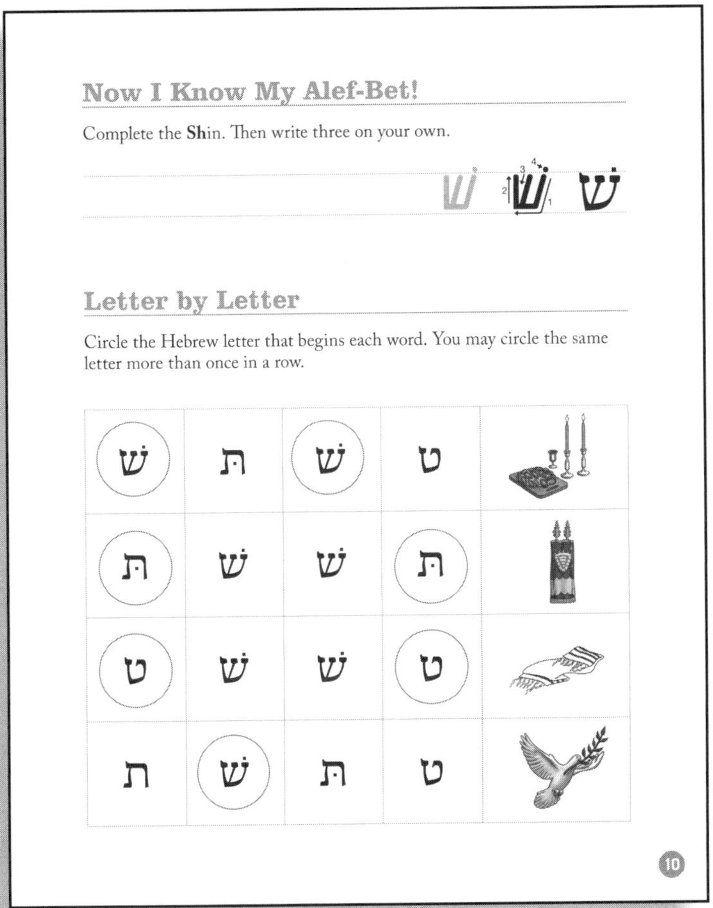

Now I Know My Alef-Bet!

Complete the **Shin**. Then write three on your own.

שׁ שׁ שׁ

Letter by Letter

Circle the Hebrew letter that begins each word. You may circle the same letter more than once in a row.

שׁ	תּ	שׁ	ט	
תּ	שׁ	שׁ	תּ	
ט	שׁ	שׁ	ט	
ת	שׁ	תּ	ט	

10

Letter by Letter

This activity reinforces the key words students have learned so far. At the same time, it gives them practice in auditory segmentation of the initial sound of each word, and making an association between the sound and the letter that represents it. Invite a volunteer to read the instructions. Complete the first item together as an example. Ask a volunteer to identify the first key word pictured. (שַׁבָּת) Then ask what sound begins the key word. (*sh*) Finally, tell the class to circle all of the letters on that line that represent the sound. (שׁ) If the class has difficulty, complete one or more additional examples until you feel confident that they understand the concept.

Allow students to complete the rest of the activity independently. Circulate to provide assistance as needed.

students that there is one day every week when we greet people with a special wish for peace and perfection. Ask them if they know which day that is. (שַׁבָּת)

Introducing the Key Words and Deducing Their Sound-Symbol Associations

Place the Shabbat items on a table and ask students to join you. Using your index finger, draw a circle in the air around all of the items and say שַׁבָּת. Ask the class to repeat the word after you.

Next, hold up the model dove, and say: שָׁלוֹם. Ask the class to repeat the word. Introduce the new letter using the "Multisensory Approach to Hebrew Sound-Symbol Associations" described on page 12. In order to create a kinesthetic link between the letter shape and its sound place your index finger against your lips and make the sound "sh." Ask students to repeat this action. At some point during the lesson, you can ask the class to recite the blessings and enjoy the juice and challah.

Letter Hint & Color the Letter

Distribute crayons or colored pencils. Ask a volunteer to read the sentence in the Letter Hint. Write the שׁ on the board and invite a volunteer to turn it into a ship and draw the "sun" dot on the correct side. Give students time to color in the letter.

Now I Know My Alef-Bet!

Ask students to trace the letter on the first line with their fingers and then in pencil while saying the sound that the letter represents. (*sh*) Next, ask them to write three examples of the letter in pencil while repeating the letter's sound. Repeating the letter's sound provides an auditory reinforcement for the visual and kinesthetic activity.

I Can Understand Hebrew!

Remind students that there is one day every week when we greet people with a special wish for peace and perfection. Read the phrase at the top of the page aloud. Ask students when they would use this greeting. (*Friday night, Saturday morning, Saturday afternoon,* שַׁבָּת)

Ask a volunteer to read the instructions and allow students to complete the activity with a partner. Provide assistance as needed, especially for students who have had difficulty with the oral language presentations. This may be an ideal time to enjoy the Shabbat treats.

Note: One or more alert students might notice that שַׁבָּת looks different when it appears in the phrase: שַׁבַּת שָׁלוֹם! Explain that the vowels change slightly when a word becomes part of a phrase; in this case, it means "a Shabbat of peace!"

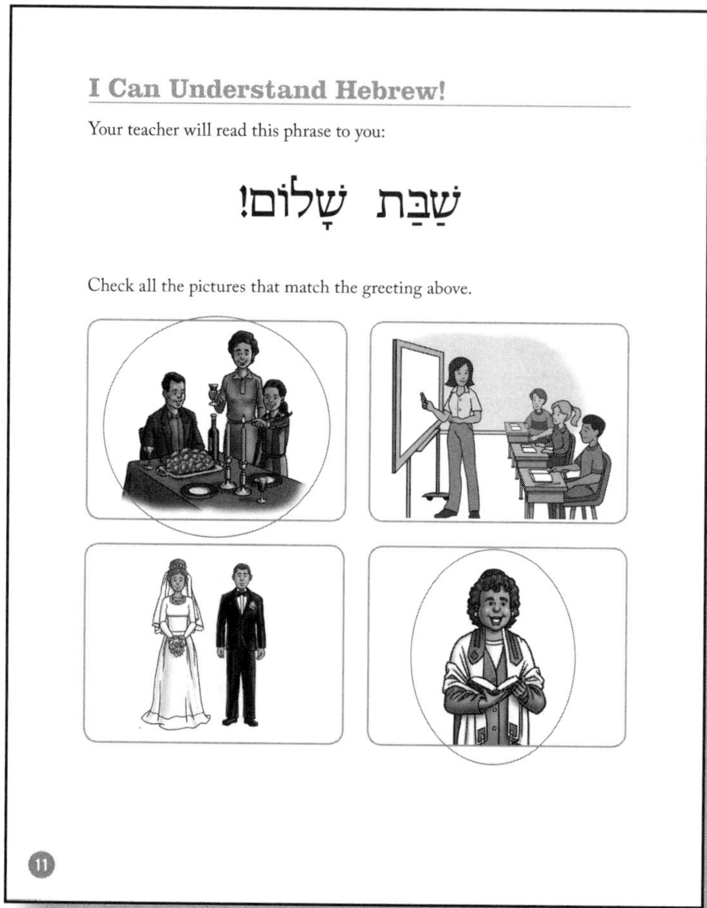

I Can Understand Hebrew!

Your teacher will read this phrase to you:

שַׁבַּת שָׁלוֹם!

Check all the pictures that match the greeting above.

11

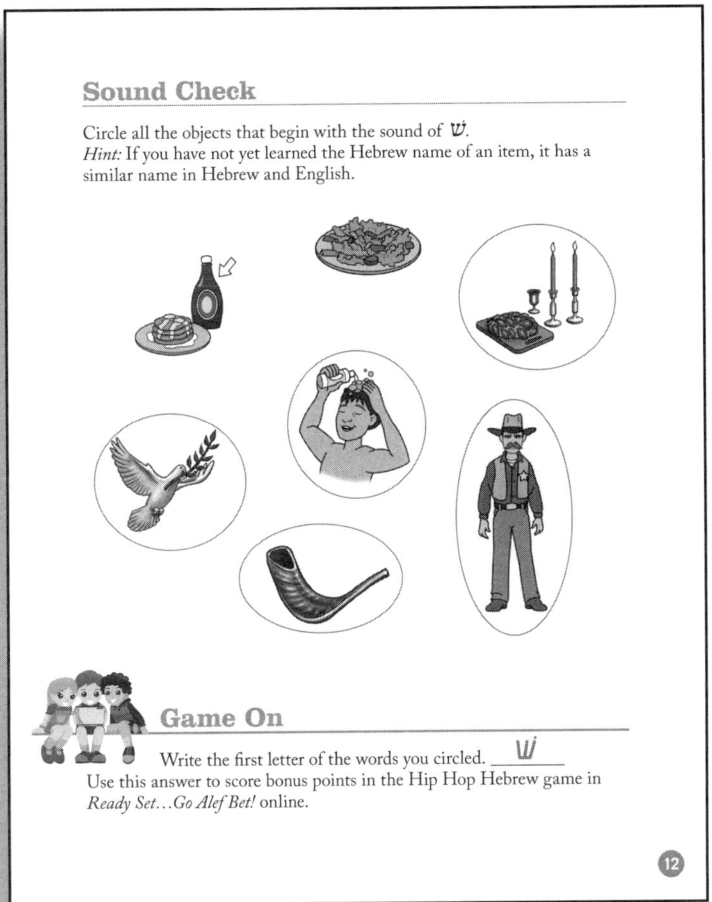

Sound Check

Circle all the objects that begin with the sound of שׁ.
Hint: If you have not yet learned the Hebrew name of an item, it has a similar name in Hebrew and English.

Game On

Write the first letter of the words you circled. שׁ

Use this answer to score bonus points in the Hip Hop Hebrew game in *Ready Set...Go Alef Bet!* online.

12

provide assistance as needed, paying attention especially to those students who had difficulty with the oral presentation.

Game On

Ask a volunteer to write the letter that begins each of the words he or she circled on the board. Ask the rest of the class if they came up with that letter or with something else. If there is a dispute about the answer, review as a class.

Ask students to complete Lesson 2 in the digital companion at home. Remind them to play the Hip Hop Hebrew game when they have completed the lesson. You might ask students to print out or e-mail their lesson summaries to you when they have completed all the activities in the lesson. Or you can assess their progress in the Behrman House Online Learning Center.

Challenge students to come to the next class with answers to the questions below. They will find the answers in Lesson 2 of the digital companion. Consider sending home a sheet with these questions, or e-mail them to parents, when you assign the lesson in the digital companion. Ask students to write the answers on the sheet and return it, with a parent's signature, at the next class.

Sound Check

This activity provides students with practice in segmenting the initial phoneme of several words using cognates (words that sound similar in Hebrew and English). This activity focuses on initial phonemes again, as it is easier to isolate the initial sound of each word. At the same time, it provides students with practice in making fine auditory distinctions. The sounds *s* and *sh* are quite similar, and some students confuse them. If a student struggles with this activity, it may indicate that he or she has difficulty with auditory distinctions and may need additional practice in this area.

Begin by providing students with the Hebrew pronunciation of each item in the activity. (See "Cognates" on page 25.) Ask students to point to each item as you say its Hebrew name. Circulate to make sure that everyone can complete this crucial first step.

Next, ask a volunteer to read the instructions at the top of the page. Since students may still be unfamiliar with this kind of activity, work through a couple of examples together. Ask a volunteer to identify the item at the top of the activity. (סָלָט) Tell the class to listen for the first sound in the word then ask the volunteer to say it clearly. Ask the class what sound they heard at the beginning. (*sh*) Ask students to look at the Hebrew letter in the instruction, and say, "Is the first sound in סָלָט the same sound as the one represented by the letter שׁ?" Once students understand that the sounds are not the same, repeat this procedure with a second example using the item at the bottom of the page.

If more practice is needed, move to the item in the middle of the activity, and repeat the procedure. Encourage all the volunteers to use the Hebrew pronunciation. If students have difficulty distinguishing this sound (*s*) from the sound of the letter שׁ, ask them to isolate the two initial phonemes (*sh* and *s*).

Once students can distinguish the two sounds, have them complete the activity individually. Be sure to tell them that they need to say each Hebrew word out loud as they work. Circulate to

1. What does the שׁ do in the Letter Hint? (*it bobs on the water*)
2. What letter begins two words in the "Letter by Letter" activity? (שׁ)

When students complete this lesson in the digital companion, and you have checked that they have done so, allow them to color in the שׁ on the Alef-Bet Chart on page 4 of their book.

Assessment

Here, as in Lesson 1, make notes concerning which students had difficulty with any of the information presented in this lesson.

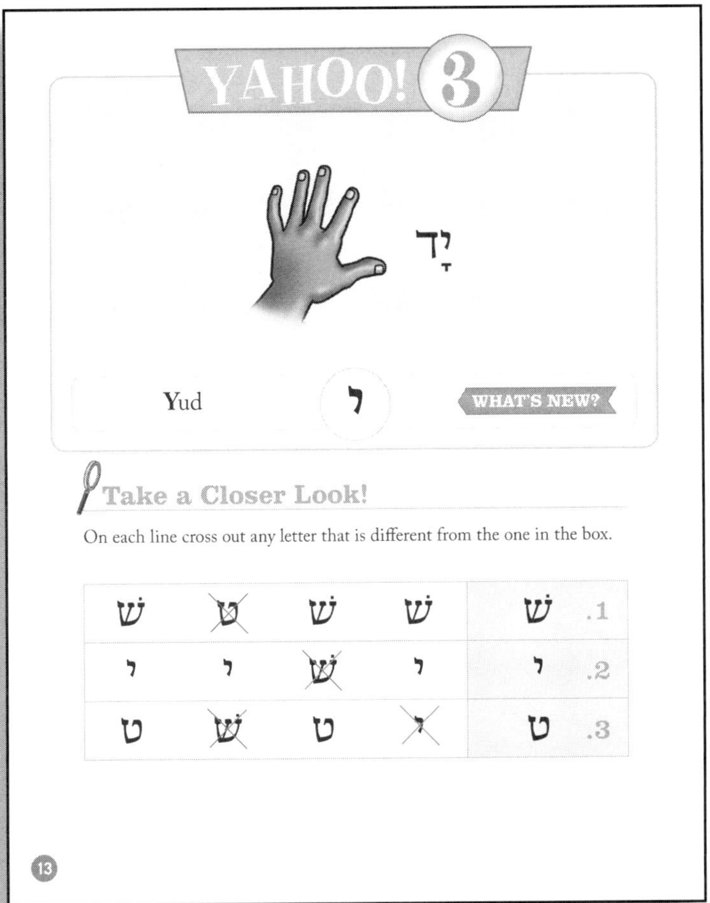

שׁ	~~ט~~	שׁ	שׁ	שׁ	.1
י	י	~~שׁ~~	י	י	.2
ט	~~שׁ~~	ט	~~י~~	ט	.3

head and pointing thumbs down. Repeat this process several times until each student who wants a turn has had one.

Review the previous vocabulary (טַלִּית, שַׁבָּת, שָׁלוֹם, עַל, תּוֹרָה,). You can review the sentences that students have already learned by saying תּוֹרָה עַל טַלִּית or טַלִּית עַל תּוֹרָה and asking students to place the objects correctly. The volunteer should say the sentence after completing the task.

Set Induction

Allow a volunteer to read the chapter title. Ask the class what sound they think they will learn in this lesson. (*y*) Next, hold up your hand, point to it and say "יָד." Ask students to repeat what you say and indicate what the word means. You can assess their understanding by pointing to your head, leg, ears, etc., as well as your hand, and asking "?יָד" for each. Once students have identified the object, repeat its name in conjunction with the adjective חֲזָקָה. Indicate the meaning of this adjective by making a muscle with your arm while you say: חֲזָקָה. This step will teach students the feminine gender of the new word יָד in a natural manner without having to provide an English translation. Ask the class to repeat the

3 Yahoo!

Pages: 13–16

Key Word: יָד

New Letter: י

Vocabulary Word: (table) שֻׁלְחָן

Cognates: גִּיטָרָה, יוֹגָה, יוֹגוּרְט, יוֹ־יוֹ גּוֹרִילָה

Recommended Materials: Phonics Flash Card #5 and at least two copies of Phonics Flash Cards #1–4; Word Picture Cards # 6 and 7 and at least 2 copies of Word Picture Cards # 1–5 (you will need multiple sets depending on how many groups of players you plan to have for the Concentration game. Each group of players will need two copies of each card.); a tallit, a model Torah, and a Torah pointer (יָד); crayons or colored pencils.

Review Activity: Play Concentration (see page 17 for instructions) using all of the letters and Hebrew words that students have studied so far. You will need two copies of each card to complete a set, and you may need two or more sets if you have a large class. Play continues until you have a winner from each group, each student has had at least one turn, or the class begins to lose interest. Ask students to answer the questions you posed at the end of the prior lesson (see page 29).

Oral Language Lesson

Begin class by taking attendance in the manner described on page 9. Introduce the terms:

מָה שְׁלוֹמְךָ? (male)

מָה שְׁלוֹמֵךְ? (female) טוֹב. טוֹב מְאוֹד.

לֹא טוֹב.

Model each question formula with a volunteer of the correct gender. Say:

שָׁלוֹם ________. מָה שְׁלוֹמְךָ? טוֹב?

טוֹב מְאוֹד? לֹא טוֹב?

Illustrate the word טוֹב with the "thumbs up" sign; illustrate טוֹב מְאוֹד with both thumbs up, and illustrate לֹא טוֹב by shaking your

word and action once they understand what it means.

Introducing the Key Words and Deducing Their Sound-Symbol Associations

Introduce the new letter using the "MultiSensory Approach to Hebrew Sound-Symbol Associations" described on page 12. You can create a kinesthetic link between the letter shape and its sound by pumping your fist while you say "*y*." Ask the class to make the shape of the י with their hands (see page 14 in the student edition) and to repeat the sound (*y*) while they do so.

Take a Closer Look!

In this activity, students focus on individual letter shapes by crossing out any letter on the line that differs from the one in the box. Since this is the first time that students have been asked to do this type of activity, do the first one together. Ask a volunteer to identify the letter in the box (שׁ) and point to the letter that is different. (ט) Allow students to complete the remaining lines individually. Circulate to provide help as needed.

Letter Hint & Color the Letter

Distribute crayons or colored pencils. Ask volunteers to read the sentence for the Letter Hint. Give students time to color in the letter.

Now I Know My Alef-Bet!

Ask students to trace the letter on the line with their fingers and then to trace it in pencil while repeating the sound that the letter represents. (*y*) Next, ask them to write three examples of the letter in pencil while repeating the letter's sound. This provides auditory reinforcement for the visual and kinesthetic activity.

Did You Know?

Hold up the Torah pointer and say "יָד." Ask the class to repeat the word. Choose a volunteer to read the sentences in the box. Show the class a picture of a Torah pointer on top of an open Torah scroll and say, "יָד עַל תּוֹרָה." Place the Torah pointer on the model Torah and ask a

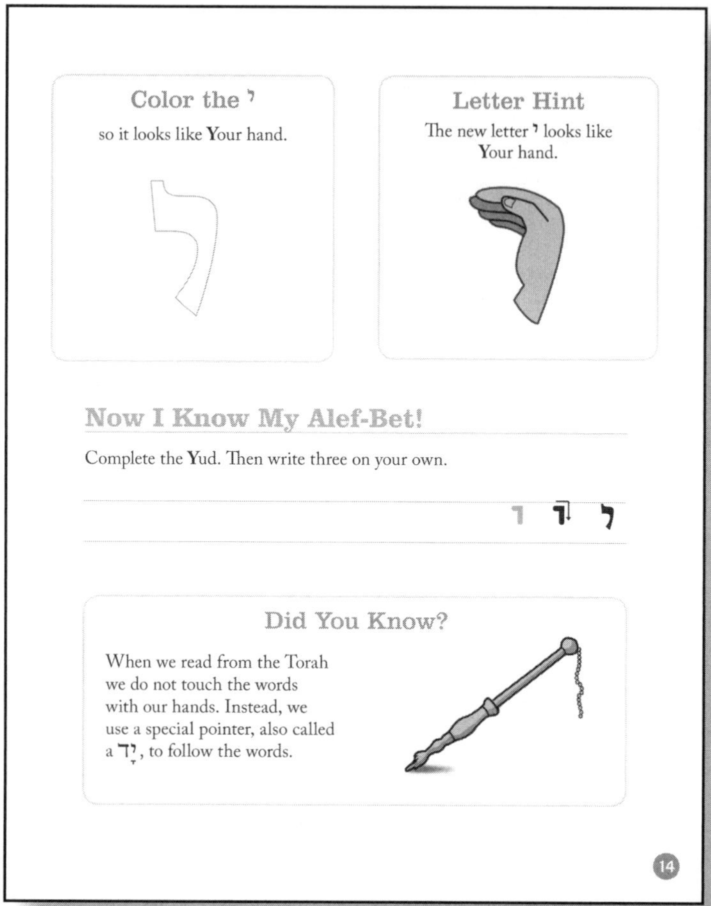

Color the י
so it looks like Your hand.

Letter Hint
The new letter י looks like Your hand.

Now I Know My Alef-Bet!
Complete the Yud. Then write three on your own.

Did You Know?
When we read from the Torah we do not touch the words with our hands. Instead, we use a special pointer, also called a יָד, to follow the words.

14

volunteer to create a Hebrew sentence that describes this arrangement. (יָד עַל תּוֹרָה.)

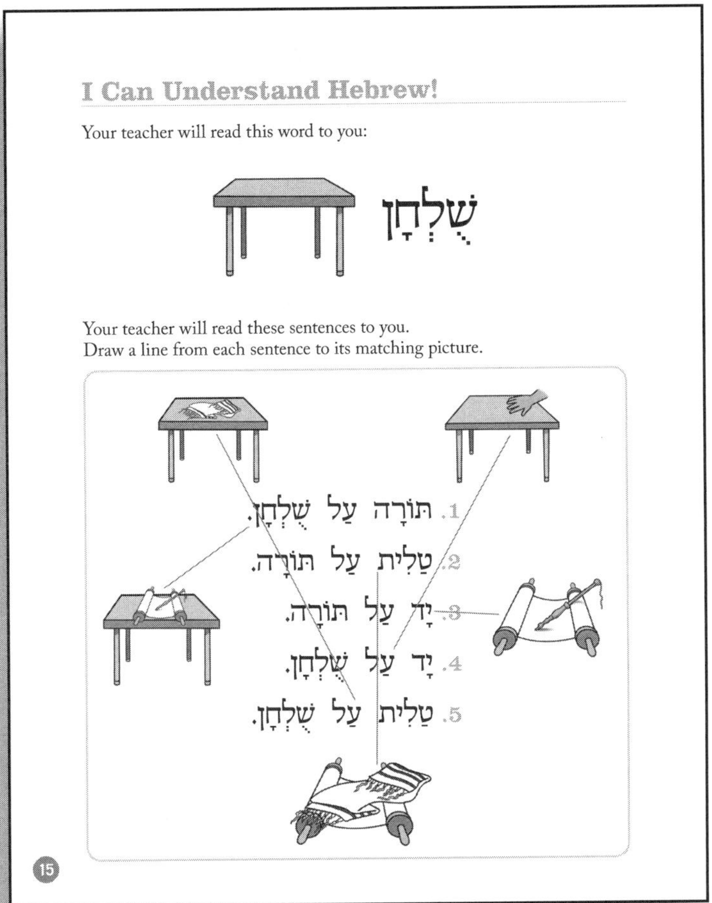

I Can Understand Hebrew!

Your teacher will read this word to you:

שֻׁלְחָן

Your teacher will read these sentences to you.
Draw a line from each sentence to its matching picture.

1. תּוֹרָה עַל שֻׁלְחָן.
2. טַלִּית עַל תּוֹרָה.
3. יָד עַל תּוֹרָה.
4. יָד עַל שֻׁלְחָן.
5. טַלִּית עַל שֻׁלְחָן.

15

I Can Understand Hebrew!

Point to the picture at the top of the page and say, שֻׁלְחָן. Ask the class to repeat after you. Next,point to a table in the room and say the word שֻׁלְחָן. Ask the class to repeat after you. Once you feel that the students understand the word, repeat the term with the adjectives גָּדוֹל (big) and קָטָן (small). This step will teach students the masculine gender of the new word שֻׁלְחָן in a natural manner without an English translation.

Place the Torah pointer on the table and ask a volunteer to create a Hebrew sentence that describes this arrangement. (יָד עַל שֻׁלְחָן.) Instruct the class to repeat the sentence if the student is correct. If the class remains silent, allow the volunteer to correct his or her sentence. Repeat this procedure by placing the tallit on the Torah, the Torah pointer on the tallit, the tallit on the Torah pointer, and so on. Repeat until each student has had the opportunity to create a Hebrew sentence.

Tell the students to look at the pictures in the box on page 15. Tell them that you are going to read a sentence and ask them to draw a line between the sentence and the picture that it describes. Read the first sentence and give the class time to find the correct picture and draw a line to it. You should repeat the sentence a few times until all of the students have completed the task. Circulate to provide assistance as needed, especially to students who have had difficulty with the oral language part. Repeat this procedure for the remaining sentences.

Sound Check

This activity provides students with practice in segmenting the initial phoneme of several cognates. At the same time, it provides practice in making fine auditory distinctions. The sounds *y* and *g* are fairly similar, and some students confuse them. Students who struggle with this activity may need individual practice with the skill.

Begin by providing students with the Hebrew pronunciation of each item in the activity. (See "Cognates" on page 30.) Ask them to point to each item as you say its Hebrew name. Circulate to make sure that everyone can complete this crucial first step.

Next, ask a volunteer to read the instructions at the top of the page. Select a volunteer to identify the item on the right side of the top row. Encourage the volunteer to use the Hebrew pronunciation. Tell the class to listen for the first sound in the word then ask the volunteer to say it clearly. Ask the class what sound they heard at the beginning. (*y*) Ask them to look at the Hebrew letter in the instruction, then ask, "Does this word begin with the sound of the letter י (*yud*-y)?"

Once students understand that the sounds are the same, allow them to complete the activity individually. Be sure to tell them that they need to say each Hebrew word out loud as they work. Circulate to provide assistance as needed, paying attention especially to those students who had difficulty with the oral presentation.

Game On

This activity is a good way to check students' answers to "Sound Check." Ask a volunteer how many words he or she crossed out. Ask the rest of the class if they came up with that number or another one. Ask for a volunteer to say the Hebrew word for the item they crossed out on the top line, and for another to name in Hebrew the item crossed out on the second line. You can also ask volunteers to name the items that were not crossed out. If there is a dispute about the number of words (2), review as a class.

Sound Check

The names of these objects sound similar in Hebrew and English. Cross out all the objects that do not begin with the sound of י.

Game On

How many objects are not crossed out? 3

Use this number to score bonus points in the Zero Gravity game in *Ready Set...Go Alef Bet!* online.

16

Have students complete Lesson 3 in the digital companion at home. Remind them to play the Zero Gravity game when they have completed the lesson. You might ask students to print out or e-mail their lesson summaries to you when they have completed all the activities in the lesson. Or assess their progress in the Behrman House Online Learning Center.

Challenge students to come to the next class with answers to the questions below. They will find the answers in Lesson 3 of the digital companion. Consider sending home a sheet with these questions, or e-mail them to parents, when you assign the lesson in the digital companion. Ask students to write the answers on the sheet and return it, with a parent's signature, at the next class.

1. How many times should you cross out the letter י in the "Take a Closer Look!" activity? (*once*)
2. What word in the "I Can Understand Hebrew!" activity has two meanings? (יָד) (*Note*: Tell students to connect the picture to the words not the words to the picture.)
3. What inventory item did you collect in the Zero Gravity game? (*yad*)

When students complete this lesson in the digital companion, and you have checked that they have done so,

allow them to color in the י on the Alef-Bet Chart on page 4 of their book.

Assessment

As with the previous lessons, make notes concerning which students had difficulty with any of the information presented in this lesson.

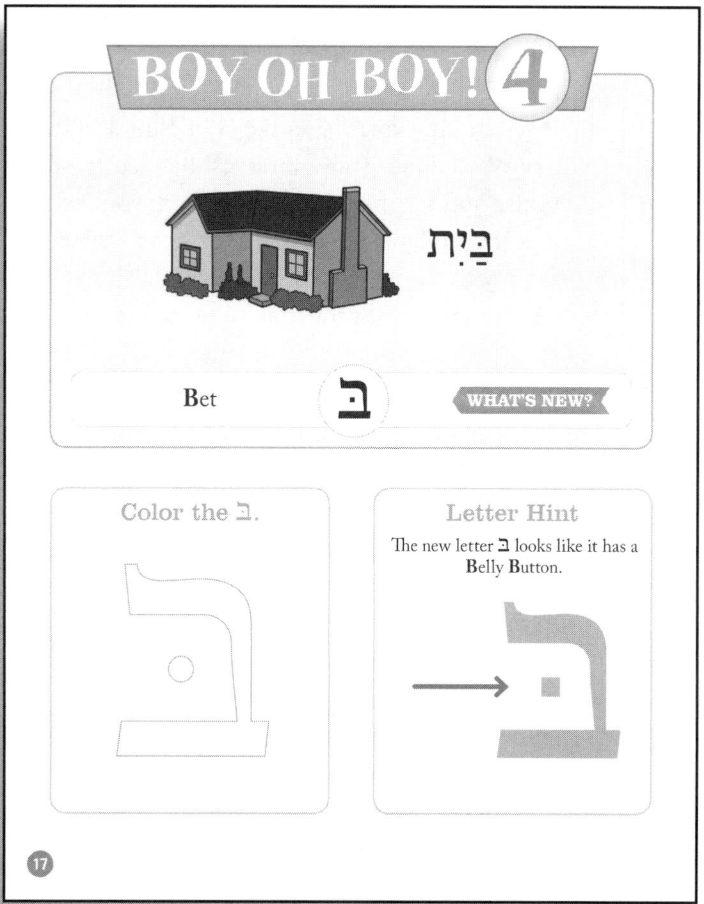

4 Boy Oh Boy!

Pages: 17–21

Key Word: בַּיִת

New Letter: בּ

Vocabulary Word: (in) בְּ־

Cognates: בֵּיסְבּוֹל, בָּנָנָה, פִּיצָה, פַּנְדָּה, בַּלּוֹן

Recommended Materials: Phonics Flash Cards #1–5 and #6–9; Word Picture Cards #1–7 and #8 and #9; a ping pong ball, a box, a tallit, a Torah pointer, a model Torah, a bottle, several art sticks or tongue depressors; crayons or colored pencils.

Review Activity: Place Word Picture Cards #1–7 on the ledge of the chalkboard or whiteboard. Point to the pictures, one at a time, and say the Hebrew word for each. Ask students to repeat after you. Ask volunteers to come up to the board. Say the Hebrew word for one of the items, and allow the volunteer to select the correct picture. If the student is correct, the class should repeat the Hebrew word. If the volunteer is incorrect, he or she will know by the class's silence and try again. Repeat until every student has had a chance. As a more difficult alternative, select a card and ask the volunteer to provide the correct Hebrew word.

Ask students to answer the questions you posed at the end of Lesson 3 (see page 33).

Oral Language Lesson

Begin class by greeting each student with שָׁלוֹם. Then take attendance in the manner described on page 9. Add to this familiar activity the introduction of another greeting, בֹּקֶר טוֹב —along with the customary response בֹּקֶר אוֹר. Review the material from the previous lesson by asking how students are

מַה שְׁלוֹמְךָ? מַה שְׁלוֹמֵךְ?

(טוֹב, טוֹב מְאוֹד, לֹא טוֹב)

Review all of the key words and vocabulary items that students have learned so far. You should also review the sentences that students have learned by asking them to use the props at hand to illustrate the meaning of a Hebrew sentence. For example, you can say: טַלִּית עַל שֻׁלְחָן. Ask a volunteer to create the correct display, repeating the Hebrew sentence either after completing the action or while performing it.

Once every student has had an opportunity to create a correct display, you can graduate them to a more difficult level by creating a display and asking volunteers to describe the result in Hebrew. For example, place the Torah pointer on the table and ask a volunteer to create a Hebrew sentence that describes this arrangement. (יָד עַל שֻׁלְחָן) Instruct the class to repeat the sentence if the student is correct. If the class remains silent, allow the volunteer to correct his or her sentence. Repeat this procedure by placing the tallit on the Torah, the Torah pointer on the tallit, the tallit on the Torah pointer, and so on.

Set Induction

Allow a volunteer to read the chapter title. Ask the class what sound they think they will learn in this lesson. (*b*) Next, write the English letter *B* and the syllable *Ba* on the board. Ask a volunteer to say the sound of each. Ask the class what the difference is between the two. (*one has a vowel sound added*

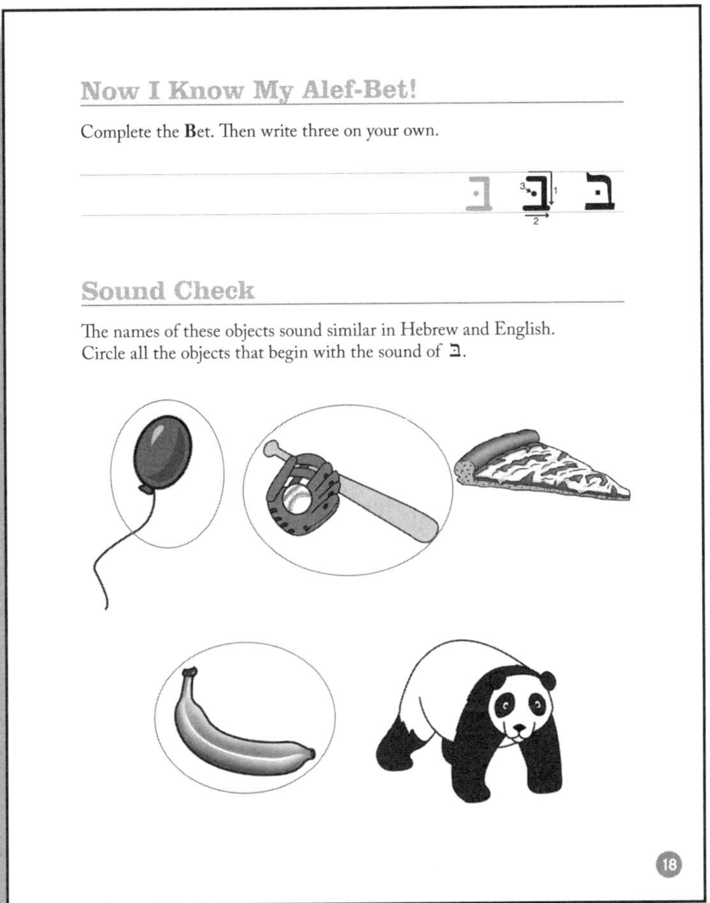

Now I Know My Alef-Bet!

Complete the **Bet**. Then write three on your own.

בּ בּ בּ

Sound Check

The names of these objects sound similar in Hebrew and English.
Circle all the objects that begin with the sound of בּ.

18

with practice in making the fine auditory distinction between the sounds *b* and *p*. Since these sounds are very similar, some students confuse them. If a students continues to struggle with this activity, provide individual practice with the skill, either with a student assistant or with a resource teacher.

Begin by providing students with the Hebrew pronunciation of each item in the activity. (See "Cognates" on page 35.) Ask them to point to each item as you say its Hebrew name. Circulate to make sure that everyone can complete this crucial first step. Next, ask a volunteer to read the instructions in the middle of the page. If students have become proficient with this type of activity, allow them to compete it on their own. If they have struggled with previous Sound Check activities, ask a volunteer to identify the item on the right side of the top line, encouraging the student to use the Hebrew pronunciation. Tell the class to listen for the first sound in the word then ask the volunteer to say it clearly. Ask the class what sound they heard at the beginning. (*p*) Ask them to look at the Hebrew letter in the instruction, and ask them, "Does this word begin with the same sound as the letter בּ?" Once students understand that the sounds are not the same, do another example using the center item on the top line, then allow them to complete the activity individually. Be sure to *and one does not*) Tell students that in this lesson they are going to learn a new Hebrew letter *and* their first Hebrew vowel sounds, and both the letter and the vowel sound can be found in the Key Word בַּיִת. Show students the picture of a house and say the word: בַּיִת. Once you feel that the students understand the word, repeat the term with the adjectives גָּדוֹל/קָטָן. This step will teach students the masculine gender of בַּיִת in a natural manner without having to provide an English translation.

Introducing the Key Words and Deducing Their Sound-Symbol Associations

Introduce the new letter using the "Multisensory Approach to Hebrew Sound-Symbol Associations" described on page 12. As an added kinesthetic association for the letter בּ, teach students the Hebrew word בַּקְבּוּק (bottle). This Hebrew word is onomatopoeic, having developed from the sound liquid makes when it is poured from a bottle. Hold the bottle upside-down and imitate the sound of pouring liquid ("b...b...b"). Ask the class to mime the action of pouring while repeating the sound.

Letter Hint & Color the Letter

Distribute crayons or colored pencils. Ask volunteers to read the sentence for the Letter Hint. Tell students to point to their belly buttons while they say the new letter's sound. Write the ב (without the dot) on the board and invite a volunteer to draw its belly button. If the student is correct, ask the class to pronounce the letter's sound. Give students time to color in the letter.

Now I Know My Alef-Bet!

Ask students to trace the letter on the line with their fingers and then to trace it in pencil while repeating the sound that the letter represents. (*b*) Next, ask them to write three examples of the letter in pencil while repeating the letter's sound.

Sound Check

This activity provides students with practice in segmenting the initial phoneme of several cognates. At the same time, it provides students

tell them that they need to say each Hebrew word out loud as they work. Circulate to provide assistance as needed, paying attention especially to those students who had difficulty with the oral presentation.

I Can Understand Hebrew!

Tell students to look at the the new vocabulary word part (prefix) and the picture that illustrates it. Read the prefix to them, and ask them to repeat it. Act out the meaning of the prefix by placing a ping pong ball in a box while you repeat the prefix. To make sure that students understand the new item, review the word עַל by placing the ball on a table as you say the word. Repeat the process of placing the ball in these two locations while you say the individual prepositions with the class repeating after you, until students can independently use each preposition to describe the location of the ball.

Then, select a volunteer to read the instructions. Ask students to look at the pictures in the first box on page 19 (upper right-hand box). Read the Hebrew sentence, and ask them to cross out the object that the sentence does not describe. (*the hand*) When the students have completed the first sentence, move on to the second allowing students to complete each of the remaining tasks independently. Circulate to assist students as needed.

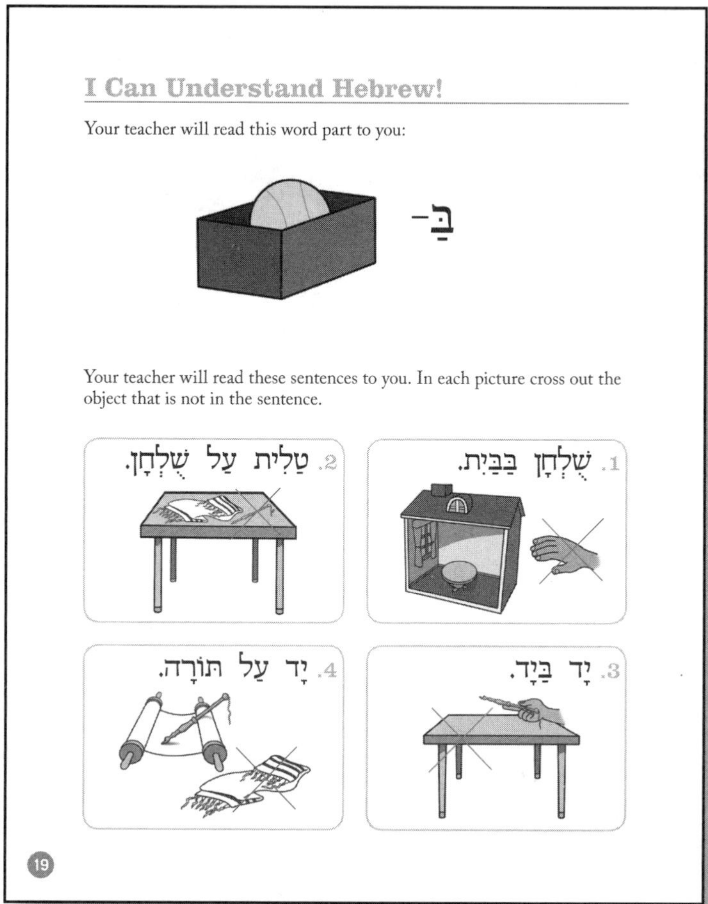
I Can Understand Hebrew!

Your teacher will read this word part to you:

-בְּ

Your teacher will read these sentences to you. In each picture cross out the object that is not in the sentence.

1. שֻׁלְחָן בַּבַּיִת.

2. טַלִּית עַל שֻׁלְחָן.

3. יָד בַּיָּד.

4. יָד עַל תּוֹרָה.

19

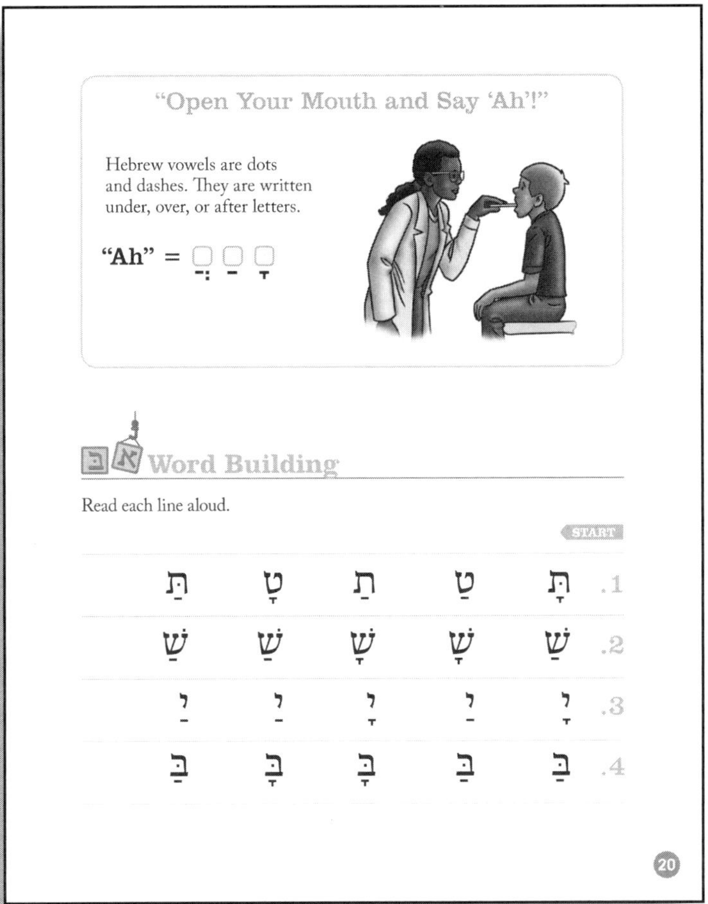

"Open Your Mouth and Say 'Ah'!"

Hebrew vowels are dots and dashes. They are written under, over, or after letters.

"Ah" = ▢ֲ ▢ַ ▢ָ

Word Building

Read each line aloud.

START

1. תָּ טַ תַ טָ תַּ
2. שַׁ שָׁ שָׁ שַׁ שַׁ
3. יָ יַ יָ יַ יַ
4. בַּ בַּ בָּ בָּ בַּ

20

ask them to read columns of syllables, which is more difficult because the letters are different.

"Open Your Mouth and Say 'Ah'!"

This is the first time that students will encounter a Hebrew vowel. Ask a volunteer to read the information in the box at the top of the page. Explain that the small orange boxes represent any Hebrew letter. Hold up the tongue depressor or art stick and tell the class that doctors often tell their patients to open our mouths and say "ah." Ask if their doctors have told them to do this. Explain that they may use a stick that looks like one of these vowels to help them look into a patient's throat. Pass a few sticks around so that students can feel their shape.

Write the vowels on the board and ask a volunteer to point to the one that looks like the doctor's stick. Next, hold up Phonics Flash Card #7 and say "ah" with the class repeating after you. Repeat this procedure with cards #7–9 until you are confident that the students recognize all three vowels.

Write a few Hebrew C-V syllables on the board, such as יָ, בַּ, שַׁ, תַּ, and so on. Invite volunteers to come up to the board. Say one of the syllables and ask the volunteer to point to it. If the student is correct the class should repeat the syllable. If the class is silent, ask the volunteer to correct the mistake. Repeat the process with a variety of syllables until every student has had at least one turn and you are confident that the class understands this simple C-V blending.

To bridge between syllable recognition and actual decoding, ask volunteers to come up to the board. Point to a syllable and ask the student to pronounce it, Again, if the student is correct, the class should repeat the syllable. If the class is silent, the student should have the opportunity to correct the error.

Word Building

Practice the basic blending skill that students have just learned by asking them to read aloud from the Word Building section at the bottom of the page. You may want to begin by asking students to take turns reading a single item. As they gain confidence, ask them to read full lines. Once students have gained confidence, you can

Hidden Picture

Pass out crayons or colored pencils. Ask a volunteer to read the instructions at the top of the page and allow students to work independently to complete the activity. Circulate to provide assistance as needed. *Note*: In the first printing of *Ready, Set...Go Alef Bet!* the following instruction is missing: Brown = "Sh."

Game On

This activity provides a mechanism for students to check their mastery of the sound-symbol associations they have made with some of the letters they've learned so far. Ask students what the picture shows. Then, ask which letter makes the first sound in that Hebrew word. (תּ) Ask students to complete Lesson 4 in the digital companion at home. Remind them to play the Wacky Wheelbarrow game when they have completed the lesson. You might ask students to print out or e-mail their lesson summaries to you when they have completed all the activities in the lesson. Or assess their progress in the Behrman House Online Learning Center.

Challenge students to come to the next class with answers to the questions below. They will find the answers in Lesson 4 of the digital companion. Consider sending home a sheet with these questions, or e-mail them to parents, when you assign the lesson in the digital companion. Ask students to write the answers on the sheet and return it, with a parent's signature, at the next class.

1. How many objects in the "Sound Check" activity begin with the letter בּ? (*three*)
2. What is the sound of the syllable that you read nine times in the "Word Building" activity? (*ta*)

When students complete this lesson in the digital companion, and you have checked that they have done so, allow them to color in the בּ on the Alef-Bet Chart on page 4 of their book.

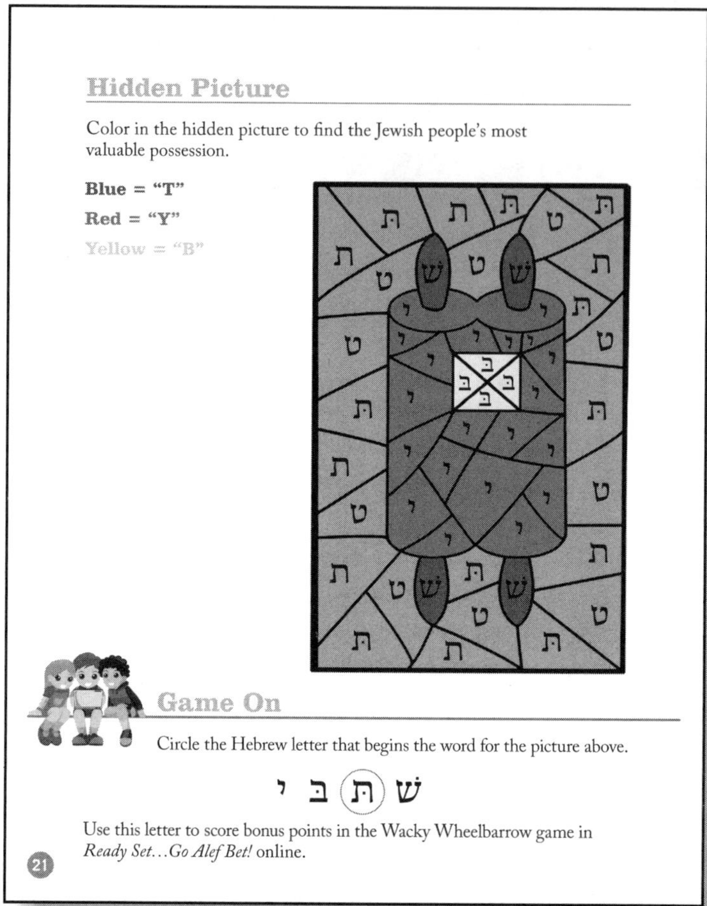
Hidden Picture

Color in the hidden picture to find the Jewish people's most valuable possession.

Blue = "T"
Red = "Y"
Yellow = "B"

Game On

Circle the Hebrew letter that begins the word for the picture above.

שׁ תּ בּ י

Use this letter to score bonus points in the Wacky Wheelbarrow game in *Ready Set...Go Alef Bet!* online.

21

Assessment

For information on assessing students' progress, see page 10. With the completion of this lesson, you can begin to administer the first oral assessment on page 137. Be sure to complete the error analysis for each student and make notes concerning students who have difficulty with oral reading. You should also make notes about students who had difficulty with any of the pre-reading skills covered in this lesson.

5 Nothing to Say

Pages: 22–25

Key Words: אַבָּא אִמָּא עִפָּרוֹן

New Letters: א ע

Recommended Materials: Phonics Flash Cards #7–11 and Word Picture Cards #10–12; a tie, a cardigan sweater, and a baby doll; a muffin tin, strips containing one letter or vowel each, and 2 sets of colored chips each in a different color; crayons or colored pencils.

Review Activity: Play Sound Toss (see page 16 for instructions), using all of the letters and vowels. Play continues until one team has three chips in one of the cups. Ask students to answer the questions you posed at the end of Lesson 4 (see page 39).

Oral Language Lesson

Begin class by taking attendance in the manner described on page 9. Teach students עֶרֶב טוֹב to say in the evening, or בֹּקֶר טוֹב along with the customary response בֹּקֶר אוֹר in the morning, and inquire how students are:

מָה שְׁלוֹמְךָ? מָה שְׁלוֹמֵךְ? טוֹב, טוֹב
מְאוֹד, לֹא טוֹב

Hold up a pencil and say, עִפָּרוֹן. Ask the class to repeat.

Review the two prepositions previously introduced (עַל and בַּ־) by saying a sentence and asking volunteers to set the props in the correct way. Sentences can include:

עִפָּרוֹן בַּיָּד.
עִפָּרוֹן עַל שֻׁלְחָן.

Volunteers should repeat the Hebrew sentence while performing the action or after completing it. Repeat several times, to provide students with ample review. Once you are satisfied that the students understand the sentences, you can increase the level of difficulty by setting up the props and asking students to provide a Hebrew sentence that correctly describes the arrangement.

Set Induction

Write the following English words on the board: Apple On Elephant

Ask students what all of these words have in common. (*they all start with vowels*) Remind students that Hebrew vowels are written as dots and dashes rather than letters. You can refer them back to page 20 if they do not remember this concept. Ask the class to divide the word "Elephant" into syllables. Once they correctly divide the word, write it in separate syllables on the board (el-e-phant). Direct the class to look at the second syllable of the word. What do they notice about it (*it is only a vowel*). Explain that Hebrew vowels cannot stand by themselves, they always need a letter to help them.

Allow a volunteer to read the chapter title. Ask the class what they think will be taught in this lesson. (*letters that don't have their own sound*) Explain that when one of those letters has a vowel with it, the only sound you hear is the vowel.

Introducing the Key Words and Deducing Their Sound-Symbol Associations

Ask for a boy to volunteer. Place the knotted necktie loosely

around his neck and ask him to hold the doll as if it were a baby. Present your actor to the class and say: אַבָּא. Ask students to repeat after you. Hold up Word Picture Card #10 and say: אַבָּא. Again, have students repeat.

Next, introduce the second key word, אִמָּא. Ask for a girl to volunteer. Drape the cardigan sweater over her shoulders and ask her to hold the doll as if it were a baby. Present your actress to the class and say: אִמָּא. Have students repeat the word. Hold up Word Picture Card #11 and say: אִמָּא. Again, have students repeat.

Tell the two actors to pass the doll back and forth while the class identifies who has the baby by using the key words אַבָּא and אִמָּא. Continue until you are sure that the class understands both words. Then, repeat the words with the adjectives טוֹב/טוֹבָה or חָזָק/חֲזָקָה. This step will teach students the genders of the new words in a natural manner.

Introduce the new letter א using the "Multisensory Approach to Hebrew Sound-Symbol Associations" described on page 12.

Next, review the key word, עִפָּרוֹן. Hold up a pencil and ask who remembers what it is called in Hebrew. Repeat this step using Word Picture Card #12. Once you feel that the students remember the word, repeat it in conjunction with the adjectives גָּדוֹל/קָטָן. This step will teach students the masculine gender of the word עִפָּרוֹן.

Introduce the new letter ע using the "Multisensory Approach to Hebrew Sound-Symbol Associations" described on page 12. Ask students what they notice about the two new letters. (*neither has a sound of its own; they make the sound of the vowel that accompanies them*) Since the new letters א and ע do not represent a sound of their own, ask students to tightly cover their mouths with their hands when you present them with the letter shapes.

Students have been introduced to the three "ah" vowels and all three can accompany א and ע. Provide students with opportunities to blend each of the new letters with those vowels.

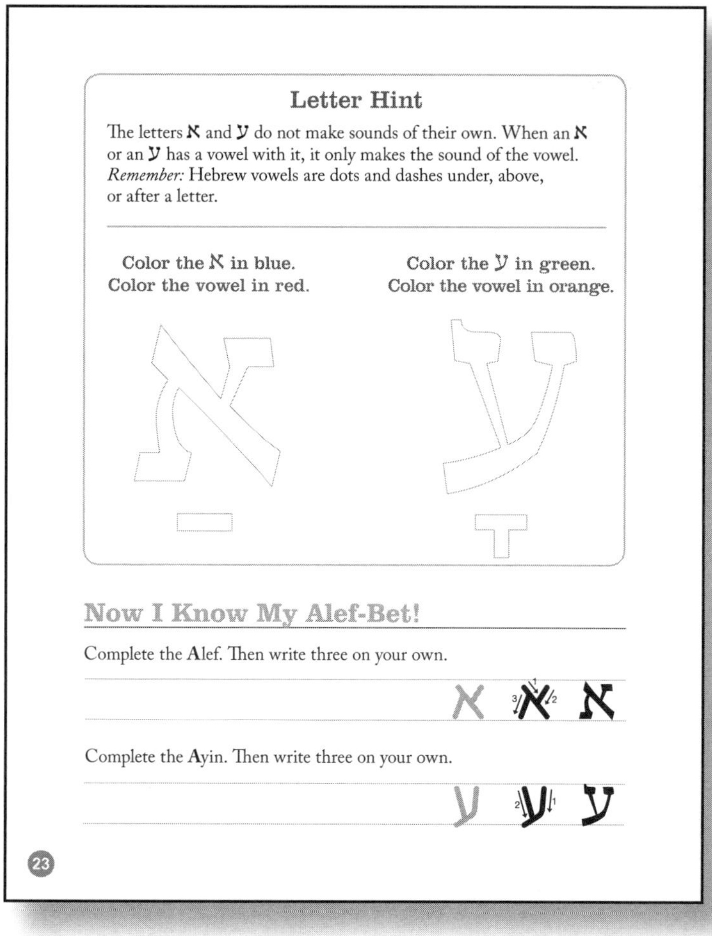
Letter Hint

The letters א and ע do not make sounds of their own. When an א or an ע has a vowel with it, it only makes the sound of the vowel. *Remember:* Hebrew vowels are dots and dashes under, above, or after a letter.

Color the א in blue. Color the vowel in red.

Color the ע in green. Color the vowel in orange.

Now I Know My Alef-Bet!

Complete the Alef. Then write three on your own.

א א א

Complete the Ayin. Then write three on your own.

ע ע ע

23

Take a Closer Look!

In this activity, students are asked to focus on individual letter shapes by crossing out any letter on the line that differs from the one in the box. Since students have had previous experience with this type of activity, ask a volunteer to read the instructions and allow students to complete the lines individually. Circulate to provide help as needed.

Letter Hint & Color the Letter

Distribute crayons or colored pencils. Ask volunteers to read the sentence in the first Letter Hint. Review the three vowels learned last lesson using Phonics Flash Cards #7–9. Give students time to color in the letters and vowels.

Now I Know My Alef-Bet!

Ask students to trace the letter on the first line, first with their fingers and then in pencil. Next, ask them to write three examples of the letter in pencil. Repeat this procedure with the letter on the second line. Since these two letters do not represent sounds on their own, students should cover their mouths with the hand they do not use for writing.

You're an Artist!

Your teacher will read these sentences to you. Draw a picture to illustrate lines 1–3.

1. שַׁבָּת בַּבַּיִת.
2. אַבָּא בַּבַּיִת.
3. אִמָּא בַּבַּיִת.
4. "שַׁבַּת שָׁלוֹם, אַבָּא."
5. "שַׁבַּת שָׁלוֹם, אִמָּא."
6. שָׁלוֹם בַּבַּיִת.

24

You're an Artist!

This activity reviews some of the Hebrew vocabulary that students have learned. Read the first three sentences and ask students where the action is taking place. (בַּבַּיִת) Ask when the story is taking place (שַׁבָּת) and who is described in the sentences. (אַבָּא and אִמָּא) You may need to reread the sentences a few times until students fully understand them. Read the final three sentences and ask how each each parent is greeted (שַׁבַּת שָׁלוֹם). Finally, ask what kind of atmosphere can be felt on שַׁבָּת. (שָׁלוֹם)

Once you are confident that students understand, ask them to draw an illustration for some part of the story. You may need to reread the entire passage several times as students complete their pictures. This will give them the opportunity to hear and recall more of the elements of the passage, which they may wish to incorporate into their drawings.

Crack the Code

This activity allows students to find letters that represent the same sound. In some instances they will simply need to find the letter that is identical to the one in the box, while other lines contain letters that represent the same sound but look quite different. Since this is a more complex activity than the previous ones that required sound-symbol associations and visual discrimination, you should work through the activity as a class.

Ask volunteers to read the little poem at the top of the page and the instructions that follow it. Call on individual students to complete a line and share which letter should be circled. Students who are struggling but who want to participate should be allowed to do lines 2 or 4, as these lines will not affect the code.

Once all of the lines have been completed, and the correct letters circled, ask students to find the letter they circled on line one and write that letter in the first space. You may need to remind them that Hebrew is written from right to left. Ask a volunteer which line provides the next clue. (*3*) Direct students to find the circled letter and write it in the middle space. Repeat for the final clue as well.

Ask if anyone can read the whole word (שַׁבָּת), and praise them for having really read their first Hebrew word!

Game On

The word that students found when they cracked the code in the previous activity provides a key for scoring extra points in the game for Lesson 5 of the digital companion. Ask a volunteer to tell you what word he or she discovered. Ask the rest of the class if they came up with that word or another one. If there is a dispute about the word (שַׁבָּת), review as a class.

Ask students to complete Lesson 5 in the digital companion at home. Remind them to play the Jungle Jump game when they have completed the lesson. You might ask students to print out or e-mail their lesson summaries to you when they have completed all the activities in the lesson. Or

Crack the Code

I'm a very special day,
For rest, for study, and for play.
Crack the code in this little game
And you will find my Hebrew name!

On each line, circle the letter that sounds the same as the one in the box.

(שׁ)	בּ	ת	ט	שׁ	.1
ט	בּ	שׁ	(י)	י	.2
שׁ	(בּ)	ת	תּ	בּ	.3
י	שׁ	(ט)	בּ	תּ	.4
(ת)	שׁ	י	בּ	ט	.5

Write the circled letters from lines 1, 3, and 5 in the numbered spaces below.

ת בָּ שַׁ
5 3 1

Game On

Use the word you filled in above to score bonus points in the Jungle Jump game in *Ready Set...Go Alef Bet!* online.

25

assess their progress in the Behrman House Online Learning Center.

Challenge students to come to the next class with answers to the questions below. They will find the answers in Lesson 5 of the digital companion. Consider sending home a sheet with these questions, or e-mail them to parents, when you assign the lesson in the digital companion. Ask students to write the answers on the sheet and return it, with a parent's signature, at the next class.

1. What letter should be crossed out twice in the "Take a Closer Look" activity? (ע)
2. Look at the last two lines of the "Crack the Code" activity. What letters all make the same sound? (ט, תּ, *and* ת)

When students complete this lesson in the digital companion, and you have checked that they have done so, allow them to color in the א and the ע on the Alef-Bet Chart on page 4 of their book.

Assessment

For information on assessing students' progress, see page 10. With this lesson, students have been introduced to all of the material that is covered in the first written

assessment, Assessment 1 on page 138. Based on the notes you have made during previous lessons, you may wish to administer this assessment to the class. If you feel that many students are not yet in command of the material, you can delay administering a formal assessment until they have completed an additional lesson or two. Continue administering the first oral assessment to students who have not yet completed it. As always, make notes on student progress, paying special attention to areas in which individual learners are having trouble.

example, you can say: עִפָּרוֹן בַּיָּד. Ask a volunteer to act out this sentence using the correct props, repeating the Hebrew sentence while performing the action or after completing it. Repeat several times asking all but the best language students to have a turn.

Sample sentences include:

טַלִּית בַּיָּד.
יָד בַּיָּד.
תּוֹרָה בַּיָּד.
עִפָּרוֹן בַּיָּד.
מְזוּזָה בַּיָּד.

Once students can respond to the sentences they hear (receptive language), reverse roles by arranging the props and asking volunteers to produce the Hebrew sentences. For example, place the tallit in your hand and ask a volunteer to create a Hebrew sentence that describes this arrangement. (טַלִּית בַּיָּד) Instruct the class to repeat the sentence if the student is correct. If the class remains silent, allow the volunteer to correct his or her sentence. Begin with the strongest language students in the class. You can drill the

6 Make Magic!

Pages: 26–30

Key Words: מְזוּזָה שָׁלוֹם

New Letters: מ/ם

Recommended Materials: Phonics Flash Cards #1–9 and #12–13 with fun tac or magnetic tape for posting on the board, Word Picture Cards #5 and 13; a tallit, a model Torah, a Torah pointer, a pencil, a mezuzah case (and parchment if possible); crayons or colored pencils

Review Activity: Play Tic-Tac-Toe (see page 16 for instructions) using all of the letters except א and ע, and all of the vowels that students have learned to date. Place the vowels and the letter ט in the center square and three of the four corners of the game. Divide the class into two teams.

Play continues over several games until each student has had at least one turn. When you redo the game board, vary the positions of the letters and vowels. After the game, ask students to answer the questions you posed at the end of Lesson 5 (see page 43).

Oral Language Lesson

Begin class by taking attendance in the manner described on page 9. Remember to add a greeting for the correct time of day, עֶרֶב טוֹב in the evening, or בֹּקֶר טוֹב with the customary response בֹּקֶר אוֹר in the morning, and inquiries into how students are:

מַה שְּׁלוֹמְךָ? מַה שְּׁלוֹמֵךְ? טוֹב,
טוֹב מְאוֹד, לֹא טוֹב

Hold up a mezuzah case and say מְזוּזָה. Ask the class to repeat. Once you feel that the students understand the word, repeat it with the adjectives גְּדוֹלָה/קְטַנָּה. This step will teach students that מְזוּזָה is a feminine word. Review the preposition -בַּ, introduced in a previous lesson, by using it with all of the appropriate key words and vocabulary items that students have learned so far. You should review the sentences that students have learned that include this preposition by creating a sentence and asking students to create the correct display. For

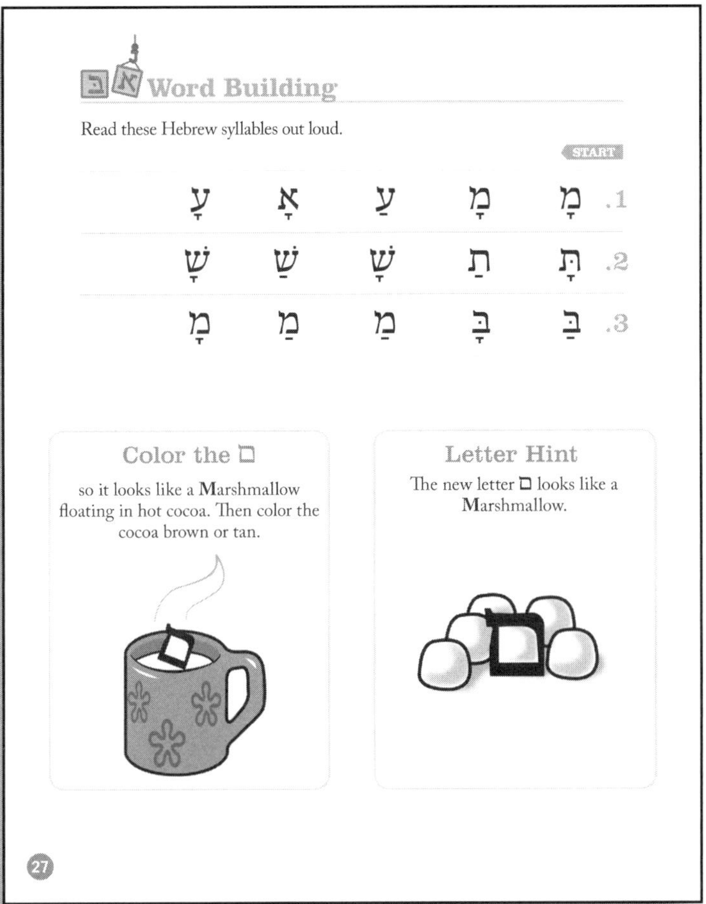

Word Building

Read these Hebrew syllables out loud.

START

עָ	אָ	עַ	מָ	מָ	.1
שָׁ	שַׁ	שָׁ	תַ	תָּ	.2
מָ	מַ	מַ	בָּ	בַּ	.3

Color the ם

so it looks like a **M**arshmallow floating in hot cocoa. Then color the cocoa brown or tan.

Letter Hint

The new letter ם looks like a **M**arshmallow.

27

same basic pattern by placing the pencil, mezuzah, model Torah, and the Torah pointer in your hand. Repeat until every student who wants the opportunity to create a Hebrew sentence has had one.

Word Building

Practice the basic blending skill that students learned in lesson 4 by asking them to read aloud from the Word Building section at the top of the page. You may want to begin by asking students to take turns reading a single item. As they gain confidence, ask them to read full lines. Then ask them to read columns of syllables, which is more difficult because the letters are different. As was the case with this activity on page 20, students are presented only with C-V syllables in this activity.

Letter Hint & Color the Letter

Ask a volunteer to read the sentence in the second Letter Hint. Write ם on the board and ask a volunteer to describe how the ם looks like a marshmallow. Give students time to color in the letter ם. Explain that ם appears only at the *end* of a word.

Set Induction

Hold up the mezuzah case and ask the class the Hebrew word for this item. Allow a volunteer to read the chapter title and ask what sound students think will be taught in this lesson. (*m*) Next, pass the מְזוּזָה around the class to allow students to feel it. If you have the parchment that goes inside the מְזוּזָה show it to the class. Ask students what other key word the parchment reminds them of. (תּוֹרָה) Tell them that the parchment inside of the מְזוּזָה contains a passage from the תּוֹרָה.

Introducing the Key Words and Deducing Their Sound-Symbol Associations

Introduce the new letter using the "Multisensory Approach to Hebrew Sound-Symbol Associations" described on page 12. Create a kinesthetic association by rubbing your stomach and say "mmm." As an alternative, ask students to use their bodies to form the letter מ by creating the yoga pose known as the camel pose. Direct the students to kneel and bend back with their arms reaching for their feet, their chests pointed toward the sky, and their heads relaxing backwards. No matter which kinesthetic association you use, ask the students to repeat the letter sound *m* while they do so.

Letter Hint & Color the Letter

Distribute crayons or colored pencils. Ask a volunteer to read the sentence in the Letter Hint at the bottom of the page. Write מ on the board and invite a volunteer to circle the part of the letter that looks like Moses climbing on the mountain. Give students time to color in the letter מ.

Now I Know My Alef-Bet!

Ask students to trace the letter on the first line with their fingers, then to trace it in pencil while repeating the sound that the letter represents. (*m*) Next, ask them to write three examples of the letter in pencil while repeating the letter's sound. Repeating the letter's sound provides an auditory reinforcement for the visual and kinesthetic activity. Repeat this procedure with the second line.

Climb the Mountain!

In Hebrew, some sounds are represented by more than one letter shape. Some letters have regular and final forms, like מ and ם. Other letters, like א and ע, are unrelated. Sometimes three different letter shapes represent a single sound, as is the case with ט, תּ, and ת. With this lesson, students have been introduced to three of these letter sets. This activity asks students to find the two letters that represent the same sound and draw a line between them. One letter is found on a mountain climber and the other on a mountain. After students complete the activity, you can explain to them that Moses and Mount Sinai contain the two forms of the new letter, מ. The Matterhorn and the Swiss Alpine climber match, while the climber in gear for extreme cold and very high altitudes matches Mount Everest.

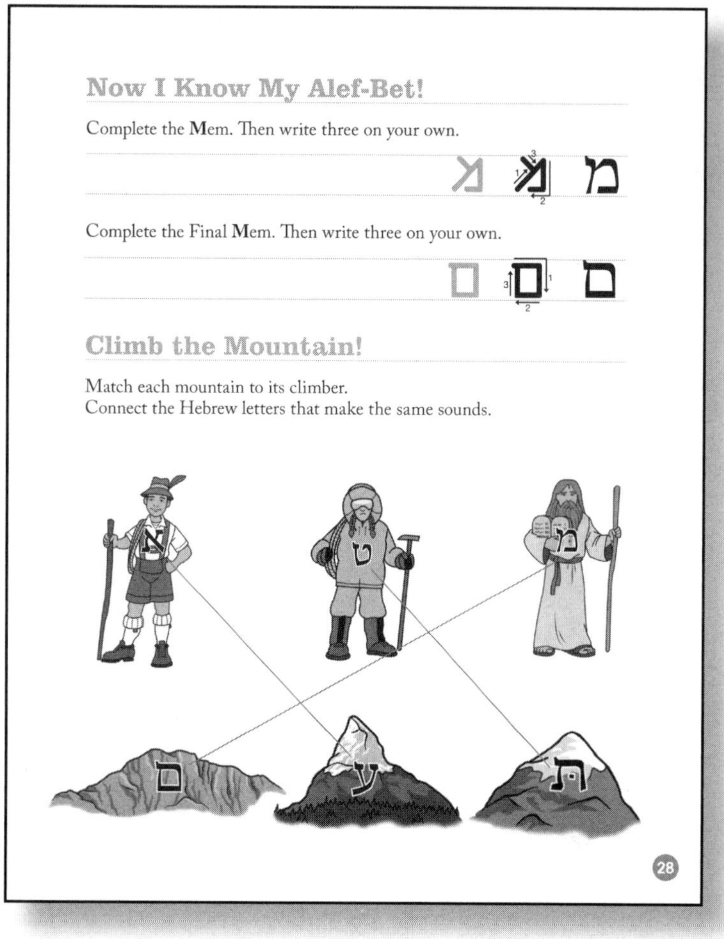
Now I Know My Alef-Bet!

Complete the Mem. Then write three on your own.

מ מ מ

Complete the Final Mem. Then write three on your own.

ם ם ם

Climb the Mountain!

Match each mountain to its climber.
Connect the Hebrew letters that make the same sounds.

28

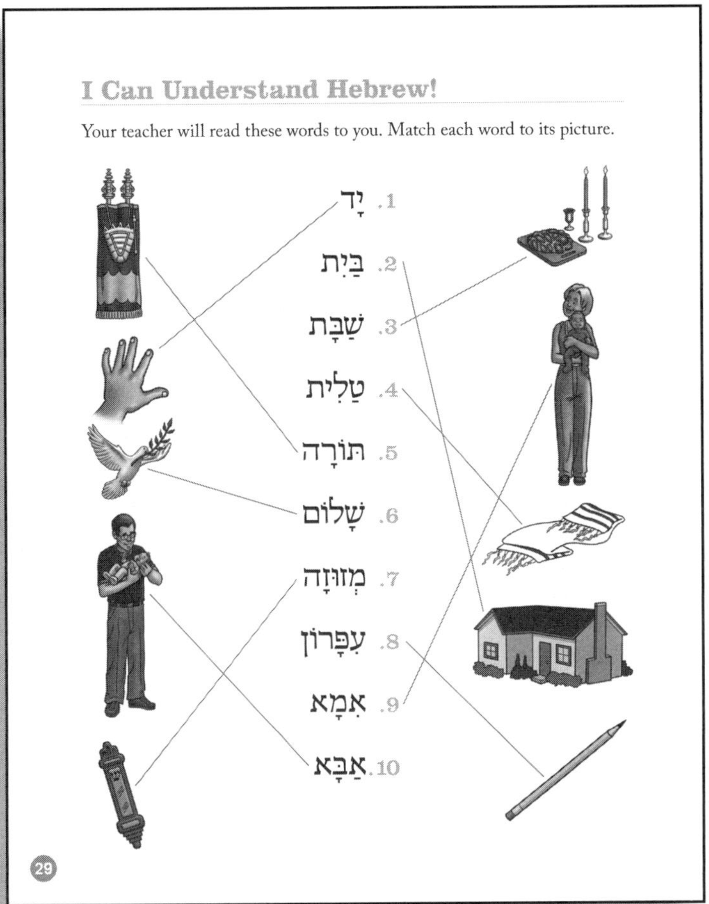

I Can Understand Hebrew!

Your teacher will read these words to you. Match each word to its picture.

1. יָד
2. בַּיִת
3. שַׁבָּת
4. טַלִּית
5. תּוֹרָה
6. שָׁלוֹם
7. מְזוּזָה
8. עִפָּרוֹן
9. אִמָּא
10. אַבָּא

29

I Can Understand Hebrew!

This activity reviews all of the key words that students have learned so far. Complete a sample together as a class. Read the first word and ask, "Who can show me their own יָד?" Allow volunteers to show the class what the word means. Then ask everyone to find the יָד drawing on the page (*second item down on the left*) and place their finger on the picture. Circulate to make sure that everyone has identified the correct picture. Ask students to draw a line between the first word and the item. When they have completed this, read the second word and ask students to find the correct picture. You may need to repeat the word several times to allow slower students to process it. Complete all ten words in this manner.

Letter By Letter

Point to the picture of the father and ask a volunteer to tell you the Hebrew word that describes the picture. (אַבָּא) Next, ask what letter that word begins with (if students have difficulty with this, refer them back to page 22 in their books). Allow students to complete the activity with a partner. In order to circle the letter, both partners have to agree on the choice. Circulate to assist as needed. If the partners can't agree on the letter, ask one of them to say the word and allow them to look back to the table of contents on page 2 to find the letter or letters that represent the first sound in the word.

Game On

This activity provides a mechanism for checking the students' answers to the Letter by Letter activity. At the same time, it provides a little additional practice with fine visual discrimination as the letters מ and ט are visually similar. Ask a volunteer which letter he or she circled three times. Ask the rest of the class if they came up with that letter or another one. If there is a dispute about the letter (ט), review as a class. You can also ask the class which letters they circled only once and which they circled twice. Ask students to complete Lesson 6 in the digital companion at home. Remind them to play the Hip Hop Hebrew game when they have completed the lesson. You might ask students to print out or e-mail their lesson summaries to you when they have completed all the activities in the lesson. Or assess their progress in the Behrman House Online Learning Center.

Challenge students to come to the next class with answers to the questions below. They will find the answers in Lesson 6 of the digital companion. Consider sending home a sheet with these questions, or e-mail them to parents, when you assign the lesson in the digital companion. Ask students to write the answers on the sheet and return it, with a parent's signature, at the next class.

1. What happens with the מ in the Letter Hint? (*Moses climbs the mountain*)
2. Which Hebrew letter should be circled twice in the first "Letter by Letter" activity? (ט)

Letter by Letter

Circle the Hebrew letter that begins each word.

Game On

Which letter did you circle three times? Draw a box around it below.

מ ט א

Use this letter to score bonus points in the Hip Hop Hebrew game in *Ready Set...Go Alef Bet!* online.

30

3. Which Hebrew letter should be circled twice in the second "Letter by Letter" activity? (א)
4. What inventory item did you collect in the Hip Hop Hebrew game? (*mezuzah*)

When students complete this lesson in the digital companion, and you have checked that they have done so, allow them to color in the מ and the ם on the Alef-Bet Chart on page 4 of their book.

Assessment

For information on assessing students' progress, see page 10. In this lesson, make notes about students who had difficulty with any of the information. You can also continue listening to individual students complete the first oral assessment.

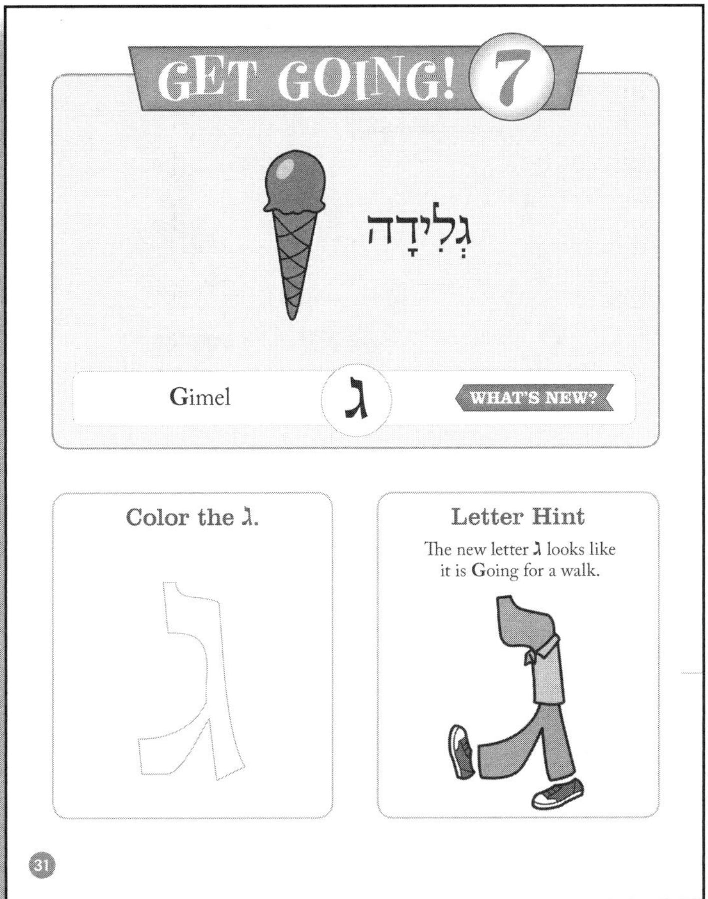

7 Get Going!

Pages: 31–35

Key Word: גְלִידָה

New Letter: ג

Vocabulary Word: (rain) גֶשֶׁם

Cognates: גּוֹלְף, קֶטְשַׁאפּ, קוֹלָה, קַנְגָּרוּ, גּוֹרִילָה, גִיטָרָה

Recommended Materials: Phonics Flash Cards #1–9 and #12–14, and Word Picture Cards #1–16; a CD player and CDs of Jewish or Israeli music; a tallit, model Torah, Torah pointer, pencil, mezuzah case, tie, cardigan sweater, baby doll, and umbrella; crayons or colored pencils.

Review Activity: Play Musical Sounds (see page 16 for instructions) using all the letters and vowels learned so far except א and ע. Continue until each student has had at least one opportunity to play. Ask students to answer the questions you posed at the end of Lesson 6 (see page 49).

Oral Language Lesson

Begin class by taking attendance as described on page 9. Review all the key words using the Word Picture Cards. Hold up a card and ask a volunteer to identify the item in Hebrew. If the class agrees that the volunteer is correct, they should repeat the word. If the class is silent, the student should try to correct his or her answer.

Next, review the two prepositions that students have previously learned (בַּ, עַל). You can ask students to create the sentences they have previously heard that include these prepositions by acting them out and asking volunteers to describe the result in Hebrew. For example, place the tallit in your hand and ask a volunteer to create a Hebrew sentence that describes this arrangement. (טַלִּית בַּיָּד) Instruct the class to repeat the sentence if the student is correct. If the class remains silent, allow the volunteer to correct his or her sentence. Repeat until each student has had the opportunity to create a Hebrew sentence. As an alternative, you can say a sentence and ask members of the class to create the correct display, repeating the sentence either while doing the task or after completing it. This is especially useful for students who are having difficulty with the oral language component, as silent comprehension is easier than active production and precedes it in natural language development. Sample sentences include:

טַלִּית בַּיָּד.
יָד עַל טַלִּית.
יָד בַּיָּד.
יָד עַל שֻׁלְחָן.
יָד עַל תּוֹרָה.
תּוֹרָה בַּיָּד.
טַלִּית עַל שֻׁלְחָן.

עִפָּרוֹן בַּיָּד.
עִפָּרוֹן עַל שֻׁלְחָן.
תּוֹרָה עַל שֻׁלְחָן.
מְזוּזָה עַל טַלִּית.
מְזוּזָה בַּיָּד.
מְזוּזָה עַל שֻׁלְחָן.

Once students can respond to the sentences they hear (receptive language), reverse roles by arranging the props and asking volunteers to produce the Hebrew sentences.

Set Induction

Allow a volunteer to read the chapter title. Ask the class what

sound they think they will learn this lesson. (*g*) Next, show the class a picture of ice cream and say: גְּלִידָה. Ask the students to repeat it. After several repetitions, ask volunteers "What is your favorite flavor of גְּלִידָה?" Teach some of the flavor names in Hebrew (e.g., תּוּת שָׂדֶה, וָנִיל, שׁוֹקוֹלָדָה—chocolate, vanilla, strawberry). Once you feel that the students understand the word גְּלִידָה, repeat it in conjunction with the adjective טוֹבָה. This step will teach students that גְּלִידָה is a feminine word. You can also teach the adjective קָרָה (cold) by miming the act of shivering.

Introducing the Key Words and Deducing Their Sound-Symbol Associations

Introduce the new letter using the "Multisensory Approach to Hebrew Sound-Symbol Associations" described on page 12. You can create a kinesthetic connection by imitating the grunts made by a gorilla. Hold up Word Picture Card #15, then bend your arms up along your sides like a gorilla while you say, "g...g!" Ask the class to repeat both the sound and the action.

As an alternative, ask students to create the letter shape through yoga. To create a ג stand with one leg slightly forward and one slightly back and arms held at an angle over the head as if preparing for a dive. No matter which kinesthetic association you use, ask the students to repeat the letter sound (g) while they do so.

Letter Hint & Color the Letter

Distribute crayons or colored pencils. Ask volunteers to read the sentence in the first Letter Hint. Write ג on the board. The class can act out the mnemonic by "going for a walk" around the classroom while repeating the letter's sound. Give students time to color in the letter.

Now I Know My Alef Bet

Ask students to trace the letter with their fingers then to trace it in pencil, while repeating the sound that the letter represents. (*g*) Next, ask them to write three examples of the letter in pencil while repeating the letter's sound.

Now I Know My Alef-Bet!

Complete the **Gimel**. Then write three on your own.

ג ג ג

Sound Check

The names of these objects sound similar in Hebrew and English. Cross out all the objects that do not begin with the new letter ג.

32

Sound Check

This activity provides students with practice in segmenting the initial phoneme of several cognates. At the same time, it provides students with practice in making fine auditory distinctions. The sounds *g* and *k* are fairly similar, and some students confuse them. Students struggling with this activity may need individual practice with the skill.

Begin by providing students with the Hebrew pronunciation of each item in the activity (גּוֹלְף, קֶטְשׁאפּ, קוֹלָה, קַנְגָּרוּ, גּוֹרִילָה, גִּיטָרָה). Ask them to point to each item as you say its Hebrew name. Circulate to make sure that everyone can complete this crucial first step. Next, ask a volunteer to read the instructions. Select a volunteer to identify the item on the right side of the top line. Encourage each volunteer to use the Hebrew pronunciation. Tell the class to listen for the first sound in the word then ask the volunteer to say it clearly. Ask the class what sound they heard at the beginning. (*g*) Ask them to look at the Hebrew letter in the instruction, and ask them, "Does this word begin with the sound of the letter ג?" Once students understand that the word begins with the ג, tell them to leave that picture as it is. Repeat this procedure for the second item on the top line. Here, students should

Word Building

Some syllables end in a vowel. Others end in a consonant. When a Hebrew syllable ends in a consonant, the consonant is the last sound you say.

Read these Hebrew syllables out loud.

START

1. בָּ בַּ בָּם אָ עַם
2. גַ גָ גָם שַׁ שָׁם
3. טַ תָּ תָּם יָ יָם
4. בָּם גַם עַם תָּם יָם
5. מַט גַת בַּת אַט תַּת

Take a Closer Look!

Circle the Hebrew letter that begins each word.

(מ) ט ע   מ (ט) ע   מ ט (ע)

33

confidence, ask them to read full lines. Once students have completed reading the syllables in rows, ask them to read columns of syllables.

Take a Closer Look!

In this activity, students are asked to segment the letter that begins each of the key words presented. At the same time, they are required to focus on individual letter shapes, distinguishing between the visually similar letters מ, ט, and ע. They are then asked to select and circle the letter that begins each word. Ask a volunteer to read the instructions and allow students to complete the activity individually. Circulate to provide help as needed.

realize that the word begins with the sound *k*. Once they understand that it begins with a different sound, ask them to cross out the picture. Allow them complete the activity individually or with a partner. Be sure to tell them that they need to say each Hebrew word out loud as they work. Circulate to provide assistance as needed, paying attention especially to those students who had difficulty with the oral presentation.

For fun, ask students to mime some of the Hebrew words they already know that begin with the *g* sound (גְלִידָה, גוֹלְף, גוֹרִילָה, גִיטָרָה). If the class is adept at discriminating between similar sounds, you can intersperse some of the words that begin with similar sounds (e.g., קַנְגָרוּ, קוֹלָה) to make the activity more challenging.

Word Building

Even though the class was introduced to a final letter in the previous lesson (ם), this is the first time that they are being asked to blend C-V-C syllables. Many beginning readers have difficulty learning how to blend the final consonant onto the end of the word. Look out for any student who adds an extra vowel sound to the end of the C-V-C syllable, reading for example *"bama"* for בָּם. Students who have difficulty with this type of blending may need additional reinforcement. Work with these students in a small group. Write pairs of syllables one above the other:

בָּגַ אַתָא יָמַ בָּתַ

בָּג אָט יָם בָּת

Model reading the first pair on the right and ask the students what is different about the two items. (*the one on top has an extra vowel*) Once students can hear the difference, focus on the second row. Read the entire line, asking the group to repeat each word after you. Then, ask individuals to read the items. If they read the item correctly, the group should repeat it.

Practice the C-V and C-V-C syllable blending skills by asking students to read aloud from the Word Building section at the top of page 33. You may want to begin by asking students to take turns reading a single item. As they gain

I Can Understand Hebrew!

Hold up Word Picture Card #16 and say: גֶּשֶׁם. Ask the class to repeat. Once you feel that the students understand the word, repeat the term with the adjective קַר. This step will teach students that גֶּשֶׁם is a masculine word.

Next, ask for a boy to volunteer. Place the knotted necktie loosely around his neck and ask him to hold the doll as if it were a baby. Present your actor to the class and say: אַבָּא. Ask students to repeat after you. Next, ask for a girl to volunteer. Drape the cardigan sweater over her shoulders and ask her to hold the doll as if it were a baby. Present your actress to the class and say: אִמָּא. Have students repeat the word. Open the umbrella and hand it to the boy and say, אַבָּא בַּגֶּשֶׁם.

Ask the class to repeat the sentence until most of the students understand it. Then, hand the umbrella to the girl and say: אִמָּא בַּגֶּשֶׁם. Repeat the sentence with the students joining in until you feel they understand it.

Ask a new volunteer to read the instructions in the middle of page 34. Remind the students that you will read the sentences from right to left. Read the first sentence and ask the class to circle the picture that matches it. You may need to repeat the sentence several times until all of the students understand it. Repeat the process for the three remaining sentences. Circulate to provide assistance as needed.

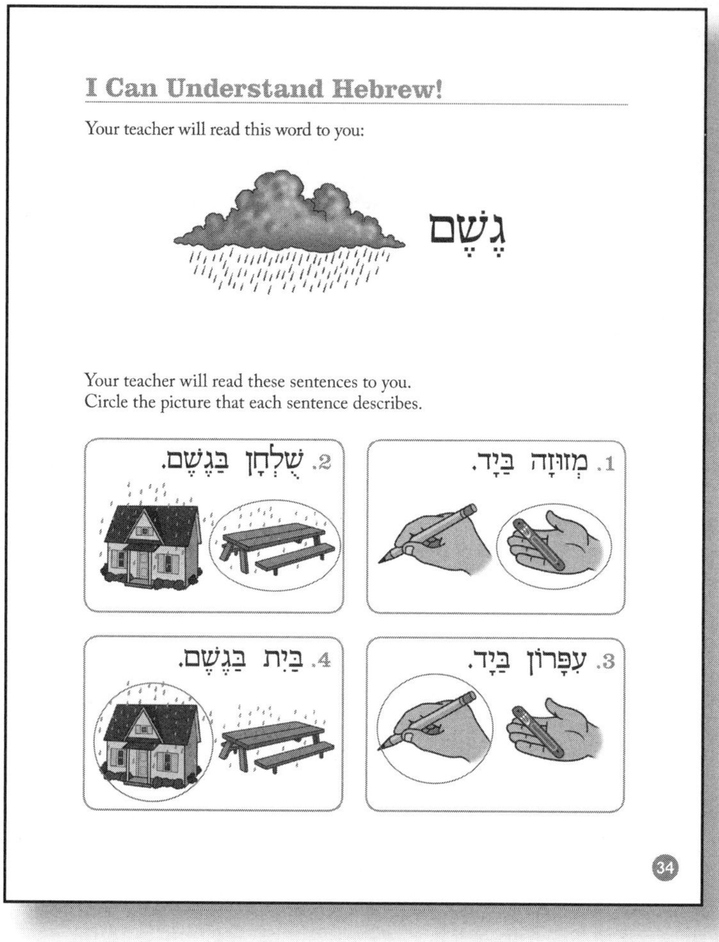

I Can Understand Hebrew!

Your teacher will read this word to you:

גֶּשֶׁם

Your teacher will read these sentences to you.
Circle the picture that each sentence describes.

1. מְזוּזָה בַּיָּד.

2. שֻׁלְחָן בַּגֶּשֶׁם.

3. עִפָּרוֹן בַּיָּד.

4. בַּיִת בַּגֶּשֶׁם.

34

End Game

Say the Hebrew name of each picture out loud.
Listen for the sound at the end of the word.
Circle all the items that end with the sound of "M."

Hint: You can look back at the words on pages 9, 22, and 34. All the other words are similar in Hebrew and English.

Game On

How many objects did you circle? 2

Draw a shape around the Hebrew letter that ends the words you circled.

שׁ (ם) ת

Use this letter to score bonus points in the Zero Gravity game in *Ready Set... Go Alef Bet!* online.

35

their progress in the Behrman House Online Learning Center.

Challenge students to come to the next class with answers to the questions below. They will find the answers in Lesson 7 of the digital companion. Consider sending home a sheet with these questions, or e-mail them to parents, when you assign the lesson in the digital companion. Ask students to write the answers on the sheet and return it, with a parent's signature, at the next class.

1. What does the ג do in the Letter Hint? (*it goes for a walk*)
2. What letter ends every syllable on line 4 of the "Word Building" activity? (ם)

When students complete this lesson in the digital companion, and you have checked that they have done so, allow them to color in the ג on the Alef-Bet Chart on page 4 of their book.

Assessment

For information on assessing students' progress, see page 10. Make notes concerning which students had difficulty with any of the information presented in this lesson. At this point, you should complete administering the first oral evaluation, making sure that every student has completed it.

End Game

It is easiest to isolate the initial sound of a word and most difficult to segment a sound from the middle of a word. Since students have had a fair amount of practice with initial segmentation, this activity focuses on final phonemes. At the same time, it provides students with practice in making fine auditory distinctions. The sounds *m* and *n* are quite similar, and some students have difficulty distinguishing between them. If a student struggles with this activity, it may indicate that he or she has difficulty with auditory distinctions and needs additional practice in this area.

Because this is the students' first exposure to segmenting phonemes in a new position, work through all of the items together. Begin by asking a volunteer to say the Hebrew name of the item on the right side of the top row. Tell the class to listen for the last sound in the word and ask the volunteer to say it clearly. Next, select a volunteer to read the instructions at the top of the page. Ask the class what sound they heard at the end. (*n*) Work as a class through the rest of the examples, encouraging volunteers to use the Hebrew pronunciation for all of the cognates in this activity. Circulate throughout to provide assistance as needed, paying attention especially to those students who had difficulty with the initial examples and those who have had difficulty with previous auditory discrimination or segmentation activities.

Game On

This activity provides a mechanism for checking the students' answers to the End Game activity. Ask a volunteer how many objects he or she circled. (2) Ask the rest of the class if they arrived at that number or another one. Ask a volunteer to identify the sound that ends the circled words, and tell the students to draw a circle around each item that ends with the sound *m*. Assign Lesson 7 in the digital companion for students to complete at home. Remind them to play the Zero Gravity game when they have completed the lesson. You might ask students to print out or e-mail their lesson summaries to you when they have completed all the activities in the lesson. Or assess

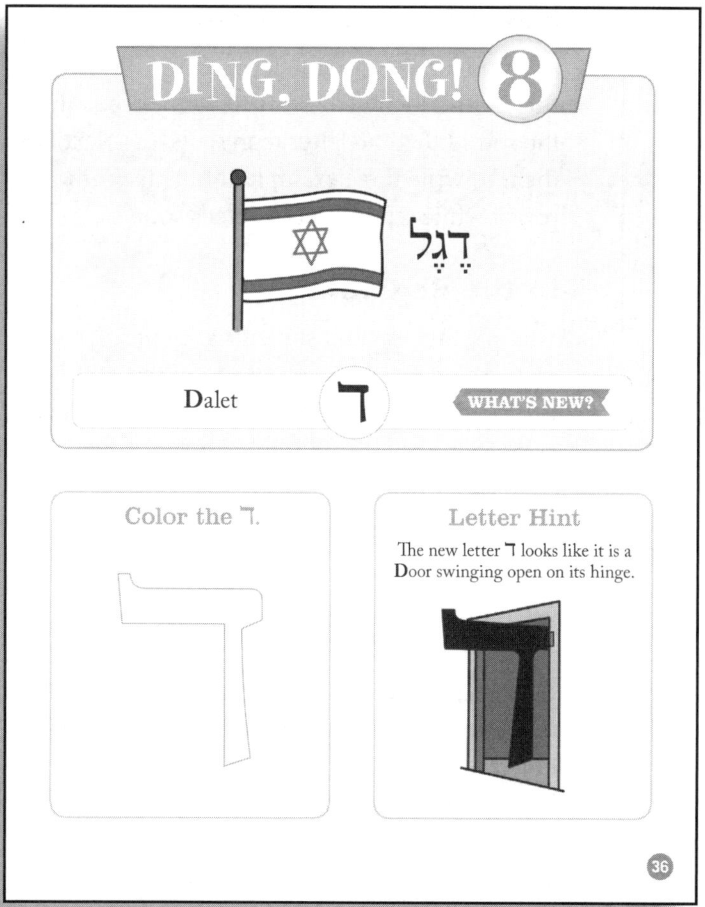

8 Ding, Dong!

Pages: 36–40

Key Word: דֶּגֶל

New Letter: ד

Vocabulary Words: (water) מַיִם, (fish) דָּג

Recommended Materials: Phonics Flash Cards #1–14 and #15–17, and Word Picture Cards #1–16 and #17–19; prepared Bingo cards and a pile of beans for each student; pictures of a pencil in water; a family, a fish, and a dolphin swimming (samples can be found on Google Images); large bottle or pitcher of water and cups; crayons or colored pencils.

Review Activity: Play Bingo (see page 17 for instructions) using cards divided into three rows and three columns filled with the letters that students have learned so far. Play continues until a winner can be declared. You can play a second round if the class is especially interested. Ask students to answer the questions you posed at the end of Lesson 7 (see page 54).

Oral Language Lesson

Begin class by taking attendance in the manner described on page 9.

Introduce ?מָה and ?מָה זֶה. Hold up the pencil and pose the question: ?מָה זֶה

Pause for 3–5 seconds then answer the question: .זֶה עִפָּרוֹן

Repeat until you feel that the class understands the question and the answer. Use the same process for שֻׁלְחָן, בַּיִת, and גֶּשֶׁם using Word Picture Cards #7, 8, and 16.

Set Induction

Allow a volunteer to read the chapter title. Ask the class what sound they think they will learn in this lesson. (*d*) Next, show students a small flag or a picture of a flag and say: דֶּגֶל. Ask students to repeat the word. Once you feel that the students understand the word, repeat it with the adjectives גָּדוֹל/קָטָן. This step will teach students that דֶּגֶל is a masculine word.

Introducing the Key Words and Deducing Their Sound-Symbol Associations

Introduce the new letter using the "Multisensory Approach to Hebrew Sound-Symbol Associations" described on page 12. Ask students to close their eyes and listen, then hold up a single sheet of paper and tap your fingers on it to create the sound of a drum. After a few seconds, say the sound *d...d* in sync with the pattering of your fingers on the paper. Ask the class to repeat the new sound while they create the sound of drumming. As an alternative, ask students to create the letter shape using their bodies. To create the ד ask students to stand with their feet together while they extend the left arm straight out from shoulder while bending the right arm at the elbow and placing their right hands behind their heads. No matter which kinesthetic association you use, ask the students to repeat the letter sound (*d*) while they do so.

Letter Hint & Color the Letter

Distribute crayons or colored pencils. Ask volunteers to read the sentence in the Letter Hint. Write ד large on the board and invite a volunteer to circle the hinge at the top of the letter. Give students time to color in the ד.

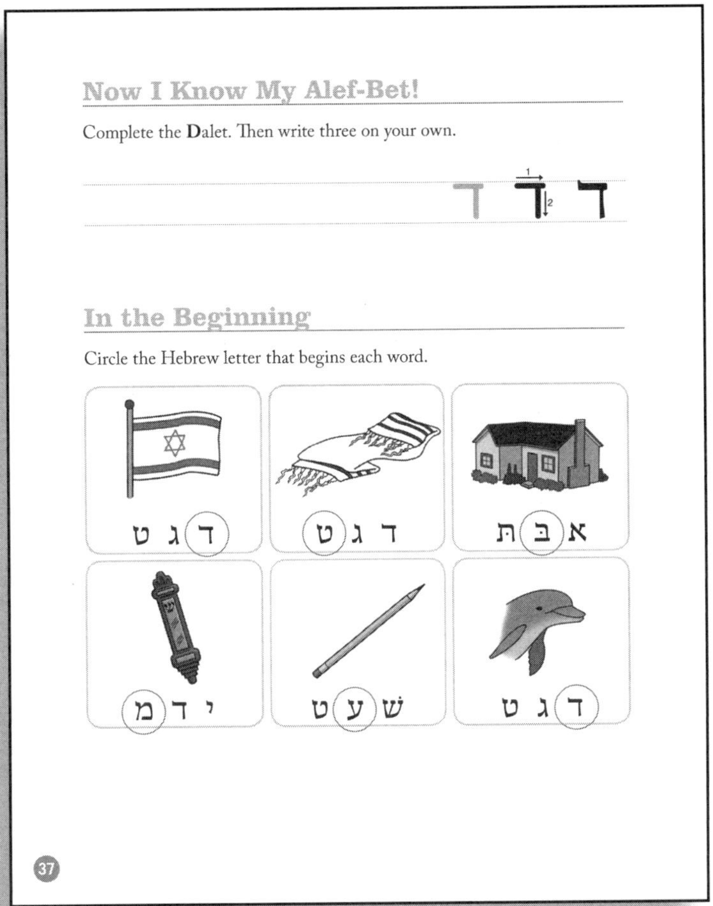
Now I Know My Alef-Bet!

Complete the **D**alet. Then write three on your own.

In the Beginning

Circle the Hebrew letter that begins each word.

ד ג ט | ד ג ט | א ב ת

י ד מ | שׁ ע ט | ד ג ט

37

Now I Know My Alef-Bet!

Ask students to trace the letter, first with their fingers and then with a pencil, while repeating the sound that the letter represents. (*d*) Next, ask them to write three examples of the letter in pencil while repeating the letter's sound.

In the Beginning

This activity provides students with practice in segmenting the initial phoneme of several key words and one cognate. It then provides students with practice in sound-symbol associations.

Ask volunteers to read the instructions and to identify the Hebrew name of the item on the right side of the top line. (בַּיִת) Tell the class to listen for the first sound in the word then ask the volunteer to say the word clearly. Ask the class what sound they heard at the beginning. (*b*) Ask them to look at the Hebrew letters below the object and ask them, Which letter does this word begin with? (בּ) If students have trouble, repeat this procedure for the middle item on the top line. Once they understand what they need to do, allow them to complete the remainder of this activity individually or with a partner. Circulate to provide assistance as needed. Pay close attention to students who confuse visually similar letters (like בּ/ת, ט/ע, and י/ד) and those that sound similar (ד/ט).

"Whoo-Whoo!"

This section presents students with the second vowel sound, *oo*. Like the "ah" that students encountered earlier, this sound can be represented by more than one symbol, in this case ▪ֻ and וּ. Make the sound of a train whistle. (*oo*) Tell students to look at the picture of the train, and especially at the speech bubble coming from its whistle. Ask them to point to the vowel on the right and say "oo." Repeat for the vowel on the left. You may want to remind students that the box represents any Hebrew letter. Next, ask students to draw the vowels in the air with their fingers while saying their sounds. Hold up three Tinkertoy spools evenly spaced and connected in a straight line with two medium rods and say "oo." Pass the Tinkertoys around so that students can feel their shape. Remind them to hold them at an angle pointing downward from left to right.

Write the vowels on the board, point to one and ask a volunteer to point to the one that looks like the Tinkertoys. Next, point to the first vowel and say "oo" with the class repeating after you. Repeat this procedure with both new vowels until you are confident that the students recognize them. Write a few Hebrew C-V syllables on the board, such as עֻ, גוּ, מוּ, יוּ, בַּ, שֻׁ, תוּ, and so on, leaving plenty of space between them. Invite volunteers to come up to the board. Say one of the syllables and ask the volunteer to point to it. Repeat the process with a variety of syllables until every student has had at least one turn. Then, write these C-V syllables scattered between the syllables you already have on the board: מָ, טָ, בַּ, אֲ, and so one. Repeat the drill as above mixing the syllables and allowing volunteers to identify them until you are confident that the class has a good grasp of all of the vowels and understands simple C-V blending.

Next, review C-V-C blending using a mixture of the vowels students know. These syllables should all end with a ם, as that is the only position in which this letter form can appear. Many beginning readers have difficulty learning how to blend the final consonant onto the end of the word and may need additional drill to master

"Whoo-Whoo!"

"OO" = וּ ◻ֻ

Word Building

Read each line aloud. *Remember*: When a syllable ends with a consonant, the consonant is the last sound you say.

START

גַ	מָ	בַּ	עֲ	דַ	.1
גֻ	מֻ	בּוּ	אוּ	דוּ	.2
מוּ	עֻ	גֻ	דֻ	יוּ	.3
מַם	יָם	גַם	עַם	דָם	.4
מוּם	יוּם	גֻ	אֻ	דֻ	.5

38

this skill. Pay attention for any student who adds an extra vowel sound to the end of the C-V-C syllable, reading for example *"bama"* for בָּם. Students who have difficulty with this type of blending may need additional reinforcement, preferably in a small group.

To bridge between syllable recognition and actual decoding, ask volunteers to come up to the board. Point to a syllable and ask the student to pronounce it. If the student is correct, the class should repeat the syllable. If the class is silent, the student should have the opportunity to correct the error.

Word Building

Ask a volunteer to read the directions for this activity, then have students take turns decoding. You may want to begin by asking students to read single items. As they gain confidence, ask them to read full lines. Once students can read whole lines of syllables, ask them to read columns of syllables to provide variety.

I Can Understand Hebrew!

Your teacher will read these words to you:

מַיִם

דָּג

You're an Artist!

Your teacher will read these sentences to you. Draw in what is missing from each picture.

1. בַּיִת בַּגֶּשֶׁם.

2. דָּג בַּמַּיִם.

3. דּוֹלְפִין בַּמַּיִם.

4. אַבָּא בַּגֶּשֶׁם. אִמָּא בַּגֶּשֶׁם.

39

I Can Understand Hebrew!

Take out a pitcher or bottle of water and a cup. Fill the cup with water and say: מַיִם. Sip the water from the cup, repeating the word מַיִם while pointing to the water in the cup. Pour a cup of water for each student and give each a cup, saying מַיִם each time you do. Hold up Word Picture Card #18 and say: מַיִם. Next, hold up Word Picture Card #19 and say: דָּג. Repeat this new word until you feel that the students understand it. You should also repeat it in conjunction with the adjectives גָּדוֹל/קָטָן. This step will teach students that דָּג is masculine.

Once students understand both new words, hold up a picture of a family swimming, point to the father, and say (with the class repeating):

אַבָּא בַּמַּיִם.

Point to the mother and say (with the class repeating):

אִמָּא בַּמַּיִם.

Hold up the picture of a fish swimming and ask:

מַה בַּמַּיִם? (דָּג בַּמַּיִם.)

Select volunteers to respond. Repeat the question alternating between the pictures of the dolphin, the fish, and the mother and father in water.

You're an Artist!

Ask a volunteer to read the directions. Tell the students to complete the pictures as you read the sentences. Start with number 1, and read the sentence. You may need to repeat it several times while the students complete their drawings. Circulate, providing assistance as necessary. Continue until every student has completed all four drawings.

End Game

In this activity, students are given additional practice in segmenting the final phoneme of several key words, a skill that is more difficult than segmenting initial phonemes. At the same time, it provides students with practice in making the fine auditory distinction between *t* and *d*. Since this is the second time that students have had practice with this pair of similar sounds, a student who struggles with this activity may have significant difficulty with auditory discrimination and should receive additional practice in this area. This is especially true for students who had the same kind of trouble with either the Sound Check activity on page 8 or the End Game activity on page 35.

Ask a volunteer to read the directions at the top of the page. Work through one example together.

Ask a volunteer to identify the items on the top right. Tell the class to listen for the last sound in the word שַׁבָּת. (*t*) Next, ask which of the letters under the picture represent the sound "*t*." Allow students to work in pairs to complete the remaining examples. Circulate to provide assistance as necessary.

If any student has difficulty identifying the letter that represents the correct sound, ask him or her to isolate the sound using the mnemonics taught for each of the letter choices.

If the student has difficulty isolating the final sound, does not recall the mnemonics, or has forgotten the Hebrew terms for the items pictured, he or she may need one-on-one assistance in mastering Hebrew pre-reading skills.

Game On

This activity provides a mechanism for checking the students' answers to the End Game activity. Ask volunteers how many times they circled the שׁ, בּ, י, ג, ת, ם, ע, and ד. After the volunteer answers for each letter, ask the rest of the class if they came up with these numbers or other ones.

Ask students to write the correct answer to Game On on the line provided. (ד) Assign Lesson 8 in the digital companion for students to complete

End Game

Say the Hebrew name of each picture out loud. Listen for the sound at the end of the word. Then circle the Hebrew letter that ends the word.

Hint: You can look back to the Key Words on pages 5, 9, 13, and 17.

י ד ת ם   שׁ ב ת ד

ג ע ד ת   ת ב י ג

Game On

Write the letter that was circled only once in the activity above.

ד

Use this letter to score bonus points in the Wacky Wheelbarrow game in *Ready Set...Go Alef Bet!* online.

40

at home. Remind them to play the Wacky Wheelbarrow game when they have completed the lesson. You might ask students to print out or e-mail their lesson summaries to you when they have completed all the activities in the lesson. Or assess their progress in the Behrman House Online Learning Center.

Challenge students to come to the next class with answers to the questions below. They will find the answers in Lesson 8 of the digital companion. Consider sending home a sheet with these questions, or e-mail them to parents, when you assign the lesson in the digital companion.. Ask students to write the answers on the sheet and return it, with a parent's signature, at the next class.

1. What does the ד do in the Letter Hint? (*it swings like a door on its hinge*)
2. What vowel sound is found in every syllable on lines 2, 4, and 6 of the "Word Building" activity? (*oo*)
3. What letter ends only one word in the "End Game" activity? (ד)

When students complete this lesson in the digital companion, and you have checked that they have done so, allow them to color in the ד on the Alef-Bet Chart on page 4 of their book.

Assessment

For information on assessing students' progress, see page 10. With this lesson, students have learned all the items tested in the second oral assessment on page 137. Evaluate a few volunteers on this second assessment, asking them to read the syllables aloud while you complete the error analysis. You will also want to make notes concerning which students had difficulty with any of the information presented.

9 Keep Cool!

Pages: 41–44

Key Words: כִּפָּה קִדּוּשׁ

New Letters: כּ ק

Vocabulary Words: (class) כִּתָּה, (female teacher) מוֹרָה

Recommended Materials: Phonics Flash Cards #18 and #19, and Word Picture Cards #20–23; a picture of a seagull; a muffin tin and strips containing one letter or vowel each; 2 sets of colored chips each in a different color; a kippah and a Kiddush cup; crayons or colored pencils.

Review Activity: Play Sound Toss (see page 16 for instructions) using all of the letters and vowels that students have learned so far. Focus especially on ם, מ, ד, ג, עֱ, אֲ, and ט. Play continues until each student has had at least one turn. Ask students to answer the questions you posed at the end of Lesson 8 (see page 59).

Oral Language Lesson

Begin class by taking attendance in the manner described on page 9. Inquire how students are doing:

מָה שְׁלוֹמְךָ? מָה שְׁלוֹמֵךְ? טוֹב, טוֹב מְאוֹד, לֹא טוֹב, לֹא רָע, מְצוּיָּן, בְּסֵדֶר

Be sure to include: the polite response:

__________ תּוֹדָה, וְאַתָּה/וְאַתְּ?

Review the question מָה זֶה?

Introduce the pronoun זֹאת and contrast it with זֶה:

מָה זֶה? זֶה עִפָּרוֹן.
מָה זֹאת? זֹאת תּוֹרָה.

After introducing the concept, review by creating sentences and asking students to create the correct display. For example, you can say: זֶה שֻׁלְחָן. Ask a volunteer to act out this sentence by pointing out or holding up the correct object. Once you are confident that students have grasped the usage of זֶה and זֹאת, allow students to create their own sentences. Ask a volunteer to select an object and hold it up or point it out to the class. Allow students to call out מָה זֶה? or מָה זֹאת? The volunteer then responds using the correct form,

__________ זֶה or __________ זֹאת

The student who calls out the correct question first gets to take the next turn to select an object.

Set Induction

Allow a volunteer to read the chapter title. Ask the class what sound they think they will learn in this lesson. (*k*) Next, ask students if they know the Hebrew name of the special Jewish head covering. (כִּפָּה) You may need to give them the hint that the word begins with the sound *k*. Ask when they see people wearing a כִּפָּה. (*when they study or pray, in the synagogue, all the time*) Show a כִּפָּה to the class and ask them to repeat the word. Once you feel that the students understand the word, repeat it with the adjective גְּדוֹלָה/קְטַנָּה/יָפָה. This step will teach students that כִּפָּה is a feminine word.

Next, ask if anyone knows the Hebrew name of the prayer we say over wine or grape juice—a word that also begins with the sound *k*. (קִדּוּשׁ) You can pass a Kiddush cup around the

Color the ק.

Letter Hint

The new letter ק looks like a **C**ane to lean on.

Now I Know My Alef-Bet!

Complete the **K**af. Then write three on your own.

כּ כּ כּ

Complete the **K**oof. Then write three on your own.

ק ק ק

42

Letter Hint & Color the Letter

Select volunteers to read the sentences in the boxes containing the Letter Hint and the coloring activity. Give students time to color in the כּ and the ק.

Now I Know My Alef-Bet!

Ask students to trace the letter on the first line with their fingers and to trace it in pencil, while repeating the sound that the letter represents. (*k*) Next, ask them to write three examples of the letter in pencil while repeating the letter's sound. Ask students to follow the same procedure with the letter ק.

class to strengthen the students' understanding of the new word.

Introducing the Key Words and Deducing Their Sound-Symbol Associations

Introduce the new letter using the "Multisensory Approach to Hebrew Sound-Symbol Associations" described on page 12. Create a kinesthetic link between the letter shape and its sound by imitating the cry of a seagull. Show the class a picture of a seagull then flap your arms while you say, "Ka...Ka!" Ask the class to repeat the action and the sound. As an alternative, ask students to create the letter shape using their bodies. The pose for ק is a variation of the classic "tree pose" in yoga. It requires students to stand on their left legs with their right legs bent and the right foot resting against the left knee. They should also place their hands together in front. You can also distribute clay or play dough to the students and allow them to form the letters in three dimensions. No matter what activity you use, ask the students to repeat the letters' sound, *k*, while they do the activity.

Letter Hint & Color the Letter

Distribute crayons or colored pencils. Ask volunteers to read the sentence in the box containing the Letter Hint. Write כ on the board and invite a volunteer to add the "cough drop." Ask a volunteer to read the directions in the other box. Before coloring in the letter, ask the class to turn the page.

I Can Understand Hebrew!

Introduce the two new vocabulary words, מוֹרָה and כִּתָּה. Hold up Word Picture Card #22 and say מוֹרָה, asking the class to repeat as soon as they understand. Point to the picture at the top of page 43 and say מוֹרָה, asking the class to repeat. If you are a female teacher, introduce yourself by saying:

שְׁמִי ________. אֲנִי מוֹרָה.

If you are male, say:

שְׁמִי ________. אֲנִי מוֹרֶה.

Once you feel that the students understand the word, repeat it with the adjective טוֹבָה. This step will teach students that מוֹרָה is a feminine word.

Next, hold up Word Picture Card #23 and say, כִּתָּה, asking the class to repeat the word. Point to the picture of the classroom and say כִּתָּה again, asking the class to repeat. Once you feel that the students understand the word, repeat it with the adjectives גְּדוֹלָה/קְטַנָּה. This step will teach students that כִּתָּה is a feminine word.

Next, you can ask questions like:

מִי בַּכִּתָּה? (אֲנִי בַּכִּתָּה, מוֹרָה בַּכִּתָּה אַתָּה/אַתְּ בַּכִּתָּה)

Ask the question until every student has had at least one turn answering. For variety, you can also ask the question:

מָה בַּכִּתָּה? (שֻׁלְחָן, עִפָּרוֹן, דֶּגֶל בַּכִּתָּה)

Once you feel that the students understand the new vocabulary, ask a volunteer to read the directions. Read each sentence and ask students to put a check next to it only if the sentence describes the picture. You may need to repeat the sentences several times as students work through them. Circulate to provide assistance as needed.

I Can Understand Hebrew!

Your teacher will read these words to you:

כִּתָּה מוֹרָה

Your teacher will read these sentences to you.
Check ✓ every sentence that describes the picture.

1. מוֹרָה בַּכִּתָּה. ✓
2. גְּלִידָה בַּיָּד.
3. אַבָּא בַּכִּתָּה.
4. עִפָּרוֹן בַּיָּד.
5. בַּיִת בַּגֶּשֶׁם.
6. דָּג בַּכִּתָּה.
7. עִפָּרוֹן עַל שֻׁלְחָן. ✓
8. דָּג עַל שֻׁלְחָן.

43

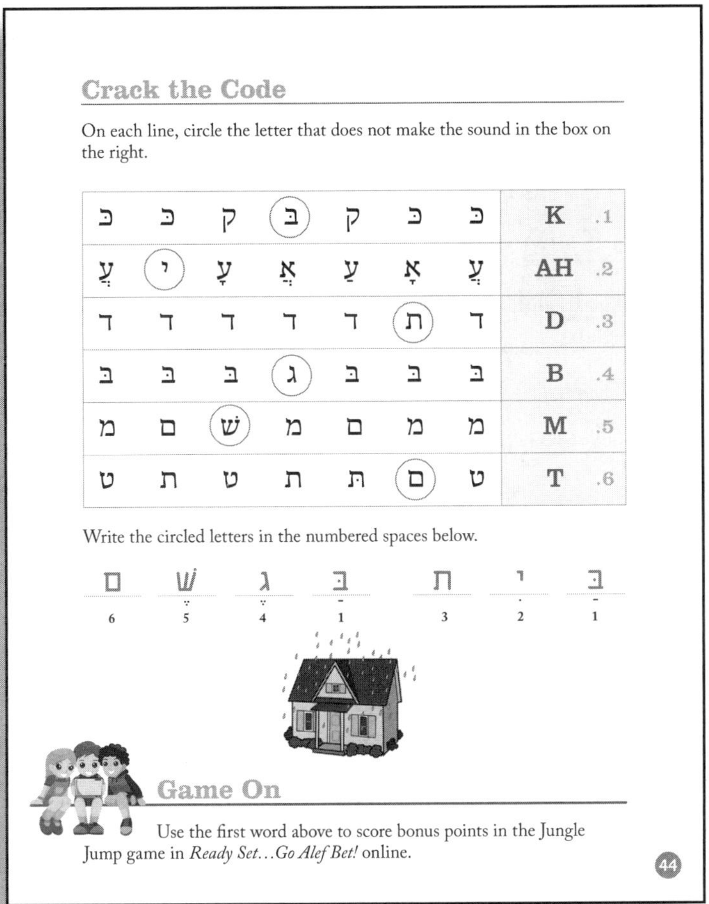

Crack the Code

On each line, circle the letter that does not make the sound in the box on the right.

כ	כ	ק	(ב)	ק	כ	כ	K	.1
עָ	(י)	עָ	אָ	עָ	אָ	עָ	AH	.2
ד	ד	ד	ד	ד	(ת)	ד	D	.3
בּ	בּ	בּ	(ג)	בּ	בּ	בּ	B	.4
מ	ם	(שׁ)	מ	ם	מ	מ	M	.5
ט	ת	ט	ת	תּ	(ם)	ט	T	.6

Write the circled letters in the numbered spaces below.

ם	שְׁ	גְ	בְּ	ת	י	בּ
6	5	4	1	3	2	1

Game On

Use the first word above to score bonus points in the Jungle Jump game in *Ready Set...Go Alef Bet!* online.

44

As an additional assignment, ask students to find out what their Hebrew names are so that they can tell you the next time they come to class.

When students complete this lesson in the digital companion, and you have checked that they have done so, allow them to color in the כ and ק on the Alef-Bet Chart on page 4 of their book.

Assessment

For information on assessing students' progress, see page 10. Continue listening to students as they read the second oral assessment on page 137, completing an error analysis for each one. Continue to make notes concerning which students had difficulty with any of the information presented in this lesson.

Crack the Code

This activity provides students with a review of sound-symbol associations. Line 1 also provides practice with fine visual discrimination (ב/כ), and line 3 provides practice in fine auditory discrimination (*t*/*d*). Ask a volunteer to read the directions at the top of the page, and complete line 1 together. Allow students to complete the remaining lines individually or in pairs. Circulate to provide assistance as needed. When the students have finished all six lines, tell them to write the letters they circled in the correct numbered spaces. Then tell them that they have created a caption for the picture. Ask volunteers to describe the picture in Hebrew.

Game On

Ask a volunteer to read the directions at the bottom of the page. Assign students to complete Lesson 9 in the digital companion at home. Remind them to play the Jungle Jump game when they have completed the lesson. You might ask students to print out or e-mail their lesson summaries to you when they have completed all the activities in the lesson. Or assess their progress in the Behrman House Online Learning Center.

Challenge students to come to the next class with answers to the questions below. They will find the answers in Lesson 9 of the digital companion. Consider sending home a sheet with these questions, or e-mail them to parents, when you assign the lesson in the digital companion. Ask students to write the answers on the sheet and return it, with a parent's signature, at the next class.

1. What does the כ do in the Letter Hint? (*it sucks on a cough drop*)
2. What does the ק do in the Letter Hint? (*looks like a cane*)
3. What vowel is found in every syllable on lines 1 and 3 of the "Word Building" activity? (*ah*)
4. What two letters make the sound of "k" in the "Crack the Code" activity? (כ *and* ק)
5. What inventory item did you collect in the Jungle Jump game? (*kippah*)

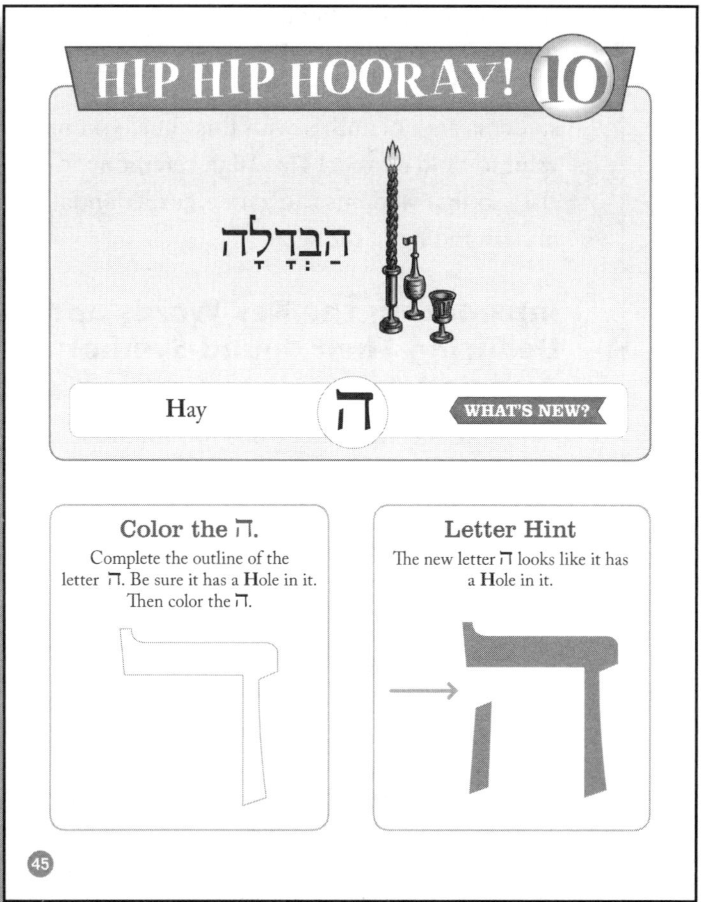

create the correct display. For example, you can say: זֶה שֻׁלְחָן. Ask a volunteer to act out this sentence by pointing to or holding up the correct object or Word Picture Card. Volunteers should repeat the sentences while they are completing the action or after they have completed it. Once the volunteer has successfully identified the object, point to it and ask the class, מָה זֶה?. Encourage the class to respond with the correct answer. Repeat several times. Once you are confident that students have grasped the usage of זֶה and זֹאת, you can allow students to create their own sentences. Begin with your strongest language students. Ask a volunteer to select a card or an object and hold it up or point it out to the class. Allow students to call out מָה זֶה? or מָה זֹאת?. The volunteer then responds using the correct form, ________ זֶה or ________ זֹאת. The student who called out the correct question first gets to select the next object.

Set Induction

Ask students if they know what we call the short ceremony that ends Shabbat (הַבְדָּלָה, which means "separation"). Havdalah separates Shabbat from the rest of the week. Bring a Havdalah set and pass the three items around, allowing

10 Hip Hip Hooray!

Pages: 45–48

Key Word: הַבְדָּלָה

New Letter: ה

Vocabulary Words: (girl) יַלְדָּה, (boy) יֶלֶד, (the) הַ־

Recommended Materials: Phonics Flash Card #20, Word Picture Cards #1, 2, 7, 8, 10–14, 16, 17, and 19–26; sets of syllable cards for Concentration; a Havdalah set (spice box, braided candle, Kiddush cup); crayons or colored pencils.

Review Activity: Play Concentration (see page 17 for instructions). Create sets of C-V and C-V-C syllable cards that make use of those letters and vowels that represent the same sounds (e.g., עַ/אָ, כֶּ/קוֹ, בַּם/בָּם, תָּג/טַג). In this version of the game, students are asked to find letters and/or syllables that sound the same. Play continues until each student has had at least one turn and all the cards have been matched. Ask students to answer the questions you posed at the end of Lesson 9 (see page 64) including asking them their Hebrew names.

Oral Language Lesson

Begin class by taking attendance in the manner described on page 9, Inquire how students are doing:

מָה שְׁלוֹמְךָ? מָה שְׁלוֹמֵךְ? טוֹב, טוֹב
מְאוֹד, לֹא טוֹב, לֹא רַע, מְצוּיָן, בְּסֵדֶר

Be sure to include the polite response:

________ תּוֹדָה, וְאַתָּה/אַתְּ?

Review the questions מִי זֶה? and מָה זֶה?

Review the pronoun זֹאת and contrast it with זֶה:

מִי זֶה? זֶה ________.
מִי זֹאת? זֹאת ________.
מָה זֶה? זֶה עִפָּרוֹן.
מָה זֹאת? זֹאת תּוֹרָה.

After introducing the concept, you can review it by creating sentences and asking students to

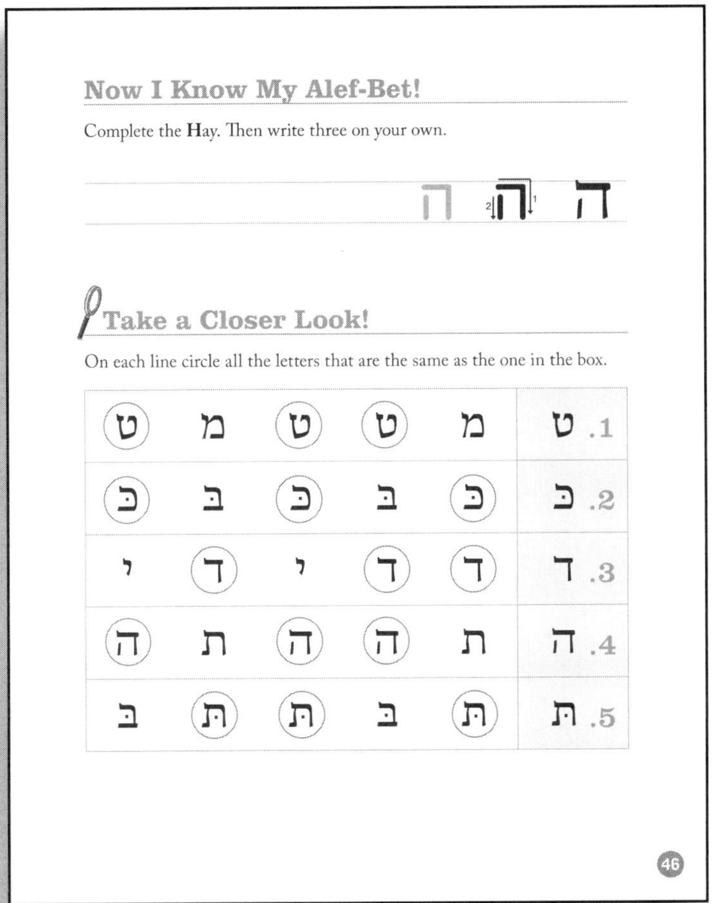

Now I Know My Alef-Bet!

Complete the Hay. Then write three on your own.

ה ה ה

Take a Closer Look!

On each line circle all the letters that are the same as the one in the box.

ט	מ	ט	ט	מ	ט .1
כּ	ב	כּ	ב	כּ	כּ .2
י	ד	י	ד	ד	ד .3
ה	ח	ה	ה	ח	ה .4
בּ	תּ	תּ	בּ	תּ	תּ .5

46

students to handle them. Select a volunteer to read the chapter title. Ask the class what sound they think will be taught in this lesson. (*h*) If students are unfamiliar with this ritual you may want to hold a model Havdalah ceremony in class so that students can gain an experiential understanding of the service.

Introducing the Key Words and Deducing Their Sound-Symbol Associations

Introduce the new letter using the "Multi-Sensory Approach to Hebrew Sound-Symbol Associations" described on page 12. You can create a kinesthetic connection by imitating the panting sound that a hot or thirsty dog makes. Show the class a picture of a dog with its tongue hanging out, then say, "h...h...h!" Ask the class to repeat both the sound and the action. As an alternative, ask students to create the letter shape using clay or play dough. No matter what kinesthetic association you use, ask the students to repeat the letter sound (h) while they do so.

Letter Hint & Color the Letter

Distribute crayons or colored pencils. Ask volunteers to read the sentence in the Letter Hint. Write a ד on the board and invite a volunteer to complete the letter ה. Select a second volunteer to draw an arrow pointing to the hole in the letter. Give students time to complete and color in the ה.

Now I Know My Alef-Bet!

Ask students to trace the letter with their fingers and to trace it in pencil, while repeating the sound that the letter represents. (*h*) Next, ask them to write three examples of the letter in pencil while repeating the letter's sound.

Take a Closer Look!

This activity provides visual discrimination practice for all three categories of visually similar letters. Lines 2, 3, and 4 require students to distinguish between pairs that are identical except for one small difference (כּ/ב, ח/ה, and ד/י). Line 1 contains letters that share an overall shape, making it difficult to tell them apart at a glance (ט/מ), and line 5 contains letters that look similar when rotated (תּ/בּ).

Ask a volunteer to read the instructions and ask students to complete the activity individually. Students who have difficulty differentiating between letters that are identical except for one small difference may benefit from tactile reinforcement, such as making letters from clay or closing their eyes while they explore sandpaper letters that have been pasted onto smooth paper. Students who are having difficulty with letters that share an overall shape may need to be reminded that Hebrew reading requires us to look closely at every letter and vowel. Be sure to circulate, both to provide assistance and to determine which students need more practice in this area.

I Can Understand Hebrew!

Introduce the three new vocabulary words at the top of page 47. Begin with יֶלֶד and יַלְדָּה using Word Picture Cards 25 and 26. Hold up each card and and say its word, asking the class to repeat as soon as they understand. Point to the pictures on the top of the page and say each word, asking the class to repeat. Once you feel that the students understand both words, repeat them with the adjectives גָּדוֹל/קָטָן and גְּדוֹלָה/קְטַנָּה. This step will teach students the genders of the new words.

Review the term מוֹרָה. If you are a female teacher, introduce yourself by saying:

שְׁמִי ________. אֲנִי מוֹרָה.

If you are a male teacher, introduce yourself by saying:

שְׁמִי ________. אֲנִי מוֹרֶה

Allow students to use these sentence patterns to introduce themselves and identify whether they are boys or girls.

שְׁמִי ________. אֲנִי יֶלֶד.

שְׁמִי ________. אֲנִי יַלְדָּה.

The prefix הַ־ should simply be translated as "the," as there is no direct way to deduce the word's meaning. You can explain to the class that Hebrew does not use a word for "the." Thus יֶלֶד means a boy, while הַיֶּלֶד means "the boy."

You're an Artist!

Ask a volunteer to read the instructions. Read sentence #1. Direct the class to look at the illustration on the bottom of page 43, which illustrates sentences 1 and 5 on page 47. If your classroom has a flag, you can ask a volunteer to point to it after you read sentence #6. The same applies for sentence #7, as a volunteer can place a pencil on the table to illustrate that sentence. Allow students to draw a picture. While they are working, you can repeat the sentences, as this will help to reinforce the students' familiarity with them. You can even begin to read them a bit faster each time, to acquaint students with the near-native pace of spoken Hebrew.

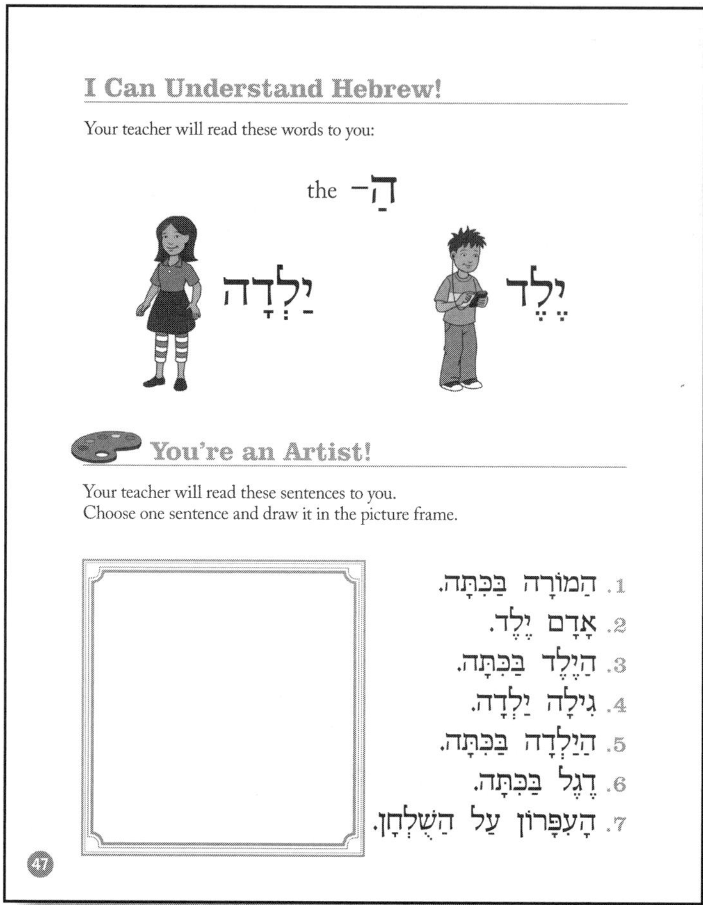

I Can Understand Hebrew!

Your teacher will read these words to you:

the הַ־

יַלְדָּה

יֶלֶד

You're an Artist!

Your teacher will read these sentences to you.
Choose one sentence and draw it in the picture frame.

1. הַמּוֹרָה בַּכִּתָּה.
2. אָדָם יֶלֶד.
3. הַיֶּלֶד בַּכִּתָּה.
4. גִּילָה יַלְדָּה.
5. הַיַּלְדָּה בַּכִּתָּה.
6. דֶּגֶל בַּכִּתָּה.
7. הָעִפָּרוֹן עַל הַשֻּׁלְחָן.

47

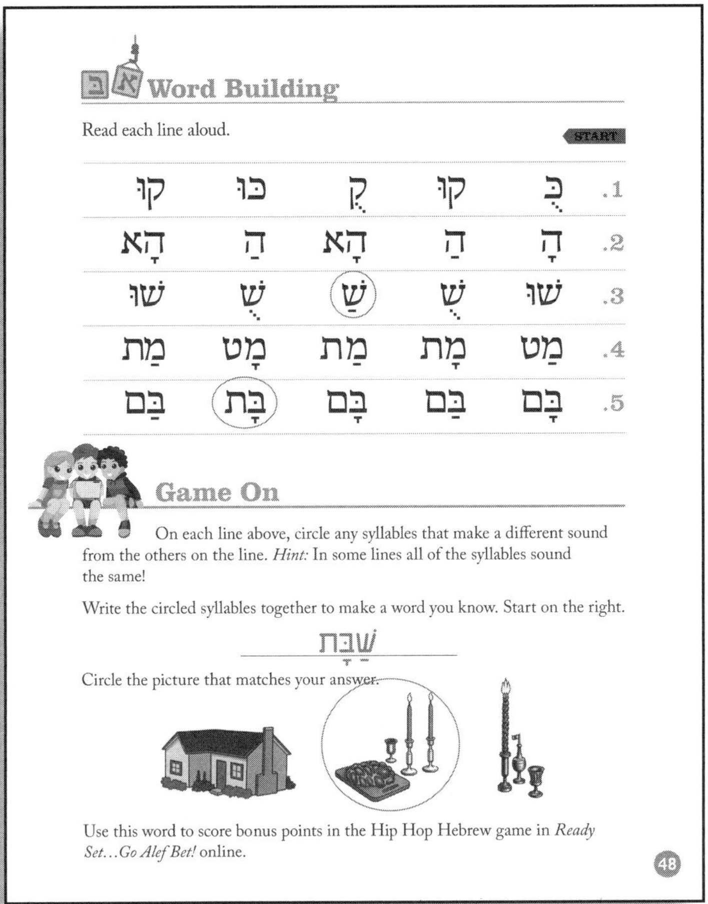

Word Building

Read each line aloud.

START

1. כֶּ קוֹ קֶ כּוֹ קוֹ
2. הָ הַ הָא הַ הָא
3. שׁוֹ שֶׁ (שַׁ) שֶׁ שׁוֹ
4. מַט מָת מַת מָט מַת
5. בָּם בַּם בָּם (בָּת) בַּם

Game On

On each line above, circle any syllables that make a different sound from the others on the line. *Hint:* In some lines all of the syllables sound the same!

Write the circled syllables together to make a word you know. Start on the right.

שַׁבָּת

Circle the picture that matches your answer.

Use this word to score bonus points in the Hip Hop Hebrew game in *Ready Set...Go Alef Bet!* online.

48

1. What letter should be circled four times in the "Take a Closer Look" activity? (ד)
2. What sound ends every syllable in line 5 of the "Word Building" activity? (*t*)

When students complete this lesson in the digital companion, and you have checked that they have done so, allow them to color in the ה on the Alef-Bet Chart on page 4 of their book.

Assessment

For information on assessing students' progress, see page 10. Make notes concerning which students had difficulty with any of the information presented in this lesson. With the completion of this lesson, students have been introduced to all of the material that is covered in Assessment 2 on page 139. Based on the notes you have made during previous lessons, you may wish to administer this assessment to the class. If you feel that many students are not yet in command of the material, you can delay administering a formal assessment until they have completed an additional lesson or two. You can also continue listening to individual students complete the second oral assessment on page 137.

Word Building

This activity is a simple review of the vowels students have learned so far, along with the C-V and C-V-C patterns they have learned. Ask a volunteer to read the directions for this activity, and then have students take turns reading. You may want to begin by asking students to read single items. As they gain confidence, ask them to read full lines. Once students can read whole lines of syllables, ask them to read columns of syllables.

Game On

The final activity for this lesson serves to build a bridge between C-V and C-V-C blending and the blending of two-syllable words. It also provides additional practice with simple blending as students are asked to reread each of the lines in the Word Building section above. This they should do individually, reading each syllable aloud as quietly as they can. As they read a line, they must determine if all the syllables sound the same or if one is different. If they identify one that differs from the rest on the line, they should circle that syllable. Once they have completed all of the lines, they should write the two syllables together on the blank line to create a single word. As a self-checking mechanism, students need to read the word they have created and then circle the picture that it describes.

Tell students to complete Lesson 10 in the digital companion at home. Remind them to play the Hip Hop Hebrew game when they have completed the lesson. You might ask students to print out or e-mail their lesson summaries to you when they have completed all the activities in the lesson. Or assess their progress in the Behrman House Online Learning Center.

Challenge students to come to the next class with answers to the questions below. They will find the answers in Lesson 10 of the digital companion. Consider sending home a sheet with these questions, or e-mail them to parents, when you assign the lesson in the digital companion. Ask students to write the answers on the sheet and return it, with a parent's signature, at the next class.

tSUPER TZADEE 11

מִיץ צְדָקָה

WHAT'S NEW? TZadi צ Final TZadi ץ

Word Building

Read each line aloud.

START

1.	צָ	צַ	צֵ	צוּ	צוּ
2.	כַּ	קַ	כֵּ	קוּ	קֵ
3.	אָ	אוּם	גַם	שָׁם	שׁוּם
4.	צַ	צוּם	דָם	דֵ	דוּם
5.	בַּ	בּוּץ	קָץ	גָץ	קוּץ
6.	אַץ	גוּץ	מַץ	כּוּץ	מוּץ

49

come up, select a card, and pose the correct form of the question to the class. Continue until all the students who want a turn have had one. You can also add variety by asking students to introduce each other. Point to a boy and ask: מִי זֶה? Allow a volunteer to introduce the boy by saying, זֶה __________. Next, point to a girl and ask: מִי זֹאת? Allow a volunteer to introduce the girl by saying, זֹאת __________.

Divide the class into pairs, and allow each member of the pair to introduce himself or herself in Hebrew using the formula: שְׁמִי __________. Encourage students to use their Hebrew names in these introductions, if possible. Then, ask each student to introduce his or her partner to the group using the correct sentence pattern:

זֶה __________. or זֹאת __________.

Set Induction

The sound represented by the new letter צ occurs in the initial position of only two English words (tsunami and tsetse fly), both of which are borrowed from other languages. This makes it difficult for many native English speakers to produce the sound in the initial position of Hebrew words.

11 tSuper Tzadee

Pages: 49–52

Key Words: צְדָקָה מִיץ

New Letters: צ/ץ

Recommended Materials: Phonics Flash Cards #1–20 for review and #21 and #22, Word Picture Cards # 1–14 and #16–26 for review, and #27–29; a bottle or carton of juice and cups; a tzedakah box and coins; picture of an impact/impulse sprinkler; crayons or colored pencils.

Review Activity: Play at least two rounds of Around the World (see page 16 for instructions). In the first round, review all letters and vowels previously introduced, and in the second round review the key words that students have learned. Play continues until both review rounds have been completed. Ask students to answer the questions you posed at the end of Lesson 10 (see page 68).

Oral Language Lesson

Begin class by taking attendance in the manner described on page 9 and inquire how students are doing:

מָה שְׁלוֹמְךָ? מָה שְׁלוֹמֵךְ? טוֹב, טוֹב מְאוֹד, לֹא טוֹב, לֹא רָע, מְצוּיָן, בְּסֵדֶר

Be sure to include the polite response:

__________ תּוֹדָה, וְאַתָּה/אַתְּ?

Review the questions מִי זֹאת? and מִי זֶה? You should review all of the people nouns by holding up pictures and asking the correct question:

מִי זֶה? (זֶה אַבָּא.)

מִי זֹאת? (זֹאת מוֹרָה.) (זֹאת אִמָּא.)

Review the nouns: מוֹרָה, יַלְדָּה, יֶלֶד, אִמָּא, אַבָּא

In the early stages, pose the question and pause 3–5 seconds. If no one in the class can answer the question, provide the correct answer yourself. Repeat the process until most of the class can answer correctly. Once the class can answer the questions independently, allow volunteers to

Nevertheless, the sound occurs with regularity in the middle or at the end of English words.

Because it is very difficult for native English speakers to produce this sound in the initial position, in this lesson begin by introducing students to the ץ first. Bring a bottle or carton of juice to class and introduce the key word מִיץ by serving it to students and allowing them to drink it. Once you feel that the students understand the word, repeat it in conjunction with the adjective טוֹב. This step will teach students that מִיץ is a masculine word. Tell students to pay attention to the last sound in the word.

You can also introduce the sound in the middle of a word using the word פִּיצָה, showing Word Picture Card #29. Finally, introduce the word צְדָקָה by taking out a tzedakah box and placing coins in it while saying צְדָקָה. Tell the class to pay close attention to the first sound in the word, and make sure that you enunciate it clearly. Invite other students to place coins in the box while saying the key word צְדָקָה. You can provide nickels or dimes for those students who do not have coins of their own. Pay close attention to each student's pronunciation of the initial sound, providing remediation as needed. Finally, allow a volunteer to read the chapter title. Ask the class what sound they think they will learn in this lesson. (*tz*)

Introducing the Key Words and Deducing Their Sound-Symbol Associations

Introduce the new letter using the "Multisensory Approach to Hebrew Sound-Symbol Associations" described on page 12. To create a kinesthetic association, show students the picture of an impact (or impulse) sprinkler. This type of sprinkler is best known for its distinctive sound, which is caused by a spring-loaded mechanism that pushes the water out in short bursts or impulses, causing the nozzle to rotate in a circular or semicircular motion. You can find pictures of this kind of sprinkler on Google Images. Ask students to close their eyes and listen to the sound that this type of sprinkler makes,

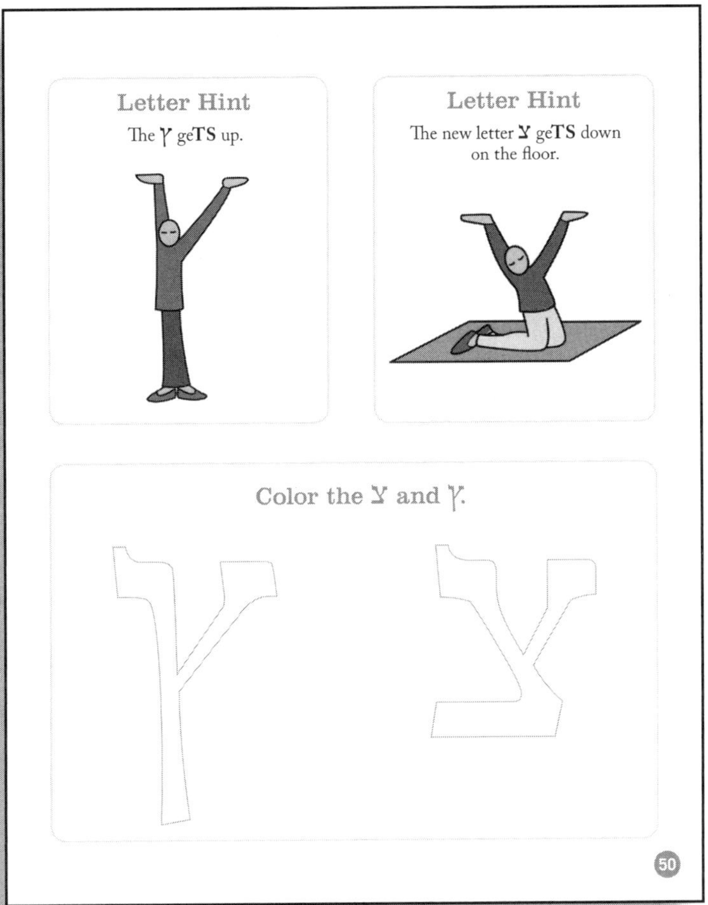

then imitate the sound by making staccato repetitions of the צ, "tz...tz...tz." Next, ask them to stand up and use their arms as the nozzle, moving them in a semicircle in front of themselves while reproducing the new letter sound. As an alternative, you can ask them to create the shapes of צ and ץ with their bodies, imitating the illustrations from the "Letter Hint" at the top of page 50 in the student text. No matter which kinesthetic association you use, ask the students to repeat the letter sound (*tz*) while they do so.

Word Building

Ask a volunteer to read the directions for this activity, and then have students take turns reading. You may want to begin by asking one student to read the first two items in a row and another to read the last three items. As they gain confidence, ask them to read full lines.

Letter Hint & Color the Letter

Distribute crayons or colored pencils. Ask a volunteer to read the sentence in the first Letter Hint. Draw two lines on the board and write the צ in between them. Invite a volunteer to draw an arrow pointing to the floor on which the צ sits.

Give students time to color in the first letter. Repeat the procedure for the ץ.

Now I Know My Alef-Bet!

Ask students to trace the letter on the first line with their fingers and to trace it in pencil, while repeating the sound that the letter represents. (*tz*) Next, ask students to write three examples of the letter in pencil while repeating the letter's sound. Repeating the letter's sound provides an auditory reinforcement for the visual and kinesthetic activity.

I Can Understand Hebrew!

This comprehension activity allows students to review the key words and one vocabulary item that they have learned so far. Read the first word and ask, "Who can show me a כִּפָּה?" Allow a volunteer to show the class what the word means. Then ask everyone to find the picture of the כִּפָּה on the page and place their finger on the picture. Circulate to make sure that everyone has identified the correct picture. When you are satisfied that each student has identified the correct item, ask them to draw a line between the first word and the item. Then read the second word and ask students to find the correct picture. You may need to repeat the word several times to allow slower students to process it. Complete all nine words in this manner.

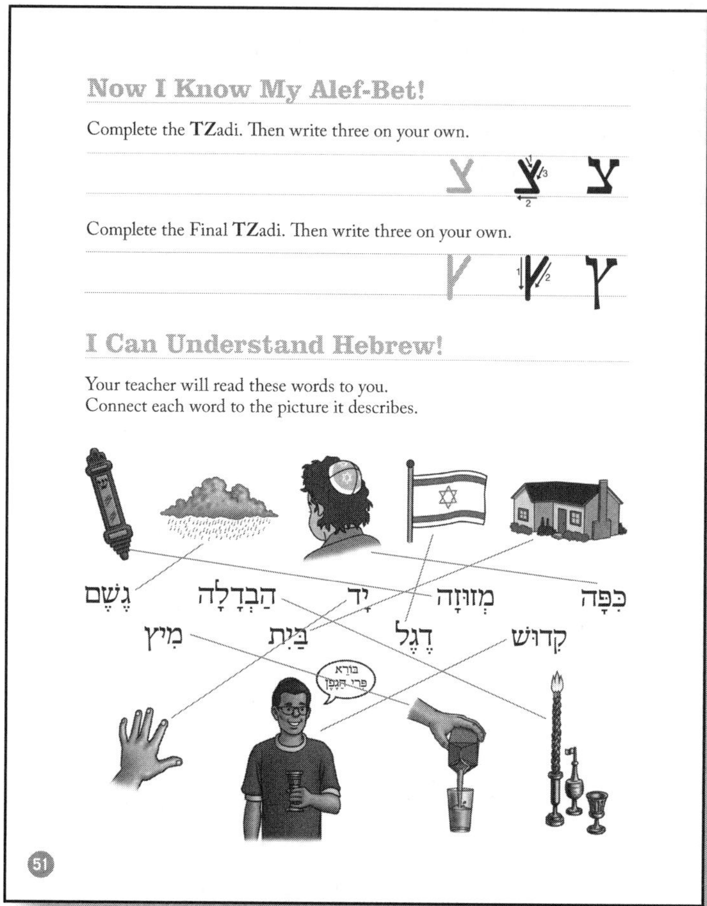
Now I Know My Alef-Bet!

Complete the TZadi. Then write three on your own.

צ צ צ

Complete the Final TZadi. Then write three on your own.

ץ ץ ץ

I Can Understand Hebrew!

Your teacher will read these words to you.
Connect each word to the picture it describes.

גֶּשֶׁם הַבְדָּלָה יָד מְזוּזָה כִּפָּה

מִיץ בַּיִת דֶּגֶל קִדּוּשׁ

51

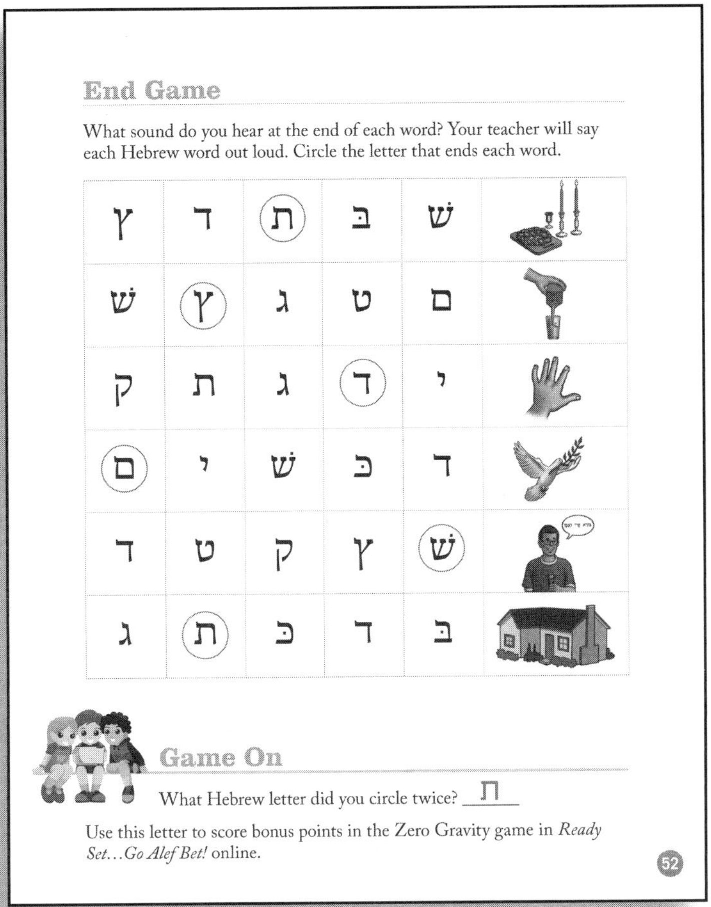

End Game

What sound do you hear at the end of each word? Your teacher will say each Hebrew word out loud. Circle the letter that ends each word.

ץ	ד	(ת)	בּ	שׁ	
שׁ	(ץ)	ג	ט	ם	
ק	ת	ג	(ד)	י	
(ם)	י	שׁ	כּ	ד	
ד	ט	ק	ץ	(שׁ)	
ג	(ת)	כּ	ד	בּ	

Game On

What Hebrew letter did you circle twice? ת

Use this letter to score bonus points in the Zero Gravity game in *Ready Set...Go Alef Bet!* online.

52

End Game

This activity provides students with additional practice in segmenting the final phoneme of several words using key words that they have learned. Begin by asking a volunteer to say the Hebrew name of the items on the right side of the top row. (שַׁבָּת) Tell the class to listen for the last sound in the word and ask the volunteer to say it clearly. Next, select a volunteer to read the instructions at the top of the page. Ask the class what sound they heard at the end. (*t*) Ask the class to find the letter that represents the sound (*t*) and to put their finger on it. Circulate to make sure that every student has identified the correct letter, providing assistance as necessary. Then ask students to circle the letter that represents the sound *t*. Allow students to work with partners to complete the activity. Circulate to provide assistance as necessary. If a student struggles with this activity, he or she may need additional practice with segmentation.

Game On

This activity provides a mechanism for checking the students' answers to the End Game activity. Ask a volunteer which letter he or she circled twice. (ת) Ask the rest of the class if they came up with the same letter or another one. If there is a dispute about which letter ends two of the words, review the whole End Game activity as a class.

Ask students to complete Lesson 11 in the digital companion at home. Remind them to play the Zero Gravity game when they have completed the lesson. You might ask students to print out or e-mail their lesson summaries to you when they have completed all the activities in the lesson. Or assess their progress in the Behrman House Online Learning Center.

Challenge students to come to the next class with answers to the questions below. They will find the answers in Lesson 11 of the digital companion. Consider sending home a sheet with these questions, or e-mail them to parents, when you assign the lesson in the digital companion. Ask students to write the answers on the sheet and return it, with a parent's signature, at the next class.

1. What do the צ and the ץ do in the Letter Hint? (*stretch their "arms" and* ץ *stands up*)
2. What letter ends ten words in the "Word Building" activity? (ץ)
3. What Hebrew letter ends a word in both "Sound Check" activities? (ת)

When students complete this lesson in the digital companion, and you have checked that they have done so, allow them to color in the צ and the ץ on the Alef-Bet Chart on page 4 of their book.

Assessment

For information on assessing students' progress, see page 10. Make notes concerning which students had difficulty with any of the information presented in this lesson, paying special attention to those who had difficulty with the correct pronunciation of the letter צ, especially in the initial position of a word. At this point, you should complete administering the second oral evaluation, making sure that every student has completed it.

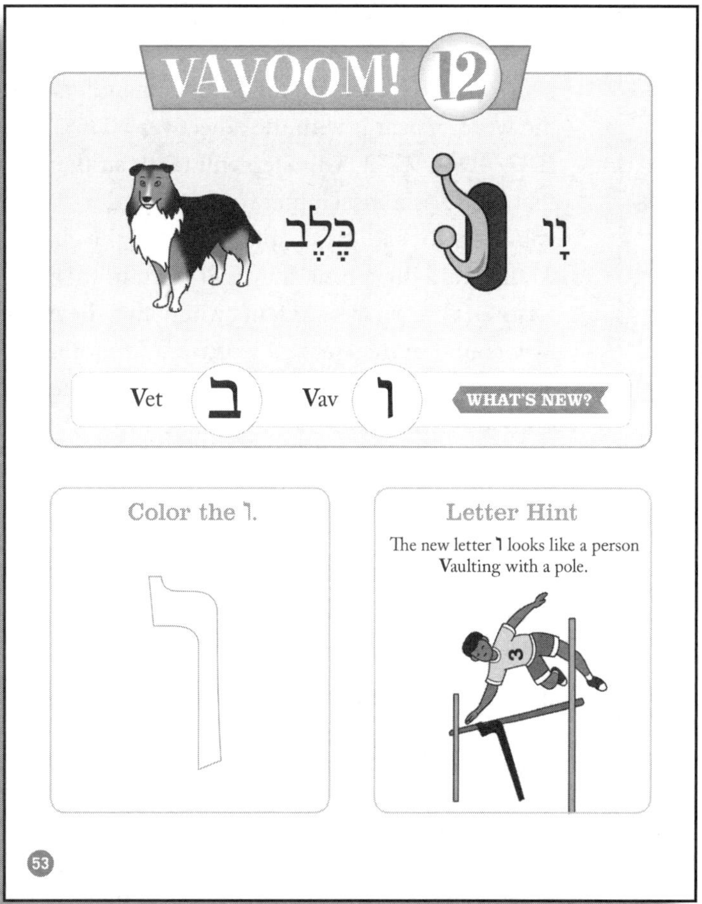

מָה זֶה? (זֶה עִפָּרוֹן.)
מָה זֹאת? (זֹאת כִּפָּה.)

Review the nouns:

יָד, בַּיִת, גְלִידָה, שֻׁלְחָן, גֶּשֶׁם, דָג, כִּתָּה, מִיץ,
דֶגֶל, טַלִּית, כִּפָּה, מְזוּזָה, תּוֹרָה

Pose the question and pause 3–5 seconds in the early stages. If no one in the class can answer the question, provide the correct answer yourself. Repeat the process until most of the class can answer correctly. Once the class can answer the questions independently, allow volunteers to come up, select a card, and pose the correct form of the question to the class. Continue until all the students who want a turn have had one.

Set Induction

Ask students, "Who has a pet?" and "Who would like to have a pet?" "What kind?" If a student owns a fish, point out that they have learned the Hebrew word for "fish," and ask who remembers what it is called. Tell the class that they are going to learn the Hebrew word for another kind of pet in this lesson. When a student identifies that he or she has or would

12 Vavoom!

Pages: 53–56

Key Words: וָו כֶּלֶב

New Letters: ב ו

Vocabulary Words: (of, belonging to) שֶׁל

Cognates: וַמְפִּיר, דוֹלְפִין, דִינוֹסָאוּרוּס, בַּבּוּן, וֵטֵרִינָר, וִיקִינְג,

Recommended Materials: Phonics Flash Cards #23 and 24, Word Picture Cards # 1, 2, 6-8, 13, 14, 16, 17, 19, 20, 23, and 28 for review, and #30, 31, and 32; cards with C-V and C-V-C syllables printed on them and Fun-Tak or magnetic tape on the back for Tic-Tac-Toe; a cup filled with water and an empty bowl; crayons or colored pencils; possibly clay or Playdough.

Review Activity: Play Tic-Tac-Toe (see page 16 for instructions) using C-V and C-V-C syllables. These syllables should be created from a mix of the letters and vowels that students have learned to date, especially ם, ג, ד, ק, כּ, ה, צ and ץ. Place C-V-C syllables, especially those containing ה, צ, and ץ, in the center square and the four corners of the game. Divide the class into two teams. Play continues until each student has had at least one turn. You may need to play multiple games to accommodate the amount of playing time necessary. When you redo the game board, use different C-V and C-V-C syllables to keep the game fresh. After the game, ask students to answer the questions you posed at the end of Lesson 11 (see page 72).

Oral Language Lesson

Begin class by taking attendance and asking students how they are doing using the Hebrew greetings that students have already learned. Model for them the use of one's Hebrew name, for example:

שָׁלוֹם. עֶרֶב טוֹב! שְׁמִי ________.
אֲנִי מוֹרָה.

Review the questions מָה זֶה? and מָה זֹאת?. You should review all of the nouns that do not refer to people by holding up pictures and asking the correct question:

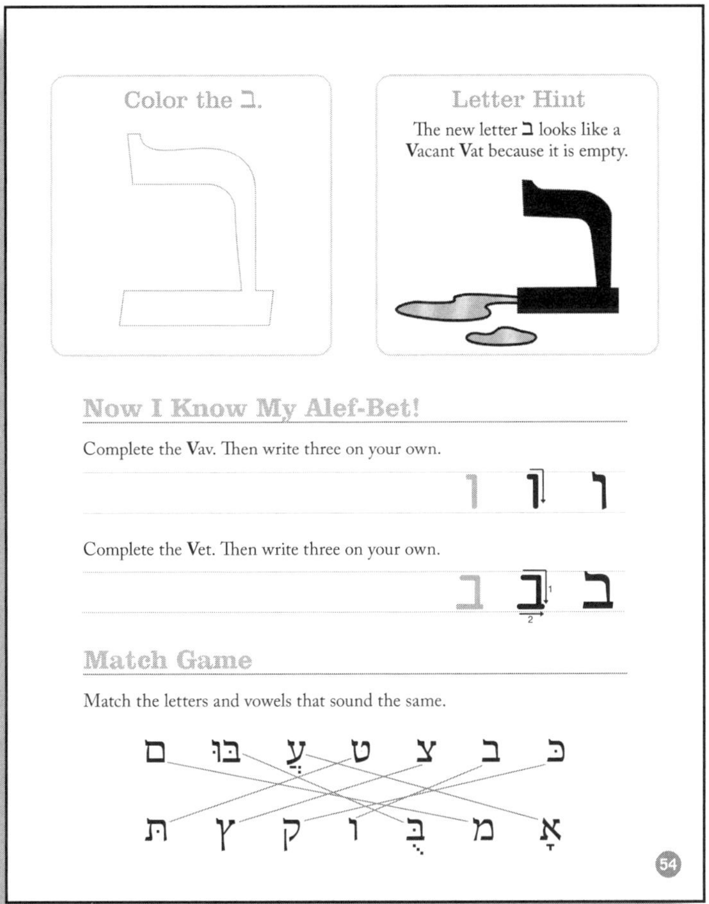

Color the ב.

Letter Hint

The new letter ב looks like a Vacant Vat because it is empty.

Now I Know My Alef-Bet!

Complete the Vav. Then write three on your own.

Complete the Vet. Then write three on your own.

Match Game

Match the letters and vowels that sound the same.

54

Letter Hint & Color the Letter

Distribute crayons or colored pencils. Select a volunteer to read the sentence in the Letter Hint. Ask a volunteer to describe how the ו looks as if it could be used for pole vaulting. Give students time to color in the first letter.

Letter Hint & Color the Letter

Hold up a cup filled with water and tell the students that you are holding a vat of water. Then, hold a plastic bowl beneath the cup and turn the cup on its side, allowing the water to drain out. Tell the class that your *vat* is now *vacant*. Select a volunteer to read the sentence in the Letter Hint. Give students time to color in the new letter, ב.

Now I Know My Alef-Bet!

Ask students to trace the letter on the first line with their fingers and to trace it in pencil, all while repeating the sound that the letter represents. (*v*) Next, ask them to write three examples of the letter in pencil while repeating the letter's sound. Repeating the letter's sound provides an auditory reinforcement for the visual and kinesthetic activity. Do the same for the letter on the second line.

like to have a dog, hold up Word Picture Card #31 and say כֶּלֶב. Ask the class to repeat the word. Once you feel that the students understand the word, repeat it with the adjectives גָּדוֹל/קָטָן/טוֹב. This step will teach students that כֶּלֶב is a masculine word. Allow a volunteer to read the chapter title. Ask the class what sound they think they will learn in this lesson. (*v*) Next, ask students where they hear the new sound in the Hebrew word כֶּלֶב. (*at the end of the word*) Introduce the key word וָו in the same way, using Word Picture Card #30 and including the adjectives גָּדוֹל/קָטָן. This step will teach students that וָו is a masculine word.

Introducing the Key Words and Deducing Their Sound-Symbol Associations

Introduce the new letter ו using the "Multisensory Approach to Hebrew Sound-Symbol Associations" described on page 12.

You can ask students to create a kinesthetic link between the letter shape and its sound using their bodies to form the letters. To create a ו, simply ask students to stand up straight with their legs together and their arms hanging straight down and pressed against their bodies. To create a ב tell students to sit on the floor with their legs stretched out in front of them. They should bend forward slightly and hold their arms out over their legs, keeping their heads up. As an alternative, you can distribute clay or Playdough and allow students to form three dimensional models of the letters. No matter which kinesthetic or tactile activity you use, ask the students to repeat the letter sound (*v*) while they do so.

Match Game

In this activity, students are asked to connect the different letters or letter-vowel combinations that represent the same sound. The ability to hear and identify homonyms is an important pre-reading skill as it demonstrates the student's ability to associate sounds with all of the symbols that can represent them.

Select a volunteer to read the directions and allow students to work on the activity in pairs.

I Can Understand Hebrew!

Introduce the Hebrew preposition that indicates possession (שֶׁל) by translating it and explaining that this is how ownership is described in Hebrew. To illustrate the term, pick up a pencil that belongs to one of the students and say:

הָעִפָּרוֹן שֶׁל __________.

Repeat this procedure several times describing who owns various pencils and asking the class to repeat after you as soon as they understand what you are saying. You can also include other items that students might own, such as כִּפָּה or דֶגֶל. Next, point to your desk and say:

הַשֻּׁלְחָן שֶׁל הַמּוֹרָה.

Once you feel that students understand the concept, allow volunteers to create their own Hebrew sentences using the same props. If the class agrees with the volunteer's statement, they should repeat it. If the class does not agree, the volunteer should attempt to correct the error. Allow several students to create phrases, then turn to the text in the book.

Select a volunteer to read the directions, then read the first sentence allowing time for students to draw a line between the phrase and the picture it describes. Circulate to provide assistance as needed. You may need to read each sentence several times for every student to complete the task.

I Can Understand Hebrew!

Your teacher will read this word to you:

of, belonging to שֶׁל

Your teacher will read these phrases to you. Match each phrase to its picture.

1. הַדָּג שֶׁל הַיֶּלֶד
2. הַדֶּגֶל בַּיָּד שֶׁל אִמָּא
3. הַכֶּלֶב שֶׁל הַיֶּלֶד
4. הָעִפָּרוֹן שֶׁל הַמּוֹרָה
5. הַדֶּגֶל בַּיָּד שֶׁל אַבָּא
6. הָעִפָּרוֹן שֶׁל הַיַּלְדָּה

55

Sound Check

The names of these objects sound similar in Hebrew and English. Circle all the objects that begin with the sound of the new letter ו.

Game On

Circle the name of the Hebrew letter that begins each word that is circled above.

דָב (וָו) בַּב

Use this letter to score bonus points in the Wacky Wheelbarrow game in *Ready Set...Go Alef Bet!* online.

56

and ask the rest of the class if they agree. If there is a dispute about the name of the letter (וָו), review as a class. Assign students Lesson 12 in the digital companion at home. Remind them to play the Wacky Wheelbarrow game when they have completed the lesson. You might ask students to print out or e-mail their lesson summaries to you when they have completed all the activities in the lesson. Or assess their progress in the Behrman House Online Learning Center.

Challenge students to come to the next class with answers to the questions below. They will find the answers in Lesson 12 of the digital companion. Consider sending home a sheet with these questions, or e-mail them to parents, when you assign the lesson in the digital companion. Ask students to write the answers on the sheet and return it, with a parent's signature, at the next class.

1. What does the ו do in the Letter Hint? (*it lifts the vaulter over the bar*)
2. What happens to the ב in the Letter Hint? (*water pours out of it*)
3. How many objects in the "Sound Check" activity begin with the letter ו? (*three*)

Sound Check

This activity provides students with practice in segmenting the initial phoneme of several cognates. At the same time, it provides students with practice in making fine auditory distinctions. The sounds *d* and *b* are fairly similar to the sound *v*, and some students may confuse them. Students who struggle with this activity may need individual practice with fine auditory discrimination.

Begin by providing students with the Hebrew pronunciation of each item in the activity. (וַמְפִּיר, דוֹלְפִּין, בָּנָנָה, דִינוֹסָאוּרוּס, בַּבּוּן, וֵטֵרִינָר, וִיקִינְג,) Ask them to point to each item as you say its Hebrew name. Circulate to make sure that everyone can complete this crucial first step.

Next, ask a volunteer to read the instructions at the top of the page. Select a volunteer to identify the item at the top. Encourage the volunteer to use the Hebrew pronunciation. Tell the class to listen for the first sound in the word then ask the volunteer to say it clearly. Ask the class what sound they heard at the beginning. (*b*) Ask them to look at the Hebrew letter in the instruction. Does this letter make the same sound as the letter ו? Once students understand that the sounds are not the same, repeat this process two more times, continuing in a clockwise direction. Students should identify that the initial sound in the second item, דוֹלְפִּין, does not match the letter, while the third item, וַמְפִּיר, does.

Allow students to complete the activity individually. Be sure to tell them that they need to say each Hebrew word out loud as they work.

Circulate to provide assistance as needed, paying attention especially to those students who have had difficulty with this type of activity previously.

Game On

This activity provides a mechanism for checking the students' answers to the Sound Check activity. Select volunteers to read the directions and each of the Hebrew syllables, and ask the class to circle the name of the letter. Allow a volunteer to read the syllable he or she circled,

4. What inventory item did you collect in the Wacky Wheelbarrow game? (*tallit*)

When students complete this lesson in the digital companion, and you have checked that they have done so, allow them to color in the ו and the ב on the Alef-Bet Chart on page 4 of their book.

Assessment

For information on assessing students' progress, see page 10. With this lesson, students have learned all the items tested in the third oral assessment on page 137. Evaluate a few volunteers on it, asking them to read the syllables aloud while you complete the error analysis. You will also want to make notes concerning which students had difficulty with any of the information presented.

הַדֶּגֶל שֶׁל אַבָּא
הַכֶּלֶב שֶׁל הַיֶּלֶד

Once you feel confident that the students understand the material, ask them to create their own sentences to describe a picture of your choosing. Finally, you can ask students to turn to page 43 and create sentences to describe the picture at the bottom of the page. Phrases can include:

הָעִפָּרוֹן שֶׁל הַיֶּלֶד
הַשֻּׁלְחָן שֶׁל הַיַּלְדָּה
הַכִּתָּה שֶׁל הַמּוֹרָה
הַשֻּׁלְחָן שֶׁל הַיֶּלֶד
הַכִּתָּה שֶׁל הַיַּלְדָּה
הַכִּתָּה שֶׁל הַיֶּלֶד

Set Induction

Tell students to think all the way back to the fall and to name one of the holidays we celebrated at that time. When a student names סֻכּוֹת ask the students to tell you what objects we use to celebrate the holiday (sukkah, etrog, lulav). When a student names the lulav, show the class Word Picture

13 Leapin' Lizards!

Pages: 57–61

Key Word: לוּלָב

New Letter: ל

Vocabulary Word: (and) וְ־

Recommended Materials: Phonics Flash Cards #25-27, Word Picture Cards #1–14, 16–28, and 30–32 for review, and #33; a round bead on a string; crayons or colored pencils; possibly clay or Playdough.

Review Activity: Play Musical Words (see page 16 for instructions) using the Word Picture Cards to review key word and vocabulary items that students have learned so far. Play continues until you have used the stack of cards at least once and every student has had the opportunity to play. Ask students to answer the questions you posed at the end of Lesson 12 (see page 76).

Oral Language Lesson

Begin class by taking attendance and asking students how they are doing using the Hebrew greetings that they have already learned. Ask some or all of the students to introduce themselves as they learned in the previous class session.

Review the preposition that indicates possession. (שֶׁל) Hold up a pencil that belongs to one of the students and say, "הָעִפָּרוֹן שֶׁל ________" Ask the class to repeat after you as soon as they understand. Continue the review by borrowing pencils from several students.

Next, ask the students to open their books to page 55. Ask them to point to the picture that you describe. Circulate to make sure that everyone has identified the correct picture and to help as needed. Phrases that you can review include:

הָעִפָּרוֹן שֶׁל הַמּוֹרָה
הַדֶּגֶל שֶׁל אִמָּא
הַדָּג שֶׁל הַיֶּלֶד
הָעִפָּרוֹן שֶׁל הַיַּלְדָּה

Card #33 and repeat the Hebrew word. Ask the class to repeat the new word. Once you feel that the students understand the word לוּלָב, repeat the term with the adjective יָפֶה. This step will teach students that לוּלָב is a masculine word. Allow a volunteer to read the chapter title. Ask the class what sound they think they will learn in this lesson. (*l*)

Introducing the Key Words and Deducing Their Sound-Symbol Associations

Introduce the new letter using the "Multisensory Approach to Hebrew Sound-Symbol Associations" described on page 12. You can create a kinesthetic link between the letter shape and its sound by asking students to create the letter shape using their bodies. To create a ל direct students to stand with their legs together and their knees bent slightly. They should then raise their arms up and out at a diagonal, as if they were about to do a dive from a standing position, while saying the sound *l*. As an alternative, you can distribute clay or Playdough and allow students to create a three dimensional model of the ל. No matter which kinesthetic or tactile activity you use, ask the students to repeat the letter sound (*l*) while they do so.

Letter Hint & Color the Letter

Distribute crayons or colored pencils. Ask volunteers to read the sentence in the Letter Hint. Draw two lines on the board and write the ל between them. Point out that the ל goes above the top line—the only Hebrew letter to do so—and invite a volunteer to circle the part that goes above the line. Give students time to color in ל.

Now I Know My Alef-Bet!

Ask students to trace the new letter first with their fingers and then with a pencil, while repeating the sound that the letter represents. (*l*) Next, ask them to write three examples of the letter in pencil while repeating the letter's sound.

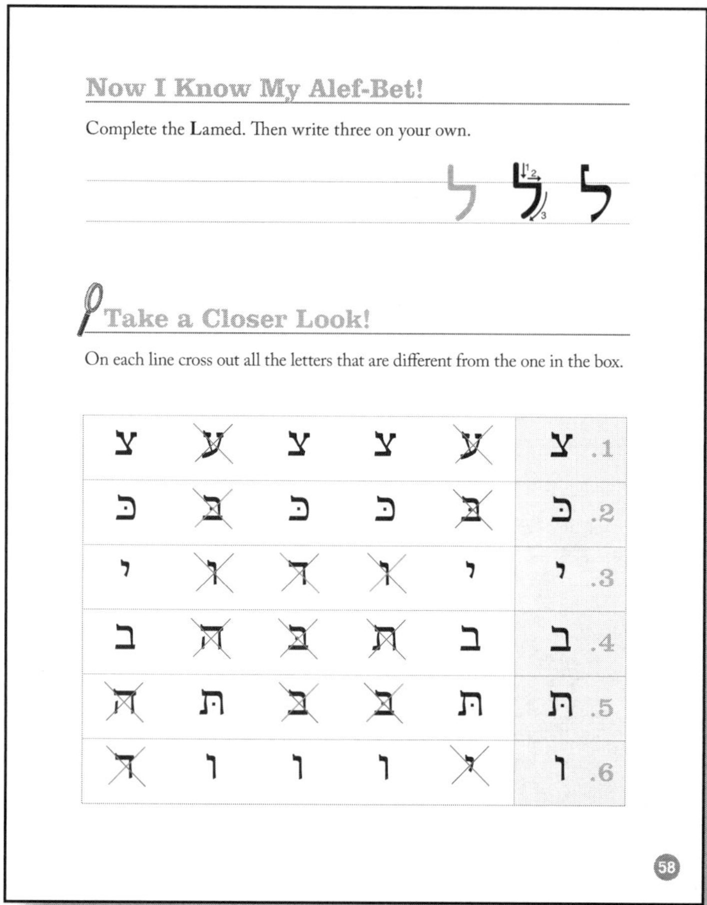

Now I Know My Alef-Bet!

Complete the Lamed. Then write three on your own.

Take a Closer Look!

On each line cross out all the letters that are different from the one in the box.

צ	ע	צ	צ	ע	צ .1
כּ	בּ	כּ	כּ	בּ	כּ .2
י	ו	ד	ו	י	י .3
ב	ה	בּ	ת	ב	ב .4
ה	תּ	בּ	בּ	תּ	תּ .5
ד	ו	ו	ו	י	ו .6

58

Take a Closer Look!

Many pairs of Hebrew letters are visually confusing.

By this point in *Ready, Set...Go Alef Bet!* students have been exposed to several such pairs of letters. This activity provides visual discrimination practice for many of these pairs. Line 1 asks students to differentiate between ע and צ. Like the מ/ט pair that was reviewed earlier, these letters share an overall shape, making it difficult to tell them apart at a glance. Lines 2, 3, and 6 deal with pairs of letters that are similar except for a single, small difference. These include pairs like כּ/בּ, י/ו, and ו/ד. Lines 4 and 5 are mixed, providing practice with some pairs of letters that are similar except for a single, small difference (specifically תּ/ה and ב/בּ), and also with those that are similar when rotated like תּ/בּ and ת/ב.

Ask a volunteer to read the instructions, then ask students to complete the activity individually. Be sure to circulate, both to provide assistance and to determine which students need more practice in this area. Pay close attention to and make note of the specific types of mistakes that individual students make.

"String the Bead!"

"EE" = ִי ִ

The new Hebrew vowel looks like a little **bead**. Color the bead.

Word Building

Read each line aloud.

START

1. תִּ שִׁי מִ עִ טִי
2. דִ כִּי לִי בִי הִי
3. דַ דֶ לָ וַ הַ
4. דָם קוּשׁ גִל עַם הִת
5. דָמִים קִדוּשׁ גַלִיל אָבִיב הִצִיל

59

To bridge between syllable recognition and actual decoding, ask volunteers to come up to the board. Point to a syllable and ask the student to pronounce it. Again, if the student is correct, the class should repeat the syllable. If the class is silent, the student should try to correct the error.

Word Building

Have students complete this activity after they have practiced the syllables written on the board. Ask a volunteer to read the directions for this activity, and then have students take turns reading. You may want to begin by asking students to read two or three items at a time, then full lines when they gain confidence. Once students can read whole lines of syllables, ask them to read columns of syllables to provide variety.

"String the Bead!"

This section presents students with the third vowel sound, *ee*. Like both of the other vowels that students encountered earlier, this sound can be represented by more than one symbol, in this case ִי and ִ. Hold up Phonics Flash Card #26 and say *ee*. Ask the class to repeat after you. Follow the same procedure with Phonics Flash Card #27. Next, ask students to draw the vowels in the air with their fingers while saying the sounds. Hold up a round bead hanging from a string. Point to the bead and say *ee*. Pass the bead around so that students can feel its shape. Remind them to hold the string up and allow the bead to hang straight down. Tell students to look at the picture of the girl at the top of page 59, and especially at the bead hanging around her neck.

Write the vowels on the board and ask a volunteer to point to the part of each that looks like a bead. Next, point to the first vowel and say *ee* with the class repeating after you. Repeat this procedure until you are confident that the students recognize them.

Write a few Hebrew C-V syllables on the board, such as לִי, וִ, כִּי, הִי, צִ, דֵ, מִי. Write them with a lot of space between each. Invite volunteers to come up to the board. Say one of the syllables and ask the volunteer to point to it. If the student is correct, the class should repeat the syllable. If the class is silent, indicating a mistake, ask the volunteer to correct the mistake. Repeat the process with a variety of syllables until every student has had at least one turn. Then, write these C-V syllables scattered between the syllables you already have on the board: מָ, טוֹ, בַּ, עֵ, and so one. Repeat the drill as above, mixing the syllables and allowing volunteers to identify them until you are confident that the class understands this simple C-V blending.

Next, review C-V-C blending using a mixture of the vowels students know. Some of these syllables should end with a ם or a ץ. Pay attention to any student who has trouble blending the final consonant onto the end of the word and adds an extra vowel sound at the end of the C-V-C syllable, reading for example *"mitza"* for מִיץ.

I Can Understand Hebrew!

Try to introduce the prefix וְ־ through a direct approach. Invite two volunteers to stand in front of the class. Point to one student and say his or her name. Point to the other and say the second student's name. Then, place the two students together and say:

__________ וְ __________.

Repeat this process using a variety of the Word Picture Cards you used in the review activity. Sample phrases include:

יֶלֶד וְיַלְדָּה
כֶּלֶב וְדָג
תּוֹרָה וְיָד
כִּפָּה וְטַלִּית
אַבָּא וְאִמָּא
עִפָּרוֹן וְשֻׁלְחָן
מוֹרָה וְכִתָּה

To make sure that students understand the new prefix, ask a volunteer to translate its meaning into English. (*and*)

Select a volunteer to read the directions at the top of page 60. Read the two sentences in box #1, and ask students to check the sentence that describes the picture. You may need to read the pair of sentences a few times to make sure that students understand them. Repeat this procedure for the other three items, circulating to provide assistance as needed.

I Can Understand Hebrew!

Your teacher will read this word part to you:

and וְ־

Your teacher will read these phrases to you.
Check the phrase that matches each picture.

.1
☑ הַבַּיִת שֶׁל אַבָּא וְאִמָּא.
☐ הַבַּיִת בַּגֶּשֶׁם.

.2
☑ הַכֶּלֶב וְהַדָּג שֶׁל הַיֶּלֶד.
☐ הַכֶּלֶב בַּמַּיִם.

.3
☑ הַיֶּלֶד וְהַיַּלְדָּה בַּכִּתָּה.
☐ הַיֶּלֶד וְהַיַּלְדָּה בַּבַּיִת.

.4
☐ הָעִפָּרוֹן עַל שֻׁלְחָן.
☑ הַטַּלִּית וְהַתּוֹרָה עַל שֻׁלְחָן.

60

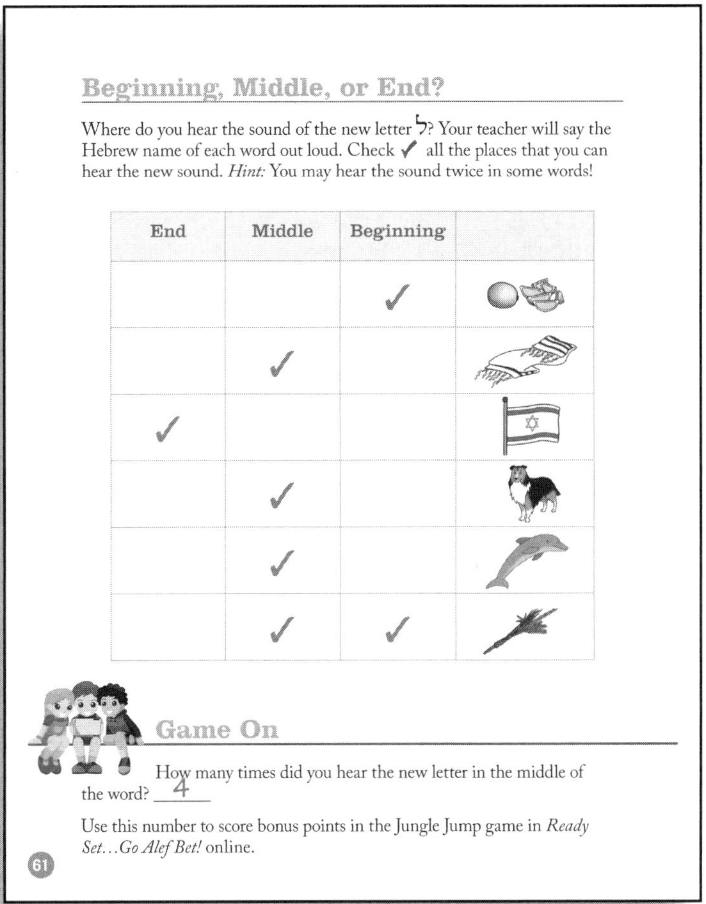

Beginning, Middle, or End?

Where do you hear the sound of the new letter ל? Your teacher will say the Hebrew name of each word out loud. Check ✓ all the places that you can hear the new sound. *Hint:* You may hear the sound twice in some words!

End	Middle	Beginning	
		✓	
	✓		
✓			
	✓		
	✓		
	✓	✓	

Game On

How many times did you hear the new letter in the middle of the word? 4

Use this number to score bonus points in the Jungle Jump game in *Ready Set...Go Alef Bet!* online.

61

Beginning, Middle, or End?

In this activity, students practice segmenting the sound of the new letter ל and identifying the various positions in which it can be found in several key words and cognates.

Ask a volunteer to read the instructions at the top of page 61. Then describe the first picture using the Hebrew pronunciation, לִימוֹן. Ask the class where they hear the sound of the new letter ל. (*the beginning*) Ask the class who agrees with the answer and who does not. You may need to repeat the word. Once the class agrees, tell them to check the box in the "Beginning" column. Since this is the students' first attempt to segment medial phonemes, complete this activity as a class. Be sure to say the cognate דוֹלְפִין with the Hebrew pronunciation.

Game On

Ask students how many times they heard the ל in the middle of a word. (*4*) If there is a dispute about the number of words, review as a class. You can also ask students which word had more than one ל in it (לוּלָב). Assign students Lesson 13 in the digital companion to complete at home. Remind them to play the Jungle Jump game when they have completed the lesson. You might ask students to print out or e-mail their lesson summaries to you when they have completed all the activities in the lesson. Or assess their progress in the Behrman House Online Learning Center.

Challenge students to come to the next class with answers to the questions below. They will find the answers in Lesson 13 of the digital companion. Consider sending home a sheet with these questions, or e-mail them to parents, when you assign the lesson in the digital companion. Ask students to write the answers on the sheet and return it, with a parent's signature, at the next class.

1. What does the ל do in the Letter Hint? (*it strikes like a lightning bolt*)
2. How many words in Word Building end with the new letter ל? (*three*)
3. Look at the second "Beginning, Middle, or End?" activity. The ל is found twice in one word. Name it. (לוּלָב)

When students complete this lesson in the digital companion, and you have checked that they have done so, allow them to color in the ל on the Alef-Bet Chart on page 4 of their book.

Assessment

For information on assessing students' progress, see page 10. Make notes concerning which students had difficulty with any of the information presented in this lesson. You can also continue listening to individual students complete the third oral assessment.

SOUNDS SUPER 14

שִׂמְחַת תּוֹרָה סֻכּוֹת

Sin שׂ Samech ס WHAT'S NEW?

Color the ס.

Letter Hint

The new letter ס looks like a Circle.

62

Finally, provide students with sentences and ask them to identify the correct pictures to indicate that they understand them. Ask them to open their books to page 11. Use the following sentences and ask students to identify the correct picture:

אַבָּא וְאִמָּא בַּבַּיִת.

הַיֶּלֶד וְהַיַּלְדָּה בַּכִּתָּה.

You can also use pictures from other pages in the book. For example, ask students to turn to page 15 and indicate the correct picture for this sentence:

הַתּוֹרָה וְהַיָּד עַל הַשֻּׁלְחָן.

On page 39, use the sentence:

אַבָּא וְאִמָּא בַּגֶּשֶׁם.

On page 60, you can use the sentence:

הַטַּלִּית וְהַתּוֹרָה עַל הַשֻּׁלְחָן.

and the phrase:

הַכֶּלֶב וְהַדָּג שֶׁל הַיֶּלֶד

Set Induction

Review the key word from the previous lesson (לוּלָב) by

14 Sounds Super

Pages: 62–65

Key Words: שִׂמְחַת תּוֹרָה סֻכּוֹת

New Letters: שׂ ס

Vocabulary Word: (Sukkah, booth) סֻכָּה

Recommended Materials: Phonics Flash Cards #28 and 29, Word Picture Cards #33-36 and cards 10, 11, 16, 23, 25, 26, 31; prepared Bingo cards with index cards for each of the syllables being reviewed and a pile of markers or beans for each student; a tallit, a kippah, a Torah pointer, and a model Torah; crayons or colored pencils.

Review Activity: Play Bingo (see page 17 for instructions) using cards divided into five rows and five columns. The center square should contain the word חָפְשִׁי ("free," pronounced "*ḥofshi*"). The remaining squares should be filled with C-V and C-V-C syllables composed of the letters and vowels that students have learned so far. Play continues until a winner can be declared. You can play a second round if the class is especially interested. Ask students to answer the questions you posed at the end of Lesson 13 (see page 82).

Oral Language Lesson

Begin class by taking attendance and asking students how they are doing, using the Hebrew greetings that students have already learned.

Review the prefix ־וְ. Hold up pictures of mother and father at the same time and say:

"אַבָּא וְאִמָּא."

Ask students to repeat the phrase as soon as they understand what you are saying. Repeat this procedure using other pairs of Word Picture Cards, such as a teacher and a classroom, a house and a mezuzah, or objects such as a Torah pointer and a model Torah, a tallit and a kippah, and so on. Model a few phrases for the students, then ask volunteers to select the correct pictures or objects when you say a phrase. Next, hold up a pair of cards and ask volunteers to create phrases that combine them.

Now I Know My Alef-Bet!

Ask students to trace the letter on the first line with their fingers and then in pencil, while repeating the sound that the letter represents. (*s*) Next, ask them to write three examples of the letter in pencil while repeating the letter's sound. Do the same for the letter on the second line.

I Can Understand Hebrew!

Review the key word סֻכּוֹת and ask students how they think this holiday got its name. (*from the word* סֻכָּה, *which means "a booth"*) Hold up Word Picture Card # 36 and say: סֻכָּה. Ask the class to repeat after you. Once you feel that the students understand the word, repeat it with the adjective יָפָה. This step will teach that סֻכָּה is a feminine word.

Hold up the pictures of the mom and dad, and say:

הַסֻּכָּה שֶׁל אַבָּא וְאִמָּא
אַבָּא בַּסֻּכָּה.
אִמָּא בַּסֻּכָּה.
הַשֻּׁלְחָן בַּסֻּכָּה.
הַיֶּלֶד וְהַיַּלְדָּה בַּסֻּכָּה.

showing Word Picture Card #33 and asking the students to name it. Ask students to identify the holiday on which we use a לוּלָב (סֻכּוֹת). You may need to ask the class to create a list of Jewish holidays until they identify the correct one. Next, ask if anyone can identify the Jewish holiday that comes right after סֻכּוֹת (שִׂמְחַת תּוֹרָה). You may need to give them a hint such as, "We read the end of the Torah and the beginning of the Torah on this holiday," or "We march around with the Torah scrolls and little flags on this holiday." Allow a volunteer to read the chapter title. Ask the class what sound they think will be taught in this lesson.(*s*)

Introducing the Key Words and Deducing Their Sound-Symbol Associations

Introduce the new letter using the "Multisensory Approach to Hebrew Sound-Symbol Associations" described on page 12. Create a kinesthetic link between the letter shape and its sound by moving your arm in an up and down motion like a snake while you say *s*. Ask the class to repeat the movement. You can also ask students to create the letter shapes through yoga poses. For example, students can create a ס by lying on their stomachs with their legs gently bent towards their heads and their arms lightly reaching back toward their feet.

Letter Hint & Color the Letter

Distribute crayons or colored pencils. Ask a volunteer to read the sentence in the Letter Hint.

Write ס on the board and invite a volunteer to draw a circle around it. Give students time to color in the first letter.

Letter Hint & Color the Letter

Ask a volunteer to read the sentence in the Letter Hint. Write a ש (with no dot) on the board and invite a volunteer to draw the ball on the seal's nose. Ask the class to repeat the sound *s* if the student is correct but to remain silent if he or she is incorrect. Allow the volunteer to correct the error. Give students time to color in the letter.

הַכֶּלֶב לֹא בַּסֻּכָּה.
הַסֻּכָּה בַּגֶּשֶׁם.

Ask the students to repeat the phrases as soon as they understand them.

Word Building

This activity reviews all three vowel sounds that students have learned. The first three lines review each vowel using the letters that students have learned most recently. Line 4 provides additional practice with C-V-C and two-syllable words. Ask students to take turns reading. You may want to begin by asking students to read single items. As they gain confidence, ask them to read full lines. Once students can read whole lines they can read columns of syllables to provide variety.

You're an Artist!

This activity reviews some of the Hebrew vocabulary and key words that students have learned. Place Word Picture Cards #10, 11, 16, 25, 26, 31, and 33 (dad, mom, rain, boy, girl, dog, lulav) on a table or on a bulletin board in front of the class. Tell the class that after you read a sentence a volunteer will select one or more of these picture cards and hold them up. If the volunteer is correct the class should repeat the sentence. If the volunteer is incorrect, the class should remain silent, allowing the volunteer to correct his or her choice.

Read the first sentence on page 64. After a student has selected the correct picture card, ask the class if the sentence already matches the picture. Since it does, no further action is necessary. Continue reading the sentences in this manner. When you arrive at a sentence that contains a missing element, allow students to add that element to the picture.

Circulate to provide assistance as needed. You may need to reread the sentences several times. This is especially true for the sentences that describe missing items.

Word Building

Read each line aloud.

1. שַׁ לָ קָ כַּ אֲ
2. שׁוּ לוּ כֻּ קוּ עֻ
3. סִ לִי קִ כִּי עִ
4. שִׁים שָׁמַיִם לוּלָב קוּם אָבִיב

You're an Artist!

Your teacher will read these sentences to you.
Draw in what is missing from the picture.

1. אַבָּא בַּסֻּכָּה.
2. אִמָּא בַּסֻּכָּה.
3. הַיֶּלֶד וְהַיַּלְדָּה בַּסֻּכָּה.
4. הַסֻּכָּה בַּגֶּשֶׁם.
5. הַכֶּלֶב בַּסֻּכָּה.
6. הַלּוּלָב שֶׁל אַבָּא בַּסֻּכָּה.

64

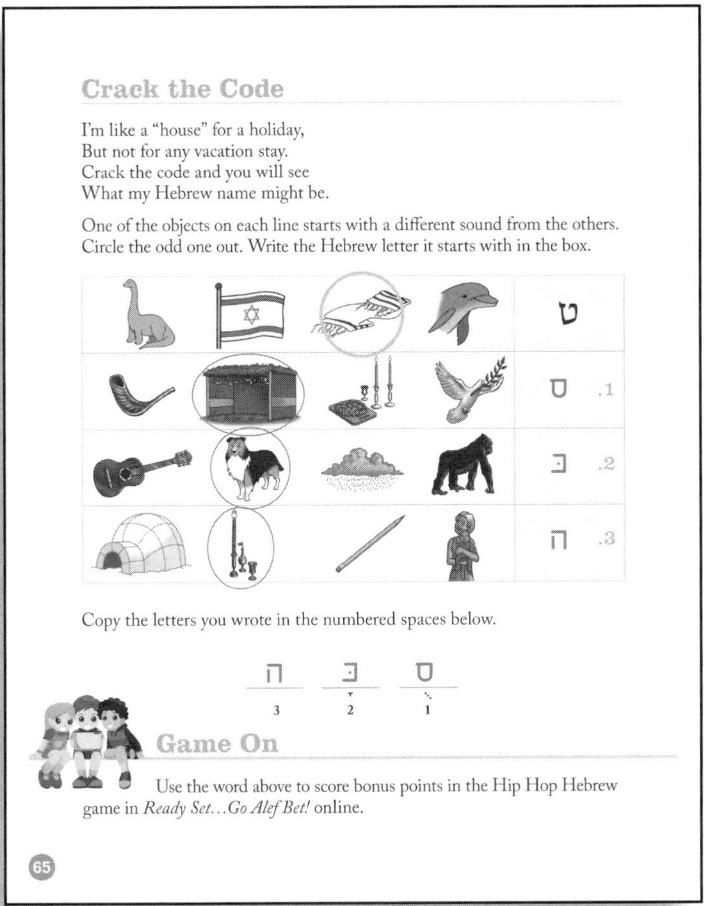
Crack the Code

I'm like a "house" for a holiday,
But not for any vacation stay.
Crack the code and you will see
What my Hebrew name might be.

One of the objects on each line starts with a different sound from the others. Circle the odd one out. Write the Hebrew letter it starts with in the box.

ט
.1 ס
.2 כ
.3 ה

Copy the letters you wrote in the numbered spaces below.

ה 3   כָּ 2   סֻ 1

Game On

Use the word above to score bonus points in the Hip Hop Hebrew game in *Ready Set...Go Alef Bet!* online.

65

completed the lesson. You might ask students to print out or e-mail their lesson summaries to you when they have completed all the activities in the lesson. Or they can assess student progress in the Behrman House Online Learning Center.

Challenge students to come to the next class with answers to the questions below. They will find the answers in Lesson 14 of the digital companion. Consider sending home a sheet with these questions, or e-mail them to parents, when you assign the lesson in the digital companion. Ask students to write the answers on the sheet and return it, with a parent's signature, at the next class.

1. What happens with the שׁ in the Letter Hint? (*the ball bounces off the seal's nose*)
2. How many words in the "Word Building" activity end with the sound of "v"? (*three*)
3. What inventory item did you collect in the Hip Hop Hebrew game? (*lulav*)

When students complete this lesson in the digital companion, and you have checked that they have done so, allow them to color in the ס and שׁ on the Alef Bet chart on page 4 of their book.

Crack the Code

This activity provides students with additional practice in distinguishing between letters that represent similar, but not identical sounds. Ask a volunteer to read the little poem at the top of the page and the instructions that follow it. Since this is an activity that provides additional practice with a skill that students have worked on previously, you should only work through the example as a class.

Call on individual students to identify the words pictured on the top line. Encourage students to use the Hebrew pronunciation of the cognates presented. Ask students to identify the sound that each item begins with and to identify the word that begins with a different sound than the others. Students must then identify the letter that the item they have circled begins with.

As you complete the first example, ask students what letter the three other items begin with and write that letter on the board (ד).

Allow students to complete the activity with a partner. Circulate to provide assistance as needed. If students have trouble deciding which letter to write for #1, refer them back to pages 9 and 63. While most students should complete lines 1 and 2 without much difficulty, they may find line 3 to be particularly challenging, as this is the first time they are asked to distinguish between an initial vowel and a voiced ה, a skill that is often difficult for beginning readers.

Once all of the lines have been completed and the correct letters filled in the blanks, ask students to copy the letters that they identified in the correct spaces. You may need to remind them that Hebrew is written from right-to-left.

Ask if anyone can read the whole word that they have written in the blank spaces (סֻכָּה), and praise them for having read a real Hebrew word!

Game On

Once students have correctly cracked the code and have found the correct Hebrew word, assign them to complete Lesson 14 in the digital companion at home. Remind them to play the Hip Hop Hebrew game when they have

Assessment

For information on assessing students' progress, see page 10. With this lesson, make notes about students who had difficulty with any of the information presented. You can also continue listening to individual students complete the third oral assessment.

Ask volunteers to hold up the correct pictures to match each sentence. They should hold up the two pictures that are linked by the conjunction וְ־ and then the card that indicates where the items can be found. They should repeat the sentence as they "illustrate" it. If they create a sentence correctly, the class should repeat the sentence. If the class remains silent, the student should attempt to correct the mistake.

Set Induction

Hold up a Shabbat candle and say, נֵר. Ask students to repeat the word as soon as they understand it. Then hold up a large candle and say, נֵר גָּדוֹל. Instruct students to repeat the phrase as soon as they understand it. Finally, hold up a birthday candle and say, נֵר קָטָן, again asking students to repeat the phrase as soon as they understand it. Teaching the noun with the adjectives shows that נֵר is a masculine word. Ask students what sound they hear at the beginning of the word. *(n)* Next, hold up a pencil and ask what this is called in Hebrew. (עִפָּרוֹן) Ask the class what sound they hear at the end of this Hebrew word. *(n)* Allow a volunteer to read the chapter title and ask what sound they think they will learn in this lesson. *(n)*

15 A Nose for News

Pages: 66–69

Key Words: נֵר עִפָּרוֹן

New Letters: נ/ן

Cognates: מִיקְרוֹפוֹן, נִיקֶל, נִנְגָּ'ה מֵיקְרוֹסְקוֹפּ

Recommended Materials: Phonics Flash Cards #30 and 31, Word Picture Cards #1, 2, 7, 8, 14, 16, 18, 19, 20, 22, 23, 25, 26, 28, 31, 36, and 37 for review, and #38 and 12; large rectangular cards with letter pairs on them for the "Same or Different?" game, a Shabbat candle, a large candle, a birthday candle, and a pencil; crayons or colored pencils.

Review Activity: Play Same or Different? (see page 17 for instructions) using single pairs of the visually similar letters students have learned so far:

שׁ/שׂ, ו/י, ב/ת, בּ/כּ, ע/צ, מ/ט,
ם/ס, ג/ו, ד/ו, ת/ה, בּ/ב, ב/ת

Be sure to include a variety of cards that contain the same letter twice (e.g., שׁ/שׁ). Play continues until all of the cards have been collected so that a winning team can be determined. Ask students to answer the questions you posed at the end of Lesson 14 (see page 86).

Oral Language Lesson

Begin class by taking attendance and asking students how they are doing using the Hebrew greetings that students students have learned.

Review any vocabulary and key words that you have not reviewed recently. Once you feel that the students recall these items, model more complex sentences than those introduced previously, such as:

הַיֶּלֶד וְהַכֶּלֶב בַּבַּיִת.
הַמּוֹרָה וְהַיַּלְדָּה בַּכִּתָּה.
הַדּוֹלְפִין וְהַדָּג בַּמַּיִם.
הַגְּלִידָה וְהַמִּיץ עַל הַשֻּׁלְחָן.
הַסֻּכָּה וְהַבַּיִת בַּגֶּשֶׁם.
הַכִּפָּה וְהַתּוֹרָה עַל הַטַּלִּית.

Introducing the Key Words and Deducing Their Sound-Symbol Associations

Introduce the new letter using the "Multisensory Approach to Hebrew Sound-Symbol Associations" described on page 12. Create a kinesthetic link between the letter shape and its sound by making the shape of the נ with your hand, placing the tip of the thumb under your nose and your fingers at the top of your nose while you say "n", Ask the class to make their noses "bigger" in the same way while saying (n). As an alternative, ask students to create the letter shapes using their bodies. To create a נ, ask students to sit on the floor with their arms at their sides and their palms pressed flat on the floor, fingers facing forward, and their legs together and stretched straight out in front. To create a ן simply ask students to stand up straight with their legs together and their arms reaching straight up over their heads. No matter which kinesthetic association you use, ask the students to repeat the letter sound *n* while they do so.

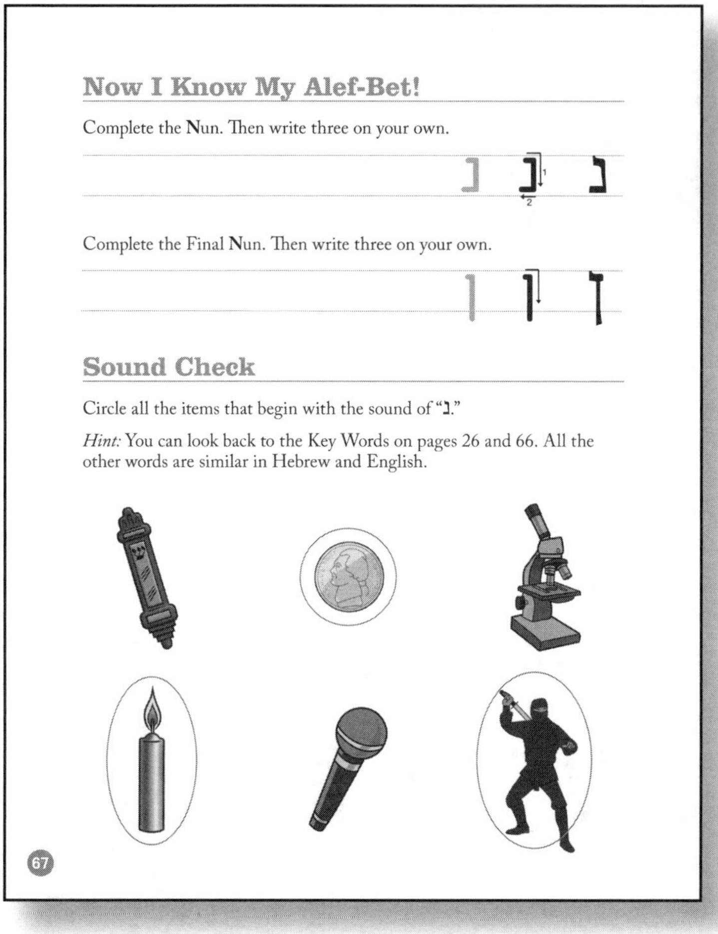
Now I Know My Alef-Bet!

Complete the Nun. Then write three on your own.

Complete the Final Nun. Then write three on your own.

Sound Check

Circle all the items that begin with the sound of "נ."

Hint: You can look back to the Key Words on pages 26 and 66. All the other words are similar in Hebrew and English.

67

Letter Hints & Color the Letters

Distribute crayons or colored pencils. Ask a volunteer to read the Letter Hint. Write נ on the board and invite a volunteer to draw eyes above it, a smile below it and a circle around it to complete it as a cartoon of a face. Next, draw the outline of a hammer and ask a volunteer to write a ן that looks like a nail below it. Give students time to color in the נ and the ן.

Now I Know My Alef-Bet!

Ask students to trace the letter on the first line with their fingers and then in pencil, while repeating the sound that the letter represents. (*n*) Next, ask students to write three examples of the letter in pencil while repeating the letter's sound. Follow the same procedure for the letter on the second line, repeating its sound as well.

Sound Check

This activity provides students with practice in segmenting the initial phoneme of several cognates. At the same time, it provides students with practice in making fine auditory distinctions. The sound *n* is fairly similar to the sound *m*, and some students may confuse them. Students who struggle with this activity may need individual practice with fine auditory discrimination.

Begin by providing students with the Hebrew pronunciation of each item in the activity. (מְזוּזָה, נִנְגָ'ה, מִיקְרוֹפוֹן, נֵר, נִיקֶל, מִיקְרוֹסְקוֹפּ) Ask students to point to each item as you say its Hebrew name. Circulate to make sure that everyone can complete this crucial first step. Next, ask a volunteer to read the instructions. Select a volunteer to identify the item on the top right. Encourage the volunteer to use the Hebrew pronunciation. Tell the class to listen for the first sound in the word then ask the volunteer to say it clearly. Ask the class what sound they heard at the beginning. (*m*) Ask them to look at the letter in the instructions, and ask them, "Does this word begin with the sound of the letter נ?" Once students understand that it does not, repeat this process with the next item on the top row. Students should identify that the initial sound (*n*) in the second item does match the letter נ, and they should circle it. Since students have had considerable practice with this kind of activity, allow them to complete it individually. Be sure to tell them that they need to say each Hebrew word out loud as they work. Circulate to

provide assistance as needed, paying attention especially to those students who have had difficulty with this type of activity previously.

I Can Understand Hebrew!

This comprehension activity allows students to review the key words and one vocabulary item that they have learned previously. Read the first word and ask, "Who can show me a נֵר?" Allow a volunteer to show the class what the word means. Then ask everyone to find the picture of the נֵר on the page (first item on the first row) and place their finger on the picture. Circulate to make sure that everyone has identified the correct picture. Then ask students to draw a line between the first word and the picture. Read the second word and ask students to find the correct picture. You may need to repeat the word several times to allow slower students to process it. Complete all three rows of words in this manner. On each row, some of the pictures do not have a word. Ask volunteers to identify those items in Hebrew. (Row 1: דֶּגֶל, אִמָּא; Row 2: יָד; Row 3: אַבָּא, כִּפָּה)

Sound Advice

This activity provides students with practice in segmenting a phoneme from the middle of words, the most difficult position from which to segment a sound. By this point in the program, students have had a fair amount of practice with segmentation from both the initial and final positions within words but have attempted segmentaion from the medial position only once. For that reason no other skills (such as visual or auditory discrimination) are reviewed in this activity.

Work through all of the items together as a class. Begin by asking a volunteer to read the instructions at the top of the page. Select a student to say the Hebrew name of the item in the box on the right side of the top row. Remind the class to listen for the consonant sound in the middle of the word and ask the volunteer to pronounce the word clearly.

Next, ask the class what sound they heard in the middle of the word. (*l*) Tell them to place their fingers on the letter that represents the *l* sound. Circulate to make sure that every student has found the correct letter, and provide assistance as needed. Complete the activity using this procedure, circulating throughout. Pay special attention to those students who had difficulty with the initial example and those who have had difficulty with previous segmentation activities. If the class can complete this activity with relative ease, you can repeat each word, asking what sound they hear at the beginning and at the end of each.

Game On

Ask a volunteer how many times they circled the following letters: ג, ד, כּ, and finally ל. Ask students to fill in the answer to the question and then to complete Lesson 15 in the digital companion at home. Remind them to play the Zero Gravity game when they have completed the lesson. You might ask students to print out or e-mail their lesson summaries to you when they have completed all the activities in the lesson. Or you can assess their progress in the Behrman House Online Learning Center.

Sound Advice

What sound do you hear in the middle of the word?
Circle the letter that is in the middle of each word.

ב	ל	ק	ג	ט	
ג	ט	כ	ל	ד	
ל	שׁ	ט	ד	ק	
ב	ג	ל	ד	כּ	
כּ	ב	ל	ס	ט	

Game On

Which letter is circled twice? ל

Use this letter to score bonus points in the Zero Gravity game in *Ready Set... Go Alef Bet!* online.

69

Challenge students to come to the next class with answers to the questions below. They will find the answers in Lesson 15 of the digital companion. Consider sending home a sheet with these questions, or e-mail them to parents, when you assign the lesson in the digital companion. Ask students to write the answers on the sheet and return it, with a parent's signature, at the next class.

1. What happens to the ן in the Letter Hint? (*it is nailed into a board*)
2. What letter is found in the middle of three words in the "Sound Advice" activity? (ל)
3. What inventory item did you collect in the Zero Gravity game? (נֵר)

As an additional assignment, ask students to bring in pictures of their pets or, for those who do not have a pet, a picture of their favorite animal.

When students complete this lesson in the digital companion, and you have checked that they have done so, allow them to color in the נ and the ן on the Alef Bet Chart on page 4 of their book.

Assessment

For information on assessing students' progress, see page 10. With this lesson, make notes concerning which students had difficulty with any of the information presented.

With the completion of this lesson, students have been introduced to all of the material that is covered in Assessment 3 on page 140. Based on the notes you have made during previous lessons, you may wish to administer this assessment to the class as a whole or only to individuals who have had difficulty with the newest letters and vowels. If you feel that many students are not yet in command of the material, you can delay administering a formal assessment until they have completed an additional lesson or two. At this point, you should complete administering the third oral evaluation, making sure that every student has completed it.

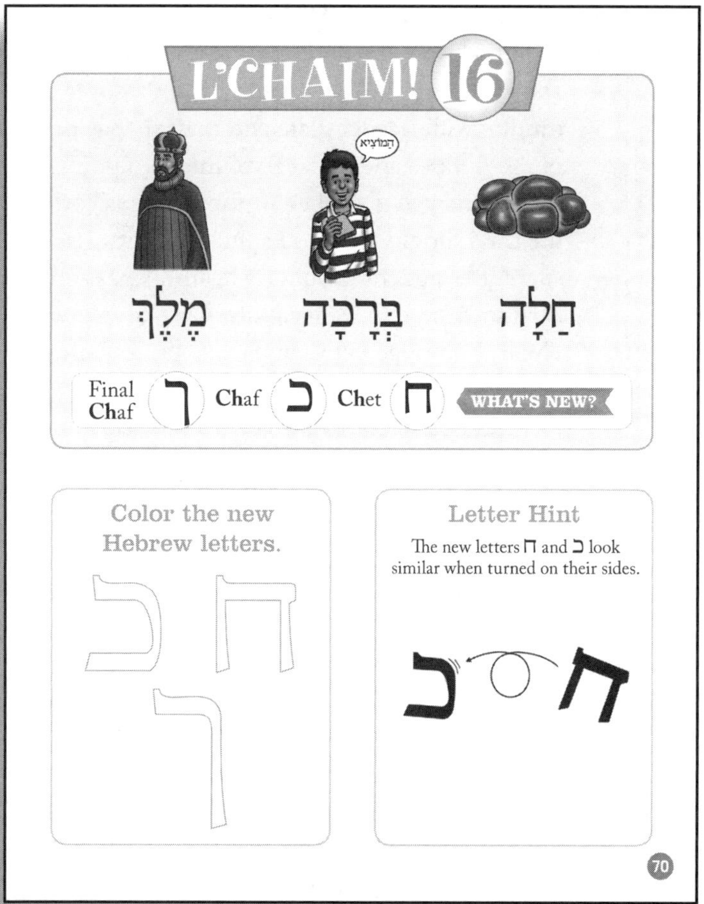

16 L'Chaim!

Pages: 70–74

Key Words: חַלָּה בְּרָכָה מֶלֶךְ

New Letters: ח כ/ך

Vocabulary Word: (cat) חָתוּל

Cognates: הִיפּוֹ, הַמְבּוּרְגֶר, חֲנֻכָּה

Recommended Materials: Phonics Flash Cards #1–31 for review and #32–34, Word Picture Cards #1–38 for review and #39–43; a Shabbat candle, a large candle, a birthday candle; a picture of the Rosh Hashanah candles with apples, honey, and/or a shofar, and Passover candles with a seder plate and matzah (available on Google images); a challah; crayons or colored pencils.

Review Activity: Play two rounds of Around the World (see page 16 for instructions). In the first round, review all of the letter and vowels sounds that students have learned so far. In the second round, review all of the key words and vocabulary items. Play continues in each round until you have gone through all of the items. Ask students to answer the questions you posed at the end of Lesson 15 (see page 91).

Oral Language Lesson

Begin class by taking attendance and asking students how they are doing using the Hebrew greetings that students have already learned.

Ask students to show you the pictures of their pets or favorite animals. Select students who have brought in pictures of animals whose Hebrew names you know and ask them to stand in front of the class. Point to one of the animals and say: "__________ שֶׁל __________ הַ." Ask the class to repeat after you as soon as they understand. Follow this procedure for each of the animals to review the preposition שֶׁל, which indicates possession. Allow any student who forgot to bring in an animal picture to use Word Picture Cards #15, 37, or 43 to practice making the sentences. Ask students to write their names on the back of the animal pictures they brought in (or on a note that can be clipped to the picture) and turn them in. For the next class, look up the Hebrew words for each of these animals and create a large label in Hebrew for each student who provided an animal. The labels need to be large enough for a bulletin board display and should say something like:

הַכֶּלֶב שֶׁל שָׂרָה or הַדָּג שֶׁל מֹשֶׁה

Next, review the key word נֵר. Hold up a candle and say נֵר, then hold up a birthday candle and say נֵר. Ask the class to repeat the word each time. Once you feel that the students recall the word, hold up a large candle and say: נֵר גָּדוֹל, with the class repeating. Then hold up the birthday candle and say, נֵר קָטָן. Once you feel that the students understand the phrases, introduce the word with the preposition that indicates possession (שֶׁל). Hold up a Shabbat candle and say, נֵר שֶׁל שַׁבָּת. Ask the students to repeat the phrase with you as soon as they understand. Next, hold up a Ḥanukkah candle and say נֵר שֶׁל חֲנֻכָּה. Again, tell the class to repeat after you as soon as they understand. Finally, show a picture of Rosh Hashanah candles with apples, honey, and/or a shofar, and Passover candles with a seder plate and matzah and say, נֵר שֶׁל יוֹם טוֹב with the class repeating as soon as they understand. You can find the pictures you need on Google Images.

Now I Know My Alef-Bet!

Complete the **Chet**. Then write three on your own.

ח ח ח

Complete the **Chaf**. Then write three on your own.

כ כ כ

Complete the Final **Chaf**. Then write three on your own.

ך ך ך

Word Building

Read each line aloud.

1. נָ כַ שַׁ חַ לָ סָ
2. נוּ חֶ סֶ כוּ טֶ צוּ
3. הִ חִ מִי כִי לִי צִ
4. דָם חַם שָׁם עַם גַם שָׁם
5. דָן כָּן מָן עָן גַן תַּן

71

their arms. No matter which kinesthetic association you use, ask the students to repeat the letter sound (*ch*) while they do so.

Letter Hint & Color the Letter

Distribute crayons or colored pencils. Ask volunteers to read the sentence in the first Letter Hint. Hold up Phonics Flash Card #32, displaying the ח, and turn it on its side to make a כ. Repeat the procedure by holding up Phonics Flash Card #33, displaying כ, then turn it on its side to make the ח. Allow one or two volunteers to repeat this action. Give students time to color all three letter shapes.

Now I Know My Alef-Bet!

Ask students to trace the letter on the first line with their fingers then in pencil, while repeating the sound that the letter represents. (*ch*) Next, ask them to write three examples of the letter in pencil while repeating the letter's sound. Direct students to do the same with the letters in the second and third lines.

Display pictures of a Shabbat table with candles; a Ḥanukkiyah; the Rosh Hashanah candles with apples, honey, and/or a shofar; and Passover candles with a seder plate and matzah. Say one of the phrases and select a volunteer to point to the picture you described. If the choice is correct, the class should repeat the phrase. If the class is silent, the student should try again. Repeat until each student who wants a turn has had one. Finally, to bridge between passive understanding and active production, point to one of the pictures and select a volunteer to provide the correct phrase for it. The class should repeat the phrase if the student is correct, and the student should try again if the class is silent. Repeat until each student who wants a turn has had one.

Set Induction

Bring in a challah, hold it up and say, חַלָּה. Ask the class to repeat the word, and pay close attention to how they pronounce the initial sound. You can tell students that this sound is hard for many people because it does not exist in English. Ask each student to say the word individually. You may need to model the act of gargling. Be prepared for laughter! Allow a volunteer to read the chapter title. Ask the class what sound they think they will learn in this lesson. (*ch*) Next, distribute pieces of the חַלָּה to every student who can correctly pronounce the Hebrew word חַלָּה.

Introducing the Key Words and Deducing Their Sound-Symbol Associations

Introduce the new letters using the "Multisensory Approach to Hebrew Sound-Symbol Associations" described on page 12. Create a kinesthetic link between the letter shape and its sound by miming a cough as if clearing your throat while saying *ch*. Ask the class to repeat this action. As an alternative you can ask students to create the letter shapes through yoga poses. For example, students can create a ח by standing with their legs together while they touch the floor with their hands. Similarly, they can create a כ by sitting on the floor with their legs and arms stretched out and their heads bent between

Word Building

This activity serves two purposes. First, it reviews all three vowel sounds that students have learned. Second, it provides students with practice in blending C-V-C syllables while requiring them to distinguish between the *m* and *n* sounds in the final position of the syllable. Line 4 drills syllables ending in ם while all of the syllables in Line 5 end in ן. Ask students to take turns reading. By this point in the year students should be able to read sets of at least three items at a time. As they gain confidence, ask them to read full lines. Once students can read whole lines, they can read columns of syllables to provide variety and an added degree of difficulty.

Sound Check

This activity provides students with practice in segmenting the initial phoneme of several key words and cognates. At the same time, it provides students with practice in making fine auditory distinctions. The sound *ch* is highly similar to the sound *h*, and many English speaking students are prone to substitute *h* for *ch*, especially in the initial position. Students who struggle with this activity may need individual practice with fine auditory discrimination.

Begin by providing students with the Hebrew pronunciation of each cognate in the activity (הִיפּוֹ, הַמְבּוּרְגֶר, חֲנֻכָּה). Point to each item as you say its Hebrew name and ask students to point to the picture in their books while repeating the Hebrew name. Circulate to make sure that everyone can complete this crucial first step. Next, ask a volunteer to read the instructions. Select a volunteer to identify the item on the top right. Encourage the volunteer to use the Hebrew pronunciation. Tell the class to listen for the first sound in the word then ask the volunteer to say it clearly. Ask the class what sound they heard at the beginning. (*h*) Ask them to look at the letter in the instruction, and ask, "Does this word begin with the sound of the letter ח?" Once students understand that it does not, repeat this process with the next item on the top row. Students should identify that the initial sound *ch* in the second item does match the

Sound Check

The names of these objects sound similar in Hebrew and English.
Circle all the objects that begin with the new letter ח.

Sounds Right

Read each Hebrew syllable out loud.
Cross out the syllable on each line that sounds different.

1. אַךְ ~~אַק~~ אָח
2. נִח נִיךְ ~~נִיק~~
3. רוּךְ ~~רֻק~~ רֻח
4. שֻׁח ~~סוּק~~ סוּךְ
5. בִּיךְ בִּח ~~בִּק~~

72

letter ח. Even though students have had considerable practice with this kind of activity, this phoneme is so problematic that you should allow students to complete the remaining examples with a partner. Be sure to tell them that they need to say each Hebrew word out loud as they work. Circulate to provide assistance and settle disputes as needed, paying attention especially to those students who have had difficulty with this type of activity previously.

Sounds Right

While students have had some practice matching single letters and C-V syllables that represent the same sound, this is the first time that they are asked to identify C-V-C syllables that sound the same and that not only use different letter and vowel forms but that sound highly similar to the syllable that is not identical. In addition, the matching syllables all contain *ch* in the final position, while the distracter ends with a *k*, the sound English readers most frequently substitute for a *ch* in the final position. Because this activity is more demanding than those previously provided, complete the entire activity as a class. Ask a student to read the instructions, then select volunteers to read individual lines. A student

I Can Understand Hebrew!

Your teacher will read this word to you:

חָתוּל

Your teacher will read these sentences to you.
Check ✓ each sentence that describes the picture in the box.

.1
☑ הַמּוֹרָה בַּכִּתָּה.
☐ הַיַּלְדָּה אוֹכֶלֶת גְּלִידָה.
☑ הַיֶּלֶד וְהַיַּלְדָּה בַּכִּתָּה.

.2
☑ שַׁבָּת בַּבַּיִת.
☑ אַבָּא, אִמָּא וְהַיַּלְדָּה בַּבַּיִת.
☑ חַלָּה וְנֵר עַל הַשֻּׁלְחָן.

.3
☐ הַיֶּלֶד וְהַיַּלְדָּה בַּסֻּכָּה.
☑ הַיֶּלֶד וְהַכֶּלֶב בַּסֻּכָּה.
☑ הַלּוּלָב בַּיָּד שֶׁל הַיֶּלֶד.

.4
☐ הֶחָתוּל וְהַכֶּלֶב בַּכִּתָּה.
☐ הֶחָתוּל וְהַכֶּלֶב בַּסֻּכָּה.
☑ הֶחָתוּל וְהַכֶּלֶב בַּבַּיִת.

73

should read the three choices aloud, and then identify the one that sounds different by saying it. The class should repeat the syllable if they agree that the choice is correct, and the students should point to the answer in their books. Circulate to make sure that every student is completing the work correctly. If the class remains silent, the volunteer should attempt to correct the error. Once the students agree, they should cross out the syllable that is different from the other two.

I Can Understand Hebrew!

Introduce the new vocabulary word by holding up Word Picture Card #42 and saying, חָתוּל. Ask students to repeat the word as soon as they understand it. Repeat it in conjunction with the adjective טוֹב. This step will teach students that חָתוּל is a masculine word. Point to the picture on the top of page 73 and ask a volunteer to identify the object in Hebrew. (חָתוּל) Next, ask questions about the pictures in the four boxes on page 73. Sample questions include:

מִי בַּכִּתָּה? (הַמּוֹרָה בַּכִּתָּה, הַיֶּלֶד בַּכִּתָּה, הַיַּלְדָּה בַּכִּתָּה)

מָה בַּכִּתָּה? (הָעִפָּרוֹן בַּכִּתָּה, הַשֻּׁלְחָן בַּכִּתָּה)

מִי בַּבַּיִת? (אַבָּא בַּבַּיִת, אִמָּא בַּבַּיִת, הַיֶּלֶד וְהַיַּלְדָּה בַּבַּיִת)

מָה בַּבַּיִת? (הַכֶּלֶב בַּבַּיִת, חָתוּל בַּבַּיִת, מִיץ וְחַלָּה בַּבַּיִת)

מִי בַּסֻּכָּה? (הַיֶּלֶד בַּסֻּכָּה)

מָה בַּסֻּכָּה? (הַכֶּלֶב בַּסֻּכָּה, הַלּוּלָב בַּסֻּכָּה)

Once you feel that the students understand the new vocabulary, ask a volunteer to read the directions. Instruct the students to put a check next to a sentence only if it describes the picture. Read the sentences in box #1. You may need to repeat the sentences several times as students work through them. Circulate to provide assistance as needed. Repeat this procedure for all four boxes.

Make the Connection

Shabbat ends when we can see three of these on Saturday evening. Draw a straight line to connect the letters that make the same sounds.
Hint: Some of the letters are in English.

What do we look for at the end of Shabbat? Three stars

Game On

Which Hebrew letter above has the sound of **ch** and comes only at the end of a word? ך

Use this answer to score bonus points in the Wacky Wheelbarrow game in *Ready Set...Go Alef Bet!* online.

74

ך on the Alef Bet Chart on page 4 of their book.

Assessment

For information on assessing students' progress, see page 10. With this lesson, students have learned all the items tested in the fourth oral assessment on page 137. Evaluate a few volunteers one at a time, asking them to read the syllables aloud while you complete the error analysis. You will also want to make notes concerning which students had difficulty with any of the information presented.

Make the Connection

This activity provides students with practice matching individual letters that represent the same sound. In each case, students will connect three letters together, and in four instances they will connect two Hebrew letters and an English letter that represent the same sound.

Ask a volunteer to read the instructions at the top of the page, then allow students to complete the activity individually. When the class has completed the activity, ask them what we need to see to know that Shabbat has ended. (*three stars*)

Game On

Select a volunteer to read the question. Ask a volunteer to write this letter on the board (ך), and take a vote to make sure that the rest of the class agrees. Assign students to complete Lesson 16 in the digital companion at home. Remind them to play the Wacky Wheelbarrow game when they have completed the lesson. You might ask students to print out or e-mail their lesson summaries to you when they have completed all the activities in the lesson. Or you can check their progress in the Behrman House Online Learning Center.

Challenge students to come to the next class with answers to the questions below. They will find the answers in Lesson 16 of the digital companion. Consider sending home a sheet with these questions, or e-mail them to parents, when you assign the lesson in the digital companion. Ask students to write the answers on the sheet and return it, with a parent's signature, at the next class.

1. What does the כ do in the Letter Hint? (*it tumbles into a* ח)
2. Look at the words you crossed out in the "Sounds Right" activity. What Hebrew letter ends all of them? (ק)
3. One animal appears twice in the "I Can Understand Hebrew!" activities. Name that animal in Hebrew. (כֶּלֶב)

When students complete this lesson in the digital companion, and you have checked that they have done so, allow them to color in the ח, כ, and

named to come forward and staple the picture of their animal above the label you indicated. You may need to point out the correct label.

Continue reviewing the preposition that indicates possession (שֶׁל). Say one of the following phrases and ask students to come forward and select the correct cards. If the student is right, the class should repeat the phrase. If the class is silent, the student should try again. Examples of phrases include:

הַכֶּלֶב שֶׁל אַבָּא
הֶחָתוּל שֶׁל אִמָּא
הָעִפָּרוֹן שֶׁל הַיַּלְדָּה
הַחַלָּה שֶׁל הַיֶּלֶד
הַכִּתָּה שֶׁל הַמּוֹרָה

Once students are able to complete this task with ease, select a couple of cards and ask two volunteers to come up. Give the cards to the first student and ask the second to create a phrase using the preposition שֶׁל. If the student creates a correct phrase, the class should repeat it. If the phrase is incorrect, the class should remain silent and the student should attempt to create a correct phrase.

17 Perfect Pitch!

Pages: 75–79

Key Words: פּוּרִים פֶּסַח

New Letter: פּ

Vocabulary Words: (salad) סָלָט (eats, fem.) אוֹכֶלֶת (eats, masc.) אוֹכֵל

Cognate: פּוֹפְּקוֹרְן

Recommended Materials: Phonics Flash Cards #35, 36, and 37, Word Picture Cards #10, 11, 12, 22, 23, 31, 39, and 42 for review, and #44–48; a muffin tin, strips containing one letter or vowel each, 2 sets of colored chips each in a different color; pictures of the Shabbat, Passover, Rosh Hashanah, and Hanukkah candles; an air popper and popcorn, bowls and napkins; a tennis ball; crayons or colored pencils; clay or Playdough.

Review Activity: Play Sound Toss (see page 16 for instructions) focusing on the letters ה, תּ/ת/ט, ח/כ/ך, נ/ן, ס/שׂ, ל, ב/ו, צ/ץ, ג, י, and שׁ, and reviewing all of the vowels that students have learned. Play continues until all of the letter and vowel sounds have been used at least once. Ask students to answer the questions you posed at the end of Lesson 16 (see page 97).

Oral Language Lesson

Before class, staple the animal labels you created to a bulletin board, allowing ample space so that students can place their pictures above the correct label.

Begin class by taking attendance and asking students how they are doing, using the Hebrew greetings that they have already learned, then review any vocabulary and key words that you have not reviewed recently.

Return the animal pictures that students brought in last session, and collect any that students have brought in this time. (You will want to add these to the display for the next session.) Go up to the bulletin board, point to one of the labels, and say: __________ שֶׁל __________ הַ

Ask the class to repeat after you as soon as they understand the phrase. Then, ask the student

Finally, display the pictures of the Shabbat, Passover, Rosh Hashanah, and Ḥanukkah candles. Say the following phrases and allow volunteers to select the correct picture to match each phrase:

נֵר שֶׁל חֲנֻכָּה
נֵר שֶׁל יוֹם טוֹב
נֵר שֶׁל שַׁבָּת

If the student is correct, the class should repeat the phrase. If the student is incorrect, the class should remain silent and the student should try again.

Set Induction

With the permission of your education director, bring an air popper and popcorn into the class. Set the machine up prior to the start of class and plug it in at the end of the oral language lesson. Tell the students to close their eyes and listen to the sound. As the kernels pop, begin to imitate the sound they make by saying *p*. Ask students to join in with you. Allow a volunteer to read the chapter title. Ask the class what sound they think they will learn in this lesson. (*p*)

Introducing the Key Words and Deducing Their Sound-Symbol Associations

Introduce the new letter using the "Multisensory Approach to Hebrew Sound-Symbol Associations" described on page 12. Create a kinesthetic link between the letter shape and its sound by creating the letter using the popcorn you've just popped. Distribute bowls of popcorn to the students and ask them to make a פּ from the popped kernels while repeating the sound *p*. Students can eat the popcorn after they've made a correct version of the letter פּ. As an alternative, you can ask students to create the letter shapes in clay or Playdough. No matter which kinesthetic association you use, ask the students to repeat the letter sound (*p*) while they do so.

Now I Know My Alef-Bet!

Complete the Pay. Then write three on your own.

Sound Check

Cross out all the items that do not begin with the sound of "פּ."

Hint: You can look back to the Key Words on pages 17 and 75. All the other words are similar in Hebrew and English.

76

Letter Hint & Color the Letter

Distribute crayons or colored pencils. Ask volunteers to read the sentence in the Letter Hint. Write the פּ on the board and invite a volunteer to pop a peppermint into its mouth using the chalk. If you have colored chalk available use pink to make the peppermint. Give students time to color in the letter.

Now I Know My Alef-Bet!

Ask students to trace the letter, first with their fingers and then in pencil, while repeating the sound that the letter represents. (*p*) Next, ask them to write three examples of the letter in pencil while repeating the letter's sound.

Sound Check

This activity provides students with practice in segmenting the initial phoneme of some key words and cognates. At the same time, it provides students with practice in making fine auditory distinctions. The sound *p* is fairly similar to the sound *b*, and some students may confuse them. Students who struggle with this activity may need individual practice with fine auditory discrimination.

"Oh, Oh—It's Over!"

"Oh" = ◌וֹ ◌ֹ

The new Hebrew vowel looks like a ball going over a letter. When you see a vowel **O**ver a letter, remember to say "**Oh**!"

Word Building

Read each line aloud.

.1	פּוֹ	לוֹ	בֹּ	גוֹ	נוֹ
.2	בּוֹ	אוֹ	טֹ	קוֹ	יוֹ
.3	פָּ	נַ	שַׁ	חָ	כִּי
.4	אָב	סוֹב	צַו	גַב	דוֹב
.5	פַּח	לָךְ	צַח	בָּךְ	סוֹךְ

77

Begin by providing students with the Hebrew pronunciation of each item in the activity. Ask them to point to each item as you say its Hebrew name. Circulate to make sure that everyone can complete this crucial first step. Next, ask a volunteer to read the instructions. Select a volunteer to identify the item on the top right. Tell the class to listen for the first sound in the word then ask the volunteer to say it clearly. Ask the class what sound they heard at the beginning. (*p*) Ask them to look at the letter in the instructions, then ask, "Does this letter make the same sound as the letter פּ?" Once students understand that the sounds are the same, they should not cross it out. Since students have had considerable practice with this kind of activity, allow them to complete it individually. Be sure to tell them that they need to say each Hebrew word out loud as they work. Circulate to provide assistance as needed, paying attention especially to those students who have had difficulty with this type of activity previously.

"Oh-Oh—It's Over!"

This section presents students with the fourth vowel sound, *oh*. Like all of the other vowels that students encountered earlier, this sound can be represented by more than one symbol, in this case ■וֹ and ■ֹ. Hold up Phonics Flash Card #36 and say *oh*. Ask the class to repeat the sound with you. Continue drilling the sound until you feel that all of the students recognize it. Repeat this procedure using Phonics Flash Card #37. Next, ask students to draw the vowels in the air with their fingers while saying their sounds. Hold a ball (about the size of a tennis ball) over your head and say *oh*. Pass the ball around so that students can feel its shape. Remind them to hold it over their heads and say *oh*. Tell students to look at the picture of the girl, and especially at the ball above her head.

Write the vowels on the board and ask a volunteer to point to the part of each that looks like a ball. Next, point to the first vowel and say *oh*, with the class repeating after you. Repeat this procedure with both new vowels until you are confident that the students recognize them. Write a few Hebrew C-V syllables on the board, such as לֹ, סוֹ, נֹ, חוֹ, בּוֹ, צֹ, כּוֹ, and so on. Write them with a lot of space between each. Invite volunteers to come up to the board. Say one of the syllables and ask the volunteer to point to it. Repeat the process with a variety of syllables until every student has had at least one turn. Then, write these C-V syllables scattered between the syllables you already have on the board: לִי, וָ, בִּי, אִי, and so on. Repeat the drill as above mixing the syllables and allowing volunteers to identify them until you are confident that the class understands this simple C-V blending. *Note*: Do NOT include any syllables that contain either ■ֻ or וּ, as this vowel sounds very similar to the new vowel, and the וֹ and וּ are also prone to confuse students because they are so similar visually.

Next, review C-V-C blending using a mixture of the vowels students know. Some of these syllables should end with a ם, ן, ץ, or a ך, as that is the only position in which these letter forms can appear. Again, do not include any syllables that contain either ■ֻ or וּ.

Word Building

This activity serves two purposes. First, it reviews three of the four vowel sounds that students have learned. The *oo* vowel is

not reviewed at this time as its sound is similar to the new vowel *oh,* and two of these vowels are also visually similar (וֹ and ֹ). For both reasons, these two vowels are also easily confused. Ask students to take turns reading. By this point in the year students should be able to read sets of at least two or three items. As they gain confidence, ask them to read full lines. Once students can read whole lines, they can read columns of syllables to provide variety.

I Can Understand Hebrew!

This activity introduces students to their first Hebrew verb, אוֹכֵל/אוֹכֶלֶת. Hold up Word Picture Card #46 and say:

הַיֶּלֶד אוֹכֵל.

Ask the class to repeat the sentence as soon as they understand it. Repeat the process with Word Picture Card #47, saying:

הַיַּלְדָּה אוֹכֶלֶת.

Invite a boy and a girl to stand in front of the class. (*Note*: Be sure to get permission from your education director for this activity as some students may have food allergies.) Give each a piece of bagel, fruit, or candy and alternate pointing to the boy and the girl as the class provides the correct sentence:

הַיַּלְדָּה אוֹכֶלֶת. or ________ אוֹכֵל.

Introduce the new vocabulary word, סָלָט. Hold up Word Picture Card #48 and say סָלָט, asking the class to repeat the word as soon as they understand it. Once you feel that the students understand the word, repeat it in conjunction with the adjective טוֹב. This step will teach students that סָלָט is a masculine word.

Next, you can ask questions like:

מִי אוֹכֵל סָלָט? (אַבָּא, הַיֶּלֶד)
מִי אוֹכֶלֶת סָלָט? (הַמּוֹרָה, אִמָּא, הַיַּלְדָּה)

Once you feel that the students understand the new vocabulary, ask a volunteer to read the directions. Read the first sentence and ask students to draw a line from the person to the food described by the sentence. Follow the same procedure for the remaining three sentences. You may need to repeat the sentences several times as students complete the activity. Circulate to provide assistance as needed.

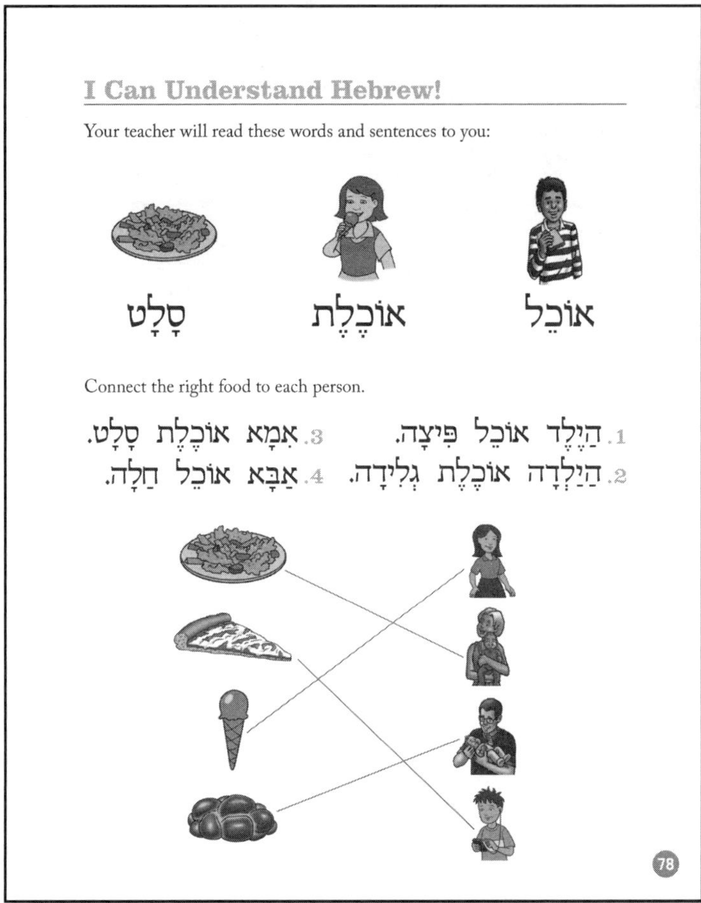
I Can Understand Hebrew!

Your teacher will read these words and sentences to you:

אוֹכֵל אוֹכֶלֶת סָלָט

Connect the right food to each person.

1. הַיֶּלֶד אוֹכֵל פִּיצָה.
2. הַיַּלְדָּה אוֹכֶלֶת גְּלִידָה.
3. אִמָּא אוֹכֶלֶת סָלָט.
4. אַבָּא אוֹכֵל חַלָּה.

78

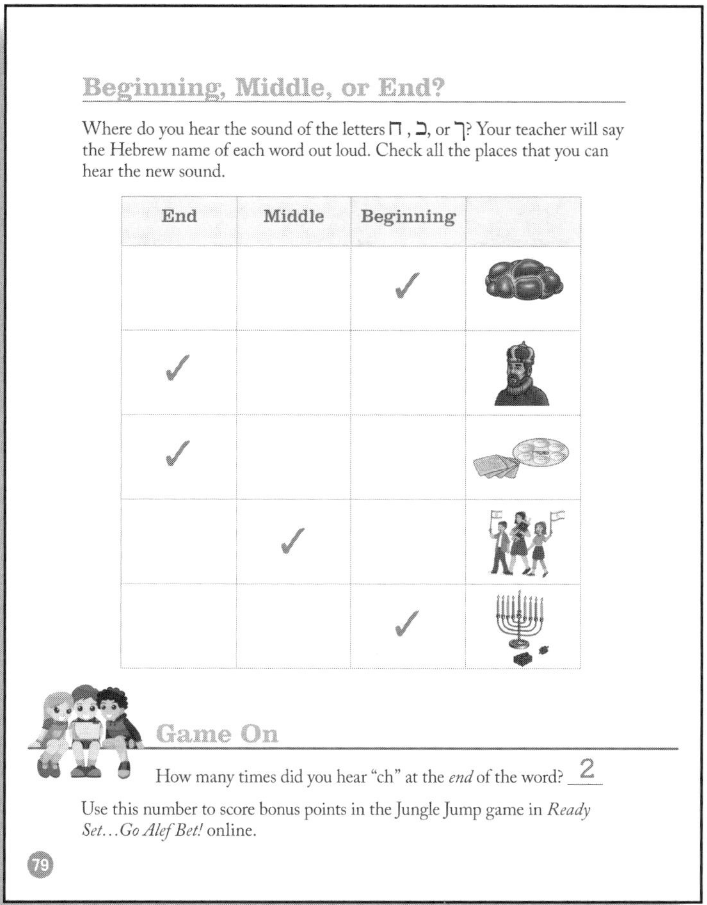

Beginning, Middle, or End?

Where do you hear the sound of the letters ח, כ, or ך? Your teacher will say the Hebrew name of each word out loud. Check all the places that you can hear the new sound.

End	Middle	Beginning	
		✓	
✓			
✓			
	✓		
		✓	

Game On

How many times did you hear "ch" at the *end* of the word? 2

Use this number to score bonus points in the Jungle Jump game in *Ready Set...Go Alef Bet!* online.

79

2. How many times can you find the *o* vowel in the "Word Building" activity? (*fifteen*)
3. In the first "Beginning, Middle, or End?" activity, how many words end with the sound of *ch*? (*two*)

As an additional assignment, ask students to bring in pictures of their favorite foods.

When students complete this lesson in the digital companion, and you have checked that they have done so, allow them to color in the פּ on the Alef Bet Chart on page 4 of their book.

Assessment

For information on assessing students' progress, see page 10. With this lesson, make notes concerning which students had difficulty with any of the information presented. You can also continue listening to individual students complete the fourth oral assessment.

Beginning, Middle, or End?

In this activity, students practice segmenting the sound of the letters ח and כ/ךְ, and identifying the various positions in which these sounds can be found in several key words and one cognate.

Ask a volunteer to read the instructions at the top of page 79. Then describe the first picture using the Hebrew pronunciation, חַלָּה. Ask the class where they hear the sound *ch*, selecting a volunteer to answer. (*the beginning*) Ask the class who agrees with the answer and who does not. You may need to repeat the word. Once the class agrees, tell them to check the box in the "Beginning" column. Even though the class has done this kind of activity once before, because of the difficulty of the phoneme *ch* and the complexity of the activity, complete it together as a class. Be sure to say the cognate חֲנֻכָּה with the Hebrew pronunciation.

Game On

Ask a volunteer how many times he or she heard the sound *ch* at the end of a word. (*two*) Allow the rest of the class to vote whether or not they agree with the answer. If there is a disagreement, review the material again. Ask students to complete Lesson 17 in the digital companion at home. Remind them to play the Jungle Jump game when they have completed the lesson. You might ask students to print out or e-mail their lesson summaries to you when they have completed all the activities in the lesson. Or assess their progress in the Behrman House Online Learning Center.

Challenge students to come to the next class with answers to the questions below. They will find the answers in Lesson 17 of the digital companion. Consider sending home a sheet with these questions, or e-mail them to parents, when you assign the lesson in the digital companion. Ask students to write the answers on the sheet and return it, with a parent's signature, at the next class.

1. What happens to one of the pink peppermints in the Letter Hint? (*it pops into the Pay's mouth*)

The girl should collect the appropriate cards, and if she is correct, the class should respond by repeating the sentence. You can repeat this process with different combinations of food words until every student has had at least one chance to participate.

Ask students to show you the pictures of their favorite foods. Select up to six students who have brought in pictures of foods whose Hebrew names you know and that you think are most appropriate to teach. Ask those students to stand in front of the class. Point to one of the foods and say its name in Hebrew. Ask the class to repeat the word as soon as they understand it.

Repeat this procedure with each food word and review them until you are confident that the class understands each word. Then, indicate a boy from the group and have him describe the food he would choose to eat by saying

אֲנִי אוֹכֵל ________.

Ask the class to repeat after you as soon as they understand:

________ אוֹכֵל ________.

Then, indicate a girl from the group and describe the food she would choose to eat by saying

18 Right On!

Pages: 80–84

Key Words: רֹאשׁ רֶגֶל

New Letters: ר

Cognates: לָמָה, לִמוֹן, רַדְיוֹ, רָקֶטָה

Recommended Materials: Phonics Flash Card #38, Word Picture Cards #14, 18, 19, 28, 29, 39, and 46–55, and possibly #1, 3, 7, 9, 12, 13, 30 and 38; sets of the cards made of pairs of C-V and C-V-C syllables that are homonyms for the Concentration game; crayons or colored pencils.

Review Activity: Play Concentration (see page 17 for instructions) using syllables that represent identical sounds made up of different letter and vowel forms. Play continues until all of the pairs have been matched and a winner can be declared. Ask students to answer the questions you posed at the end of Lesson 16 (see page 102).

Oral Language Lesson

Begin class by taking attendance and asking students how they are doing using the Hebrew greetings.

Using Word Picture Cards #14, 18, 19, 28, 29, 39, 46, 47, and 48, review all of the food and drink words that students have learned:

גְלִידָה, מַיִם, דָג, מִיץ, פִּיצָה, חַלָּה, סָלָט

as well as the verbs for eating (אוֹכֵל, אוֹכֶלֶת). You should also review the other food and drink words that students have learned that are cognates using Word Picture Cards #49–55):

קוֹלָה, בָּנָנָה, יוֹגוּרְט, תֵּה, הַמְבּוּרְגֶר, לִימוֹן, פּוֹפְּקוֹרְן

You can use all of these Word Picture Cards to review complex sentences. For example, call up a boy. Say the sentence:

________ אוֹכֵל פּוֹפְּקוֹרְן וְהַמְבּוּרְגֶר.

The boy should collect the appropriate cards, and if he is correct, the class should respond by repeating the sentence. Next, call a girl up and say:

________ אוֹכֶלֶת פִּיצָה, גְלִידָה, וְסָלָט.

Word Building

Read each line aloud.

1. רוֹ פֹּ סֹ לוֹ גוֹ נֹ
2. תֹּ בּוֹ שׁוֹ כֹּ חוֹ מֹ
3. טוֹר בּוֹר שׁוֹר קֹר כֹּר מוֹר
4. תּוּר בֶּר צוּר כּוּר חוּר מֶר
5. מָרוֹר בָּחוּר צִפּוֹר כִּנּוֹר חִבּוּר חֲמוֹר

Now I Know My Alef-Bet!

Complete the **R**esh. Then write three on your own.

ר ר ר

81

Letter Hint & Color the Letter

Distribute crayons or colored pencils. Ask volunteers to read the sentence in the Letter Hint. Write the ר on the board and direct the class to draw a round ר in the air while they say the sound *r*. Give students time to color in the letter and turn it into a round back of a head.

Word Building

This activity focuses on the use of the new letter ר in all three positions within a word. At the same time, it provides students with practice distinguishing the vowel sounds *oh* and *oo*. By this point in the year students should be able to read sets of at least three items initially. As they gain confidence, ask them to read full lines. Once students can read whole lines, they can read columns of syllables to provide variety.

Now I Know My Alef-Bet!

Ask students to trace the letter on the first line with their fingers and to trace it in pencil, while repeating the sound that the letter represents. (*r*) Next, ask them to write three examples of the letter in pencil while repeating the letter's sound.

אֲנִי אוֹכֶלֶת ________.

Ask the class to repeat after you as soon as they understand:

________ אוֹכֶלֶת ________.

Follow this procedure for each of the students whom you have selected to review the verb אוֹכֵל/אוֹכֶלֶת. Ask all of the students to hand in their pictures. Look up the Hebrew words for each of these foods and create large labels in Hebrew for food items. The labels need to be large enough for a bulletin board display. You should also create a large title for the bulletin board:

מָה אַתָּה אוֹכֵל? מָה אַתְּ אוֹכֶלֶת?

Set Induction

Ask students to tell you which holiday we celebrate by eating a round חַלָּה with apples and honey. (רֹאשׁ הַשָּׁנָה) Tell them that רֹאשׁ הַשָּׁנָה not only begins with this lesson's new letter, but it even contains one of the chapter's new key words. Select a volunteer to read the chapter title. Ask the class what sound they think they will learn in this lesson. (*r*).

Introducing the Key Words and Deducing Their Sound-Symbol Associations

Introduce the new letter using the "Multisensory Approach to Hebrew Sound-Symbol Associations" described on page 12. Create a kinesthetic link between the letter shape and its sound by miming a lion batting its paw and roaring by saying *r*. Ask the class to repeat this action. As an alternative, students can create the letter shape through a yoga pose. To create a ר, students should stand with their legs together. They should then bend at the waist with their arms arched toward the floor. No matter which kinesthetic association you use, ask the students to repeat the letter sound *r* while they do so.

Take a Closer Look!

Unlike English letters, which vary greatly in both size and shape, Hebrew letters lack distinctive features, and many of them are highly similar in appearance. For this reason Hebrew requires the reader to look closely at every letter and vowel.

By this point in *Ready, Set…Go Alef Bet!*, students have been exposed to most of the letters that are visually similar. This activity provides visual discrimination practice for many of these pairs. Line 1 asks students to differentiate between פּ and many of the letters that look similar to it, such as ט, תּ, כ, בּ. Line 2 requires students to distinguish between י and ו, נ, ג, and ר. Lines 3 and 5 provide practice distinguishing between letters that share an overall shape, such as צ/ע and ט/מ. While these letters differ more from each other than many of the other visually similar letters, their shared general shape makes it difficult to tell them apart at a glance. Lines 4 and 7 ask students to differentiate between ה, ח, ת, and כ. Line 6 requires students to distinguish שׁ from שׂ and ע, while Line 8 provides practice distinguishing between ן, ץ, ו, י, and ג.

Select a volunteer to read the instructions and ask students to complete the activity individually, as you need to assess not only which students are having difficulty with visual discrimination overall, but which category presents the most trouble for them in order to provide proper remediation. Be sure to circulate, both to provide assistance and to determine which students need more practice in this area. Pay close attention to and make note of the specific types of mistakes that individual students make.

The code and illustration activity at the bottom provide a self-checking mechanism. Tell students to write the letters they circled in their numbered spaces. Students should be able to actually read the sentence produced. If they cannot make sense of it, it means that one or more of their answers is incorrect. When students correctly read the sentence, congratulate them on having read a real sentence in Hebrew!

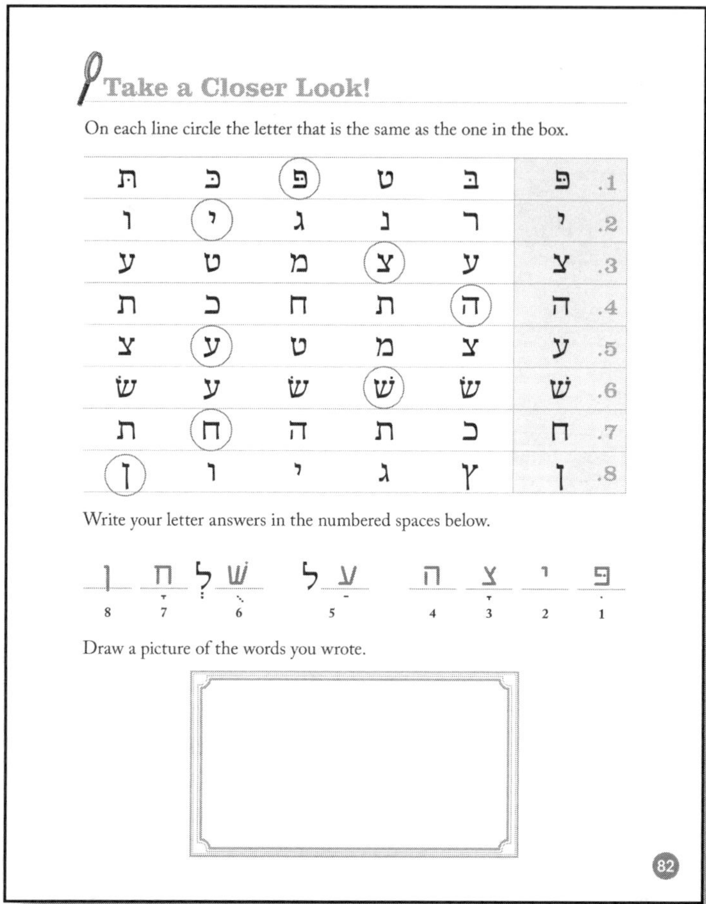

Once students have correctly completed the sentence they should say it out loud to themselves and illustrate it with a drawing. If any students struggle with the meaning of the sentence, give them Word Picture Cards #1, 3, 7, 9, 12, 13, 29, 30, and 38. Ask them to select the correct card as you read each word. Once they can find the cards, ask them to put the cards in order under each word in the book, and then to reread the sentence for themselves.

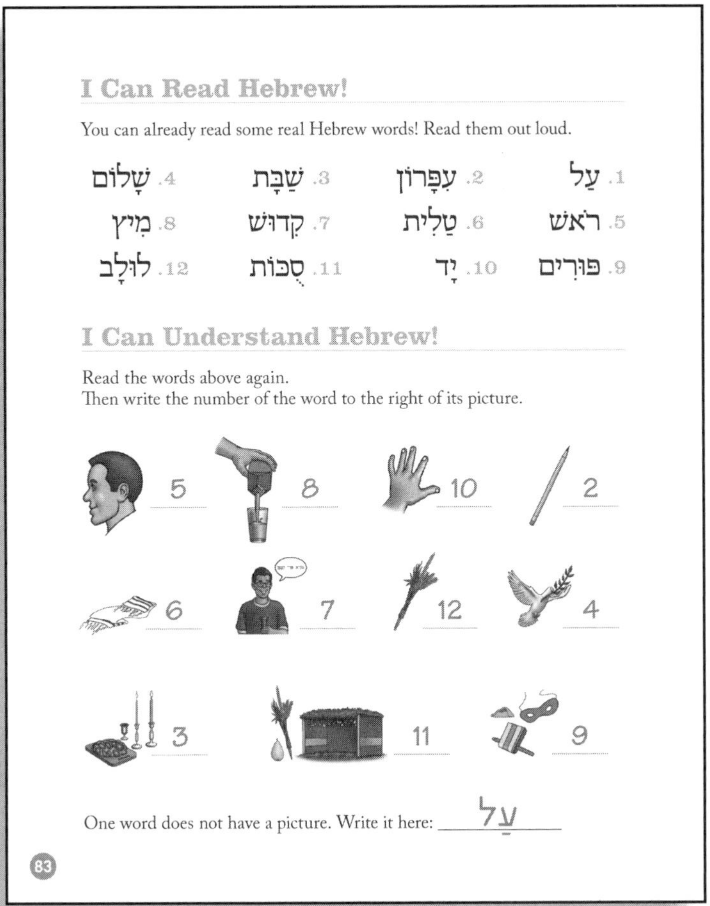

I Can Read Hebrew!

You can already read some real Hebrew words! Read them out loud.

1. עַל	2. עִפָּרוֹן	3. שַׁבָּת	4. שָׁלוֹם
5. רֹאשׁ	6. טַלִּית	7. קִדּוּשׁ	8. מִיץ
9. פּוּרִים	10. יָד	11. סֻכּוֹת	12. לוּלָב

I Can Understand Hebrew!

Read the words above again.
Then write the number of the word to the right of its picture.

One word does not have a picture. Write it here: עַל

83

I Can Read Hebrew!

As the activity on the previous page demonstrates, students can actually read—and understand—many of the words they have learned so far. This is their first opportunity to read a dozen of the words they have learned in this program. Ask volunteers to read each of the words in this activity. You may need to reread some of the words to give every student the opportunity to read a word.

I Can Understand Hebrew!

This activity builds on the previous one by giving students the opportunity to identify the meaning of the words they just read. Tell students to look at the item on the right side of the top line. Ask a volunteer to identify the item in Hebrew. (עִפָּרוֹן) If the student is correct, the class should repeat the word. Next, tell the class to reread the words above until they can find the correct word. (עִפָּרוֹן) Once they find the word and identify its number (2), tell the class to read word #3 and find its matching picture, and to write the number 3 next to it. They should continue in this manner with words 4 through 12. Allow the students to complete this activity with a partner while you circulate to provide assistance as needed. When all of the pairs have finished matching the words to their pictures, ask students to find the one word that did not have an illustration (עַל) and to write it on the blank line provided.

Sound Check

This activity provides students with practice in segmenting the initial phoneme of some key words and cognates.

Begin by providing students with the Hebrew pronunciation of each item in the activity. (See "Cognates" on page 103.) Ask them to point to each item as you say its Hebrew name. Circulate to make sure that everyone can complete this crucial first step. Next, ask a volunteer to read the instructions. Select a volunteer to identify the item on the top right. (רֶגֶל) Tell the class to listen for the first sound in the word, then ask the volunteer to say it clearly. Ask the class what sound they heard at the beginning. (*r*) Ask them to look at the letter in the instruction, and ask them, "Does this item begin with the sound of the letter ר?"

Once students understand that the sounds are the same, they should circle the item. Since students have had considerable practice with this kind of activity, allow them to complete it individually. Be sure to tell them that they need to say each Hebrew word out loud as they work. Circulate to provide assistance as needed, paying attention especially to those students who have had difficulty with this type of activity previously.

Game On

This activity provides a mechanism for checking the students' answers to the Sound Check activity. Ask a volunteer how many words he or she circled. Ask the rest of the class if they came up with that number or another one. If there is a dispute about the number of words (*four*), review as a class. Ask students to complete Lesson 18 in the digital companion at home. Remind them to play the Hip Hop Hebrew game when they have completed the lesson. You might ask students to print out or e-mail their lesson summaries to you when they have completed all the activities in the lesson. Or assess their progress in the Behrman House Online Learning Center.

Challenge students to come to the next class with answers to the questions below. They will find the answers in Lesson 18 of the digital companion. Consider sending home a sheet with

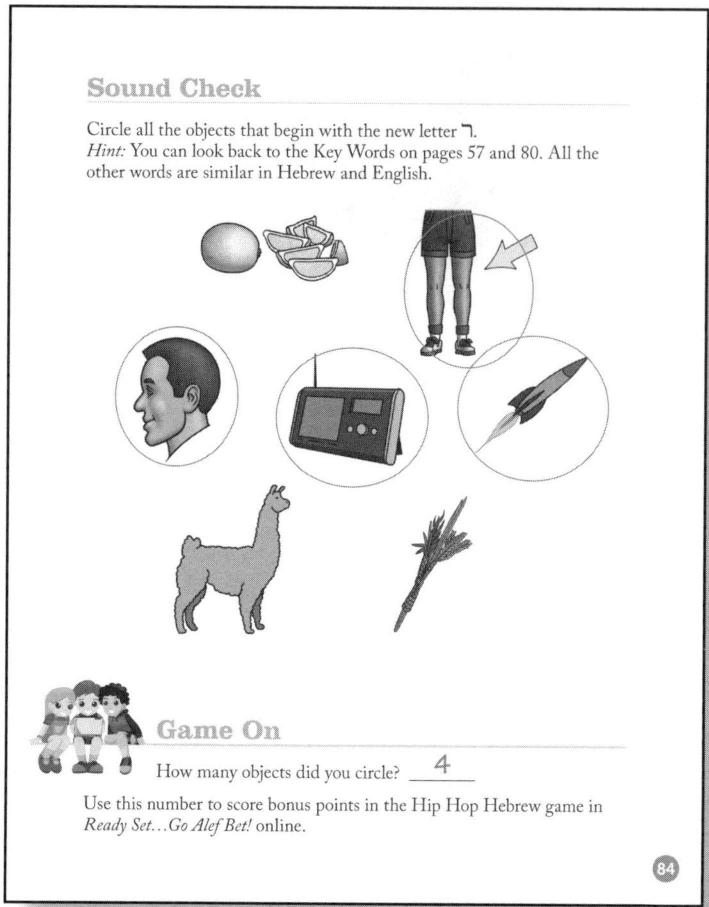

Sound Check

Circle all the objects that begin with the new letter ר.
Hint: You can look back to the Key Words on pages 57 and 80. All the other words are similar in Hebrew and English.

Game On

How many objects did you circle? 4

Use this number to score bonus points in the Hip Hop Hebrew game in *Ready Set...Go Alef Bet!* online.

84

these questions, or e-mail them to parents, when you assign the lesson in the digital companion. Ask students to write the answers on the sheet and return it, with a parent's signature, at the next class.

1. How many times does the new letter ר appear in the "Word Building" activity? (*twenty*)
2. How many words in the "Sound Check" activity begin with the letter ר? (*four*)

When students complete this lesson in the digital companion, and you have checked that they have done so, allow them to color in the ר on the Alef Bet Chart on page 4 of their book.

Assessment

For information on assessing students' progress, see page 12. Make notes concerning which students had difficulty with any of the information presented in this lesson. You can also continue listening to individual students complete the fourth oral assessment on page 137.

as well as the ones reviewed in the last lesson, until you are confident that students understand.

Set Induction

Hold up Word Picture Card #58, and say: זֶבְּרָה. Ask the class to repeat the word as soon as they understand it. Once you feel that the students understand the word, repeat it with the adjectives גְּדוֹלָה and קְטַנָּה. This step will teach students the feminine gender of the new word זֶבְּרָה. As you introduce the word זֶבְּרָה, tell students to pay attention to the first sound in the word. Allow a volunteer to read the chapter title. Ask the class what sound they think they will learn in this lesson. (*z*)

Introducing the Key Words and Deducing Their Sound-Symbol Associations

Introduce the new letter using the "Multisensory Approach to Hebrew Sound-Symbol Associations" described on page 12. Create a kinesthetic link between the letter shape and its sound by miming a person trying to swat a fly with a newspaper. Move your eyes and head from side to side, as if following the flight of a fly while saying *z*. Ask the class to repeat this action.

19 Zigs and Zags

Pages: 85–89

Key Word: זֶבְּרָה

New Letter: ז

Recommended Materials: Phonics Flash Cards #39-41, Word Picture Cards for review, and #58; prepared Bingo cards with index cards for each of the syllables being reviewed, and a pile of markers or beans for each student; a small basket and five ping-pong balls; crayons or colored pencils, including blue, green, and black.

Review Activity: Play Bingo (see page 17 for instructions) using cards divided into five rows and five columns. The center square should contain the word חָפְשִׁי ("free," pronounced *ḥofshi*). The remaining squares should be filled with C-V and C-V-C syllables composed of the letters and vowels that students have learned so far. Place special emphasis on the letters ס, נ, ן, צ, ץ, שׁ, ךְ, כ, ח, פּ, and ר, as well as the vowels ■וֹ, ■ֶ, ■ִי, and ■ִ. Play continues until a winner can be declared. You can play a second round if the class is especially interested. Ask students to answer the questions you posed at the end of Lesson 18 (see page 107).

Oral Language Lesson

Before class, staple the food pictures with their labels and the large title to a bulletin board. You may opt to make use of those that the class brought in as well as those Hebrew words (including cognates) that they have learned over the course of the program.

Begin class by taking attendance and asking students how they are doing using the Hebrew greetings that students have already learned.

Teach עַיִן, אֹזֶן, אַף, and פֶּה. Play שִׁמְעוֹן אוֹמֵר ("Simon Says") using all of these body parts, as well as the two key words they learned last lesson (רֶגֶל and רֹאשׁ) and the prepositional phrase:

יָד עַל ________.

At the end of class, review the Hebrew words for the foods you have placed on the bulletin board,

As an alternative, students can create the letter shape through a yoga pose. To create a ז students should stand up straight with their legs together. Their arms should be stretched out from their shoulder with left arm angled slightly toward the floor and the right arm angled slightly toward the ceiling. No matter which kinesthetic association you use, ask the students to repeat the letter sound *z* while they do so.

Letter Hint & Color the Letter

Distribute crayons or colored pencils. Ask volunteers to read the sentence in the Letter Hint. Draw a zigzag on the board and invite a volunteer to turn it into a ז. Give students time to color in the letter.

Now I Know My Alef-Bet!

Ask students to trace the letter with their fingers first and then in pencil, while repeating the sound that the letter represents. *(z)* Next, ask them to write three examples of the letter in pencil while repeating the letter's sound.

Hidden Picture

Pass out blue, green, and black crayons or colored pencils. Ask a volunteer to read the instructions and allow students to work independently to complete the activity. Circulate to provide assistance as needed.

Now I Know My Alef-Bet!

Complete the Zayin. Then write three on your own.

Hidden Picture

Color in the hidden picture.

Green = "G"
Blue = "CH"
White = "Z"
Black = all other sounds

86

"Egg-xactly!"

"Eh" = ▢ֱ ▢ֶ

The new Hebrew vowels look like eggs in a nest. When you see three dots or five dots under a letter, remember to say "Eh"!

Word Building

Read each line aloud.

.1 עֶ	רֶ	כֶ	נֶ	פֶּ	זֶ
.2 הֶב	לֶב	חָו	שֶׁם	פֶּן	קַב
.3 עֹז	לוּז	חוּץ	זוּז	פּוּז	רוּץ
.4 הָלוֹ	רֶלוֹ	חֱלוֹ	נֶלִי	פֶּלִי	אֶלִי
.5 אֱגוֹז	רֶמֶז	גָזוֹז	נֶשֶׁק	פֶּרֶק	מֶשֶׁק

87

volunteers to identify them until you are confident that the class understands this simple C-V blending.

Next, review C-V-C blending using a mixture of the vowels students know. Some of these syllables should end with a ם, ץ, ן, or a ךְ. Pay attention to any student who has trouble blending the final consonant onto the end of the word and adds an extra vowel sound at the end of the C-V-C syllable. Students who have difficulty with this type of blending may need additional reinforcement, preferably in a small group.

Word Building

This activity serves two purposes. First, it drills the new letter ז in all three positions within a word. Second, it reviews all of the vowel sounds that students have learned. Ask students to take turns reading. By this point in the year students should be able to read sets of at least three items. As they gain confidence, ask them to read full lines. Once students can read whole lines they can read columns of syllables to provide variety.

"Egg-xactly!"

This section presents students with the fifth and final vowel sound introduced in *Ready, Set...Go Alef Bet!* (*eh*). Like all of the other vowels that students encountered earlier, this sound can be represented by more than one symbol, in this case ▢ֶ and ▢ֱ. Hold up Phonics Flash Card #40 and say "eh." Ask students to repeat the sound, and repeat the procedure using Phonics Flash Card #41. Ask students to look at the top of page 87, put their fingers on the vowel on the right and say "eh". Repeat for the vowel on the left. You may want to remind students that the boxes represent any Hebrew letter. Next, ask students to draw the vowels in the air with their fingers while saying their sounds. Hold a small basket in front of you and invite the class to gather around it so that they can see. Place three ping pong balls in the basket and say "eh." Ask the class to repeat. Next, place five ping pong balls in the basket and say "eh." Ask the class to repeat the vowel sound. Pass the basket around and ask each student to place three or five eggs in the basket in the correct configuration while saying "eh." If the student is correct, the class should repeat the sound. If the class remains silent, the student should rearrange the basket to create the correct image of the vowel. Tell students to look at the eggs in the nests on the top of page 87.

Draw an empty nest (a simple circle will suffice) on the board and ask a volunteer to put the "eggs" in the nest. If the student is correct, the class should say, "eh." Repeat this procedure with both new vowels until you are confident that the students recognize them. Write a few Hebrew C-V syllables on the board, such as פֶּ, עֶ, זֶ, חֶ, צֶ, נֶ, שֶׁ and so on. Write them with a lot of space between each. Invite volunteers to come up to the board. Say one of the syllables and ask the volunteer to point to it. Repeat the process with a variety of syllables until every student has had at least one turn. Then, write C-V syllables composed of the same consonants with the other vowels that have been introduced. Write these new syllables between the ones that are already on the board. Repeat the drill as above, mixing the syllables and allowing

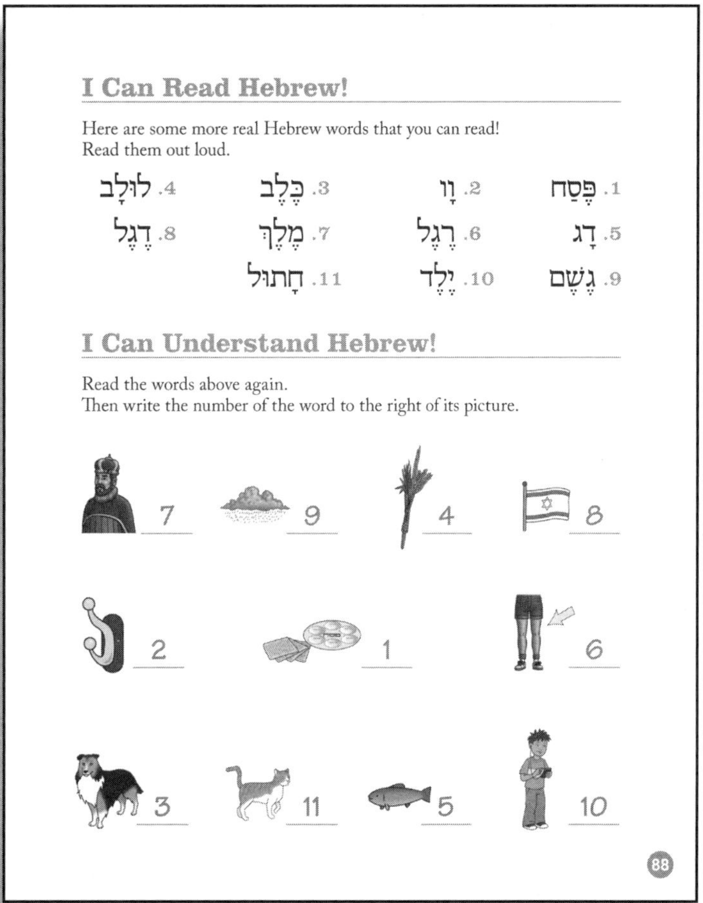

I Can Read Hebrew!

Here are some more real Hebrew words that you can read!
Read them out loud.

1. פֶּסַח 2. וָו 3. כֶּלֶב 4. לוּלָב
5. דָג 6. רֶגֶל 7. מֶלֶךְ 8. דֶגֶל
9. גֶשֶׁם 10. יֶלֶד 11. חָתוּל

I Can Understand Hebrew!

Read the words above again.
Then write the number of the word to the right of its picture.

7 9 4 8
2 1 6
3 11 5 10

88

I Can Read Hebrew!

As noted in the previous lesson, students can now read with understanding many of the words they have learned so far. This exercise provides eleven additional words for students to read with full comprehension. Ask volunteers to read each of the words in this activity. You may need to reread some of the words to give every student the opportunity to read at least once.

I Can Understand Hebrew!

This activity builds on the previous one by giving students the opportunity to identify the meaning of the words they just read. Select a student to reread word #1. (פֶּסַח) Then tell the class to find the picture that matches the word among the objects at the bottom of the page. (*in the middle of the second row*) Circulate to make sure that every student has correctly identified the meaning of the word פֶּסַח. Next, tell the class to write the number "1" on the line next to the picture of פֶּסַח. If students have difficulty with this activity, complete it as a class. If they grasp it easily, allow them to complete the page with a partner. If you choose the second option, be sure to tell the students to read each word out loud, and circulate so you can provide assistance as needed.

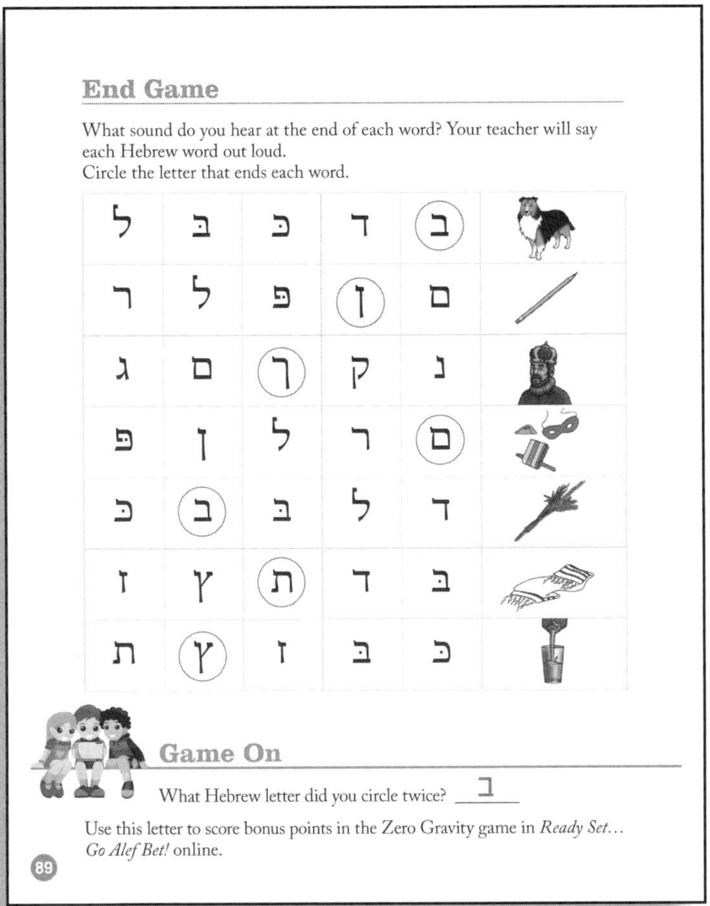

End Game

What sound do you hear at the end of each word? Your teacher will say each Hebrew word out loud.
Circle the letter that ends each word.

ל	בּ	כּ	ד	(ב)	
ר	ל	פּ	(ן)	ם	
ג	ם	(ך)	ק	נ	
פּ	ן	ל	ר	(ם)	
כ	(ב)	בּ	ל	ד	
ז	ץ	(ת)	ד	בּ	
ת	(ץ)	ז	בּ	כ	

Game On

What Hebrew letter did you circle twice? ב

Use this letter to score bonus points in the Zero Gravity game in *Ready Set... Go Alef Bet!* online.

89

mail their lesson summaries to you when they have completed all the activities in the lesson. Or assess their progress in the Behrman House Online Learning Center.

Challenge students to come to the next class with answers to the questions below. They will find the answers in Lesson 19 of the digital companion. Consider sending home a sheet with these questions, or e-mail them to parents, when you assign the lesson in the digital companion. Ask students to write the answers on the sheet and return it, with a parent's signature, at the next class.

1. How many times does the new letter ז appear in the "Word Building" activity? (*nine*)
2. How many times does the letter ל appear in the "I Can Read Hebrew" activity? (*eight*)
3. What letter ends a word on both of the "End Game" activities? (ב)

When students complete this lesson in the digital companion, and you have checked that they have done so, allow them to color in the ז on the Alef-Bet Chart on page 4 of their book.

End Game

This activity provides students with additional practice in segmenting the final phoneme of several words using key words that they have learned.

Begin by asking a volunteer to say the Hebrew name of the item on the top right. (כֶּלֶב). Tell the class to listen for the last sound in the word and ask the volunteer to say it clearly. Next, select a volunteer to read the instructions at the top of the page. Ask the class what sound they heard at the end. (*v*) Ask the class to find the letter that represents the sound *v* and to put their finger on it. Circulate to make sure that every student has identified the correct letter, providing assistance as necessary. Then ask students to circle the letter that represents the sound *v*.

If a lot of students have difficulty with this example, complete one or two more, then allow students to complete the activity individually. Remind them to say each Hebrew word out loud, and circulate to provide assistance as necessary. If a student struggles with this activity, he or she may need additional practice with segmentation.

Game On

This activity provides a mechanism for checking the students' answers to the End Game activity. Ask volunteers the following questions:

1. What is the Hebrew word for the item shown in the second line? (עִפָּרוֹן)
2. What sound do you hear at the end of עִפָּרוֹן? (*n*)
3. What letter makes the sound *n*? (ן) Make sure that every student has identified the correct letter. Repeat this procedure for the rest of the page.

Then, ask, "How many times did you circle ן? (*1*) ץ? (*1*) ך? (*1*) ם? (*1*) ת? (*1*) ב? (*2*). Select a volunteer to read the instructions and tell the students to write the letter they circled twice in the blank provided.

Ask students to complete Lesson 19 in the digital companion at home. Remind them to play the Zero Gravity game when they have completed the lesson. You might ask students to print out or e-

Assessment

For information on assessing students' progress, see page 10. Make notes concerning which students had difficulty with any of the information presented in this lesson. You should also complete administering the fourth oral assessment on page 137.

juice/water, yogurt, eggs, cream cheese, bagels, etc. Review all of the following words:

שֻׁלְחָן, עַל, גְּלִידָה, דָג, מַיִם, מִיץ, חַלָּה, אוֹכֵל,
אוֹכֶלֶת, סָלָט, הַמְבּוּרְגֶר, לְמוֹן,
פּוֹפְּקוֹרְן, תֵּה, יוֹגוּרְט, פִּיצָה, בָּנָנָה, קוֹלָה

Set Induction

Write the letter א on the board. Ask if anyone can remember the letter's name. (*Alef*). You can also bring a shofar into class and ask the students to tell you as much as they can about it (what it is called, what it is made of, when we use it, and even what it was used for in biblical times). If you know how to blow the shofar, demonstrate it for the class, or invite someone who has the skill to show the students how it's done. Select a volunteer to read the chapter title. Ask the class what sound they think they will learn in this lesson (*f*).

Introducing the Key Words and Deducing Their Sound-Symbol Associations

Introduce the new letters using the "Multisensory Approach to Hebrew Sound-Symbol Associations" described on page 12. Create a kinesthetic link between the letter shape and its

20 Fun, Fun, Fun

Pages: 90–94

Key Words: שׁוֹפָר אָלֶף

New Letters: פ/ף

Recommended Materials: Phonics Flash Cards #42 and 43, Word Picture Cards #3, 7, 14, 18, 19, 20, 28, 29, 39, 46–55 for review, and #59 and 60; large rectangular cards with letter pairs on them for the "Same or Different?" game; a balloon; crayons or colored pencils.

Review Activity: Play Same or Different? (see page 17 for instructions) using single pairs of the visually similar letters they have learned so far: (ב/ת, ח/ת, ת/ה, ד/ר, ג/ו, ם/ס, מ/ט, ע/צ, ב/כּ, כ/פּ, ו/י, נ/ג, ו/ן, ו/ז, שׁ/שׂ).

Be sure to include a variety of cards that contain the same letter twice (e.g., שׁ/שׁ). Play continues until all of the cards have been collected so that a winning team can be determined. Ask students to answer the questions you posed at the end of Lesson 19 (see page 112).

Oral Language Lesson

Begin class by taking attendance and asking students how they are doing using the Hebrew greetings.

Review the body parts you introduced in the previous session: עַיִן, אֹזֶן, אַף, and פֶּה. Play שִׁמְעוֹן אוֹמֵר using all of these body parts, as well as the two key words they learned in lesson 18 (רֶגֶל and רֹאשׁ) and the prepositional phrase:

יָד עַל ________.

At the end of this session, plan a סִיּוּם for the class to celebrate completing *Ready, Set...Go Alef Bet!* (*Note*: Be sure to get permission from your education director as some students may have food allergies.) If your class meets in the afternoon, plan a pizza party with pizza, salad, juice/water/cola, popcorn, and ice cream. If your class meets in the morning, you will want to teach them some breakfast food items, which can include ḥallah, fruit (especially bananas),

sound by blowing up a balloon, and directing the class to listen closely to the sound as you slowly release your grip on the opening and allow the air to escape very slowly. Once the balloon is empty, tell the students that they are going to imitate a balloon. To model the process for the class take a deep breath. Then expel the air slowly while you make the sound *f*. Ask the class to repeat this action. As an alternative, students can create the letter shape through a yoga pose. To create a פ, students should sit on the floor with their legs stretched out together in front of them. They should then bend forward at the waist and curve their arms around their heads pointing toward their stomachs. To create a ף, students should stand with their legs together. They should then bend forward at the waist and curve their arms around their heads pointing toward their stomachs. No matter which kinesthetic association you use, ask the students to repeat the letter sound *f* while they do so.

Letter Hint & Color the Letter

Distribute crayons or colored pencils. Ask volunteers to read the sentence in the Letter Hint. Write a פ on the board and invite a volunteer to use it to create a face. Then write a ף on the board and ask a volunteer to create a flag from it. Give students time to color in the פ and ף.

Now I Know My Alef-Bet!

Ask students to trace the letter on the first line with their fingers and to trace it in pencil, while repeating the sound that the letter represents (*f*). Next, ask them to write three examples of the letter in pencil while repeating the letter's sound. Ask them to follow the same procedure for the letter on the second line.

Match Game

With this lesson, students have learned all of the letters that have final forms. The Match Game activity provides students with practice matching the regular letters with their final forms, as well as two discrete letters that represent a single sound (שׂ/ס). This final pair is present for two reasons. First, like the letter ס, the letter שׂ is among the least common Hebrew letters, and it

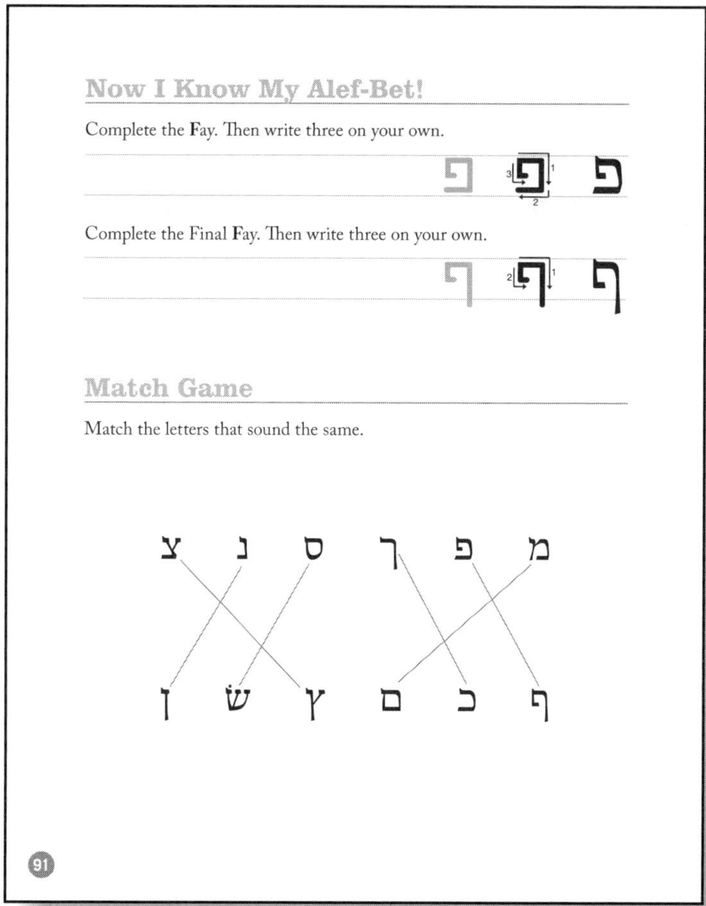
Now I Know My Alef-Bet!

Complete the Fay. Then write three on your own.

פ

Complete the Final Fay. Then write three on your own.

ף

Match Game

Match the letters that sound the same.

מ פ ך ס נ צ

ף כ ם ץ שׂ ן

91

is the one that has received the least amount of review in *Ready, Set...Go Alef Bet!* Second, some of the final letters are visually similar, such as ך and ף. The letter ס is visually similar to the ם, providing students with additional practice in fine visual discrimination.

Ask a volunteer to read the instructions, then allow students to complete the activity individually. Circulate to provide assistance as needed. When the class has completed the activity ask them to compare their answers with those of the person sitting next to them. If there is a dispute, resolve the issue with the pair.

Take a Closer Look!

Circle the "twin letters" in each row.
Then write the circled letters in the spaces at the right.

צ	(שׁ)	ע	שׂ	(שׁ)	י	ו	ז	שׁ .1
ן	י	(ו)	ז	ג	נ	(ו)	ר	ו .2
ד	ץ	(ף)	ךְ	(ף)	ן	ק	פּ	ף .3
תּ	ח	בּ	(פ)	ט	(פ)	פּ	כ	פ .4
(ח)	ה	ם	ס	ת	(ח)	ע	צ	ח .5
נ	(ר)	ן	ו	ז	ךְ	ד	(ר)	ר .6

Write your letter answers in the numbered spaces below.

ר פָ וֹ שׁ

6 4 2 1

Circle the picture that the word describes.

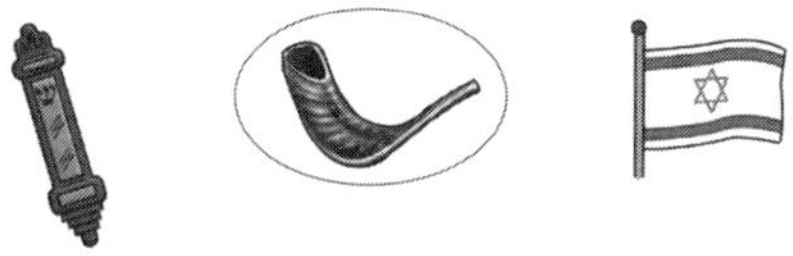

92

Take a Closer Look!

The entire focus of this activity is fine visual discrimination. Each line contains multiple pairs of letters that are visually similar. In some cases, such as lines 1, 4, 5, and 6, there are two or more types of visually similar letters, such as שׁ/שׂ and ז/ו. In these instances, students must identify the matching letters, which are camouflaged by two or more types of distracters.

Allow a volunteer to read the directions, then complete line 1 together as a class. If you are confident that most of the class can complete the activity, allow them to do so, as the end of the activity provides a self-checking mechanism. Students who may be having difficulty with this skill can complete the activity as a small group with you or a student assistant. Once students have completed lines 1-6, ask them to fill in the correct letter in each space to create a word and then circle the picture that matches the word.

I Can Read Hebrew!

As is the case with the two previous lessons, this exercise provides words that students can read with full comprehension. Unlike the previous activities of this type, this collection contains six words that end with the vowel sound "ah" and use the Hebrew letter ה, which is not vocalized. This is a concept that students have not been taught directly, and it may challenge some students. Others will have already noticed this use of the letter ה in the key words and vocabulary items they have seen. Ask a volunteer to read the directions. Then ask students to take turns reading the words in this activity. Repeat the question posed in the instructions, "What letter ends the Hebrew words that end in the sound "[ah]?" (ה).

I Can Understand Hebrew!

This activity builds on the previous one by giving students the opportunity to identify the meaning of the words they have just read. Select a student to reread word #1. (כִּפָּה) Then tell the class to find the picture that matches the word among the objects at the bottom of the page. (*at the end of the second row*) Hold up Word Picture Card #20 and ask a volunteer to identify it in Hebrew. If the student is correct, the class should repeat the word. Next, tell the class to write the number "1" in the line next to the picture of כִּפָּה. If students have difficulty with this activity, complete it as a class. If they grasp it easily, allow them to complete the page with a partner. If you choose the second option, be sure to remind them to read every Hebrew word out loud as they complete the activity, and circulate so you can provide assistance as needed.

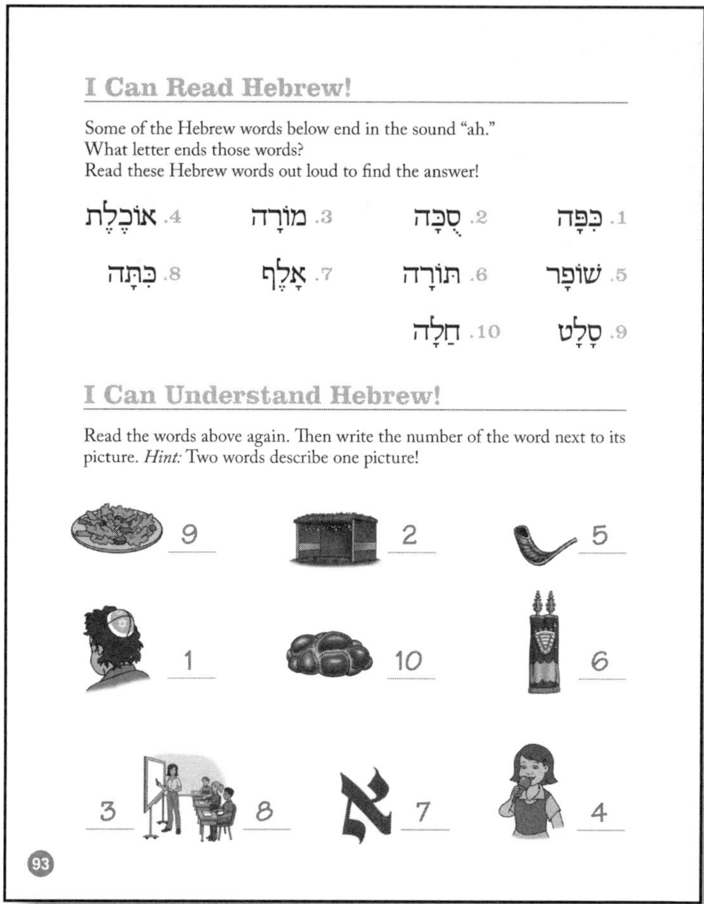

I Can Read Hebrew!

Some of the Hebrew words below end in the sound "ah."
What letter ends those words?
Read these Hebrew words out loud to find the answer!

1. כִּפָּה
2. סֻכָּה
3. מוֹרָה
4. אוֹכֶלֶת
5. שׁוֹפָר
6. תּוֹרָה
7. אָלֶף
8. כִּתָּה
9. סָלָט
10. חַלָּה

I Can Understand Hebrew!

Read the words above again. Then write the number of the word next to its picture. *Hint:* Two words describe one picture!

93

Challenge students to come to the next class with answers to the questions below. They will find the answers in Lesson 20 of the digital companion. Consider sending home a sheet with these questions, or e-mail them to parents, when you assign the lesson in the digital companion. Ask students to write the answers on the sheet and return it, with a parent's signature, at the next class.

1. One pair of letters in the "Two of a Kind" activity does not contain a final letter. What two letters make up that pair? (ס *and* שׂ)
2. How many of the letters you circled in the "Take a Closer Look" activity make the sound *f*? (*four letters, two pairs*)
3. How many words in the "I Can Read Hebrew" activity end in the letter ה? (*six*)
4. What inventory item did you collect in the Wacky Wheelbarrow game? (*shofar*)

When students complete this lesson in the digital companion, and you have checked that they have done so, allow them to color in the פ and ף on the Alef-Bet Chart on page 4 of their book.

Crack the Code

The final activity in *Ready, Set...Go Alef Bet!* requires students to crack a code by using the Picture Dictionary at the end of the book. Select a volunteer to read the instructions at the top of the page, then direct them to find the picture for word #1 in the pictionary (*page 96, first column, sixth word down*). Tell students to identify the word by pointing to it. When you are satisfied that every student has correctly identified the word, tell them to write the letters that make up the word in the blank spaces under the picture. Tell them that they should only write the Hebrew letters in the blank spaces, as the dots and dashes necessary for the vowels have already been provided. Allow students to complete this activity independently. Circulate to provide assistance as needed.

Game On

This activity provides a mechanism for checking the students' answers to the "Crack the Code" activity above. Ask a volunteer to read the directions and allow students to fill the correct letters in their numbered blanks. As with the Hebrew words in the activity above, students should write the letters only, as the correct dots and dashes for the vowels have already been included. Allow students to complete this independently, and while they are working, write a large version of the blanks with their vowel signs on the board. When everyone has finished, select a volunteer to read the phrase. If the student is correct, allow him or her to write the letters in the blank spaces you have on the board. Ask the rest of the class if they agree with the letters written. If there is a dispute about the answer, review as a class.

Assign students to complete Lesson 20 in the digital companion at home. Remind them to play the Wacky Wheelbarrow game when they have completed the lesson. You might ask students to print out or e-mail their lesson summaries to you when they have completed all the activities in the lesson. Or assess their progress in the Behrman House Online Learning Center.

Assessment

For information on assessing students' progress, see page 10. Make notes about which students had difficulty with any of the information presented in this lesson.

With the completion of this lesson, students have been introduced to all of the material that is covered in both the fifth oral assessment on page 137 and the three-part final assessment on page 141. While the previous assessments have provided you with valuable information about the progress individual students have made, the Final Assessment is more of a diagnostic tool. Share the results of this assessment with the education director and the students' teacher next year. Summer review will help prepare students for the upcoming year, when they will need to fully master Hebrew decoding. Based on the notes you have made during previous lessons, you may wish to delay administering a formal assessment until the class has had the opportunity for some additional review. While students are completing the written assessment, listen to each student read the last oral assessment individually.

CULMINATING ACTIVITIES

Just as it is important to set the stage on the first day of school, it is equally important to mark the end of this first step in the students' Hebrew education. As suggested above, in the Oral Language section for Lesson 20, you may wish to plan a סִיּוּם for the class to celebrate completing *Ready, Set...Go Alef Bet!* (see page 114).

Present students with their certificates of completion for *Ready, Set...Go Alef Bet!* You may also want to provide some light refreshments.

APPENDIX A: PHONICS FLASH CARDS BLACK-LINE MASTERS

תּ 2	ט 1
שׁ 4	ת 3
בּ 6	י 5
◌ַ 8	◌ָ 7
א 10	◌ֲ 9

מ 12	ע 11
ג 14	ם 13
וּ 16	ד 15
כּ 18	◌ֻ 17
ה 20	ק 19

ץ 22	צ 21
ב 24	ו 23
◌ִ 26	ל 25
ס 28	◌ִי 27
נ 30	שׁ 29

Card	Letter
31	ז
32	ח
33	כ
34	ך
35	פּ
36	◌ֹ
37	וֹ
38	ר
39	ז
40	◌ֶ

ֱ

41

פ

42

ף

43

APPENDIX B: WORD PICTURE CARDS BLACK-LINE MASTERS

טַלִית

1

תּוֹרָה

2

עַל

3

שַׁבָּת

4

שָׁלוֹם

5

יָד

6

שֻׁלְחָן

7

בַּיִת

8

בַּי

9

אַבָּא

10

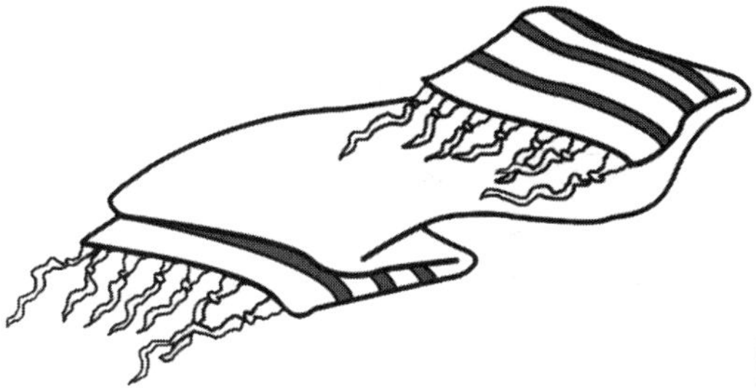

1

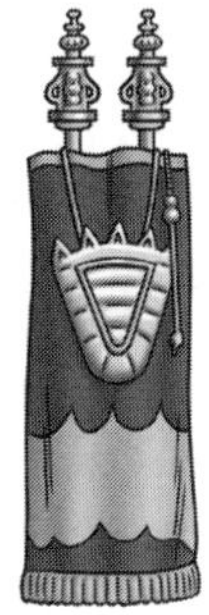

2

on

3

4

5

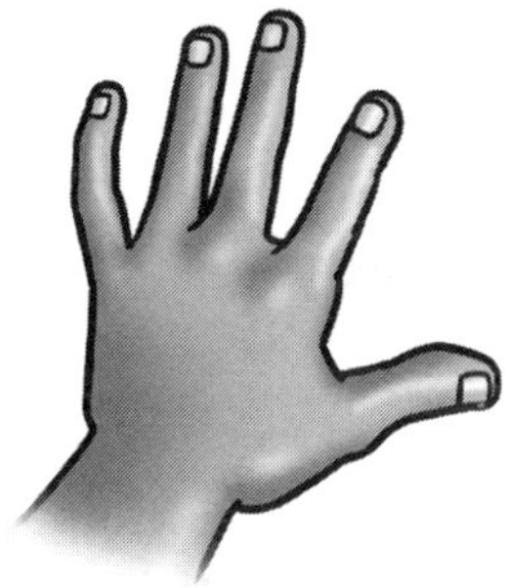

6

7

8

in

9

10

אִמָא

 11

עִפָּרוֹן

 12

מְזוּזָה

 13

גְלִידָה

 14

גוֹרִילָה

 15

גֶשֶׁם

 16

דֶגֶל

 17

מַיִם

 18

דָג

 19

כִפָּה

 20

11

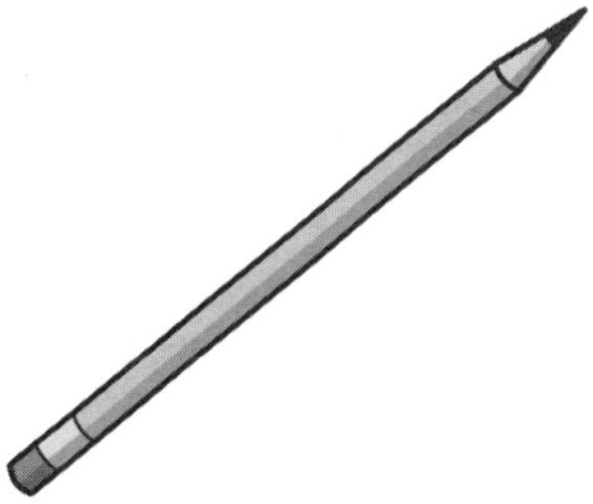

12

13

14

15

16

17

18

19

20

קִדוּשׁ

21

מוֹרָה

22

כִּתָּה

23

הַבְדָלָה

24

יֶלֶד

25

יַלְדָה

26

צְדָקָה

27

מִיץ

28

פִּיצָה

29

וָו

30

21

22

23

24

25

26

27

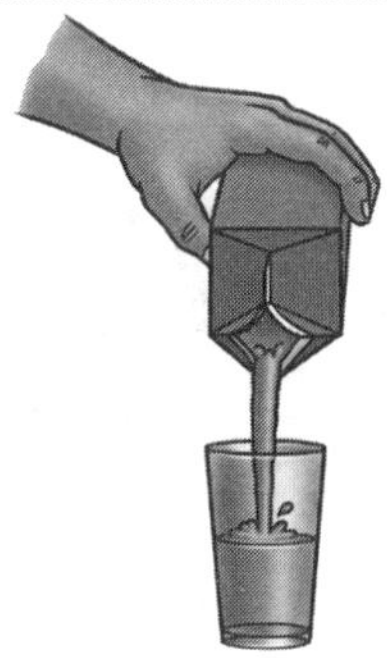

28

29

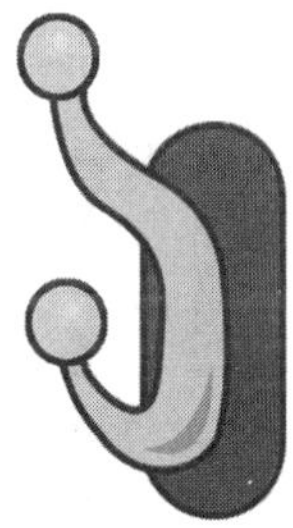

30

כֶּלֶב

Ready, Set...Go Alef Bet! © Behrman House, Inc. 31

שֶׁל

Ready, Set...Go Alef Bet! © Behrman House, Inc. 32

לוּלָב

Ready, Set...Go Alef Bet! © Behrman House, Inc. 33

סֻכּוֹת

Ready, Set...Go Alef Bet! © Behrman House, Inc. 34

שִׂמְחַת
תּוֹרָה

Ready, Set...Go Alef Bet! © Behrman House, Inc. 35

סֻכָּה

Ready, Set...Go Alef Bet! © Behrman House, Inc. 36

דוֹלְפִין

Ready, Set...Go Alef Bet! © Behrman House, Inc. 37

נֵר

Ready, Set...Go Alef Bet! © Behrman House, Inc. 38

חַלָּה

Ready, Set...Go Alef Bet! © Behrman House, Inc. 39

בְּרָכָה

Ready, Set...Go Alef Bet! © Behrman House, Inc. 40

31

of, belonging to

32

33

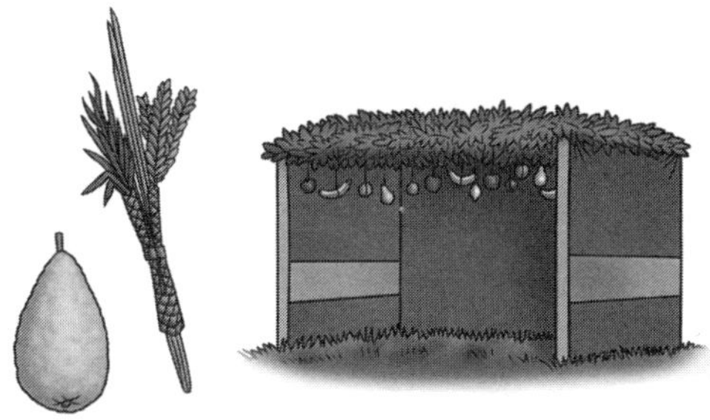

34

35

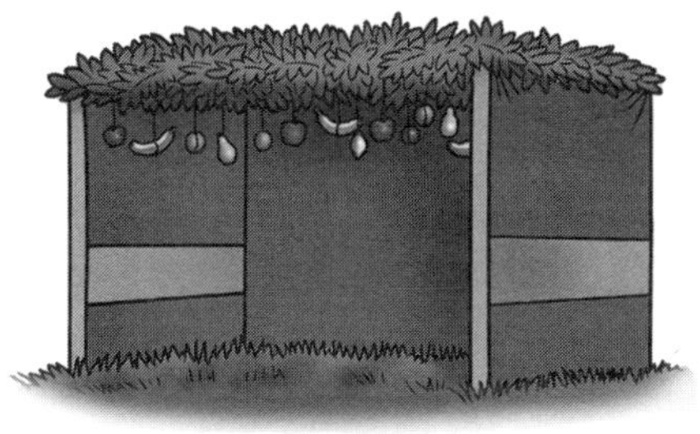

36

37

38

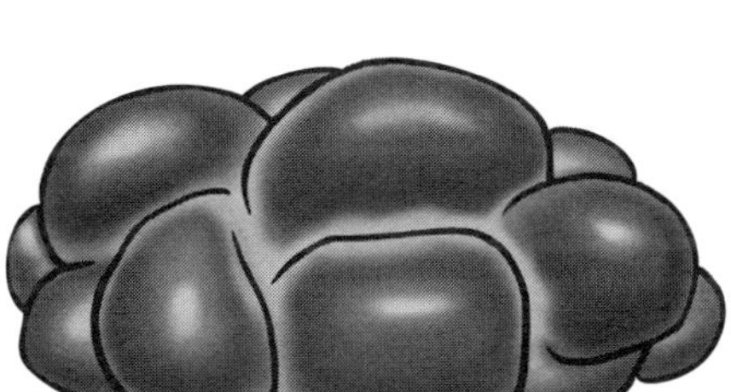

39

40

מֶלֶךְ

 41

חָתוּל

 42

קַנְגָרוּ

 43

פּוּרִים

 44

פֶּסַח

 45

אוֹכֵל

 46

אוֹכֶלֶת

 47

סָלָט

 48

קוֹלָה

 49

בָּנָנָה

 50

41

42

43

44

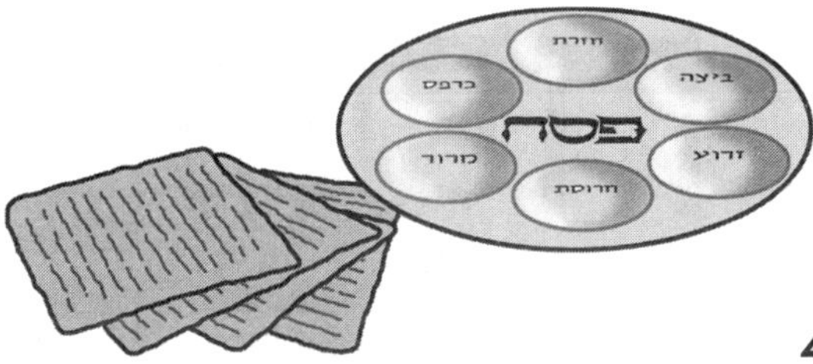

45

46

47

48

49

50

יוֹגוּרְט

 51

תֵה

 52

הַמְבּוּרְגֶר

 53

לִימוֹן

 54

פּוֹפְּקוֹרְן

 55

רֹאשׁ

 56

רֶגֶל

 57

זֶבְּרָה

 58

שׁוֹפָר

 59

אָלֶף

 60

51

52

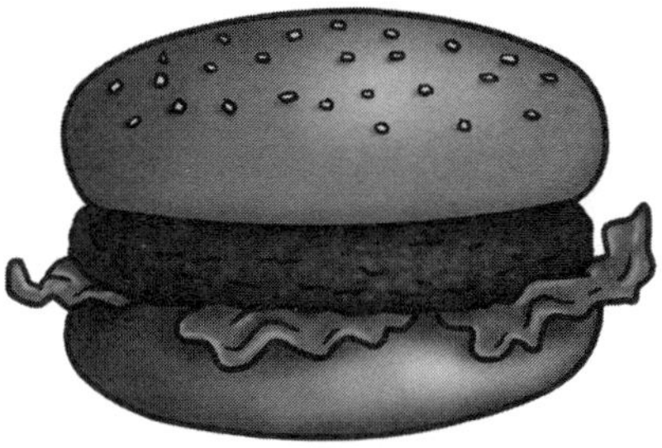

53

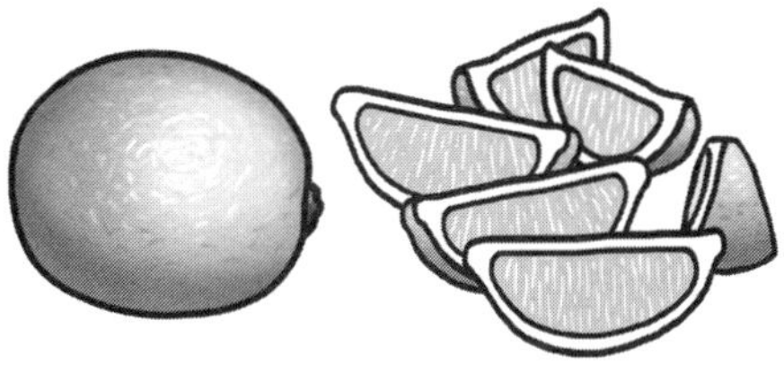

54

55

56

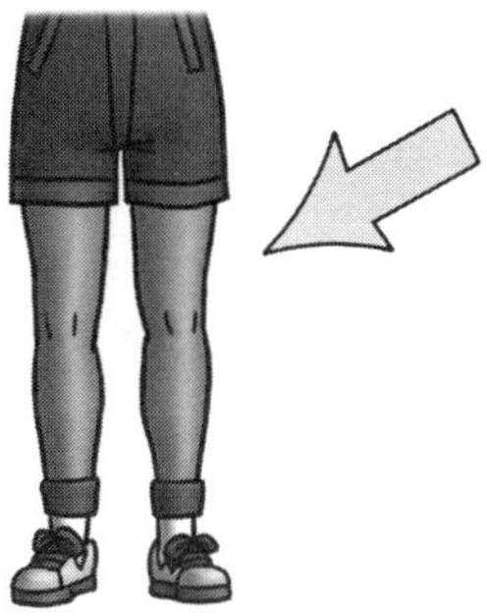

57

58

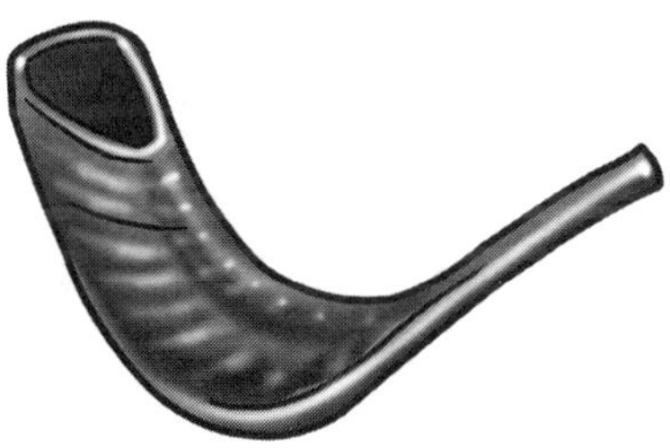

59

א

60

APPENDIX C: ASSESSMENT

ORAL ASSESSMENT

Name ______________________ Class ______________

After Lesson 20	After Lesson 16	After Lesson 12	After Lesson 8	After Lesson 4	
פֹּ	שׂ	כֶּ	אֱ	בַּ	.1
רֶ	סֶ	הֲ	עֶ	טָ	.2
זוֹ	לָךְ	צֶ	מָ	יָ	.3
הוֹד	שׁוּק	קוּ	גָ	שַׁ	.4
סוֹף	נָח	צָו	טוּ	תָּ	.5
תּוֹךְ	שִׂים	שַׁב	שֶׁ	יַ	.6
רִמוֹן	חוּץ	אָץ	דָג	תַ	.7
נֶפֶשׁ	סָכַן	גָם	בַּת	שָׁ	.8
עֱזוּז	וָדִי	בּוּץ	יָם	טַ	.9
שָׂפָם	נִגוּן	דָם	עַם	בָּ	.10
					Date
					Score

Notes: ____

____

____

____

ASSESSMENT 1

Name ______________________________ Class ________________

Circle the Hebrew letter that begins each word.

בּ	שׁ	י	תּ	
שׁ	א	תּ	בּ	
י	ט	ע	שׁ	
ע	ת	בּ	שׁ	
א	י	ע	ט	
י	בּ	א	ת	

Match the Hebrew items that make the same sound.

בַּ   י   שׁ   ט   אָ

י   שׁ   בָּ   עֲ   תּ

ASSESSMENT 2

Name ______________________________ Class ________________

Cross out all the Hebrew letters that make a different sound from the one in the box.

ע	ם	מ	ט	מ .1
ה	ד	י	א	ע .2
ת	ה	תּ	מ	ט .3
תּ	כּ	בּ	ק	כּ .4
ה	א	ת	י	ה .5

Circle the Hebrew syllables that make the same sound as the one in the box.

דַ	טַ	טֶ	דוּ	דָ .1
גֶ	גָ	גוּ	יוּ	גֶ .2
הֶ	הָ	הוּ	עֲ	הַ .3
דוּ	גֶ	קוּ	בּוּ	כֶּ .4

ASSESSMENT 3

Name ______________________ Class ______________

Circle the Hebrew letter that begins each word.

י	ו	ג	נ	
צ	שׁ	ם	ס	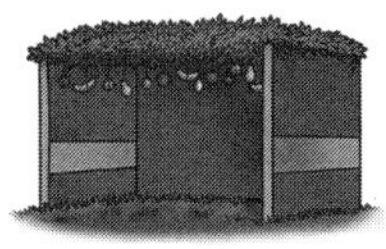
כּ	בּ	תּ	ה	
ו	נ	ג	ד	
ס	ע	צ	ט	
ע	שׂ	שׁ	צ	

Match the Hebrew letters that make the same sound.

ב   ק   שׁ   ץ   נ

כּ   ו   ן   ס   צ

FINAL ASSESSMENT PART 1

Name ______________________________ Class ________________

Circle the Hebrew letter that begins each word.

 ו ז	 צ ע	 ג נ	 ת ח
 ר ד	 ג נ	 שׂ שׁ	 מ ט
 ק ג	 מ א	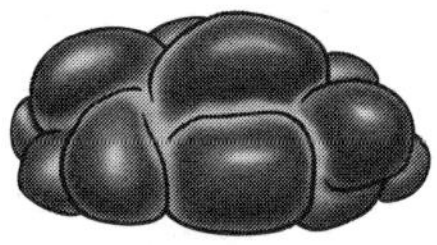 ח ה	 בּ כּ
 ר ד	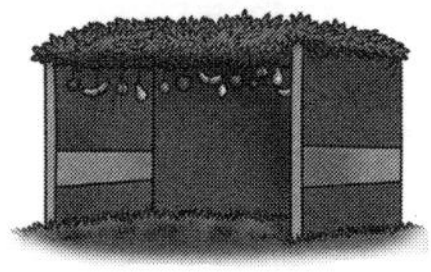 ם ס	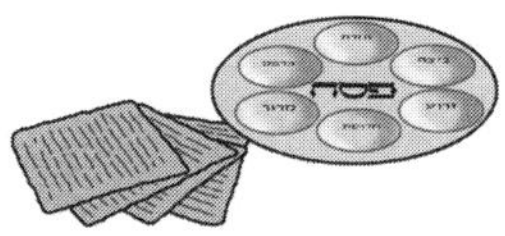 פּ פ	 ט מ
 כּ כ	 ו י	 ח ה	 ס ט

FINAL ASSESSMENT PART 2

Name ______________________________ Class ________________

Circle the Hebrew letter that ends each word.

ל	בּ	ב	כּ	
שׁ	ץ	שׁ	ן	
ן	ם	ץ	ע	
ד	ךְ	ף	ץ	
ט	ג	ד	ל	
ן	ג	ו	י	

Match the Hebrew letters that make the same sound.

ט　　שׁ　　ךְ　　ן　　ץ　　ף　　ו

ח　　ת　　ס　　צ　　נ　　ב　　פ

FINAL ASSESSMENT PART 3

Name __________________________________ Class ____________________

Circle the Hebrew letter(s) that make the same sound as the English letter.

ס מ M נ ם	ט ר D ד ת	ז צ Z ס שׁ
ו ר V ב כ	נ ו N ג ן	פ ט F ף פּ
שׁ שׂ SH ס ז	ח א H ה ת	ק כּ K ח ף
כּ ב B תּ בּ	ח כ CH ק ך	נ כּ G ג ו
ת ד T ט תּ	שׂ ם S ס שׁ	ס ל L ק ר
בּ פּ P פ כּ	א ז No Sound ע צ	ו ר R ד ל

Certificate of Completion

____

Student's Name

Has successfully completed *Ready, Set…Go Alef Bet!* and is a certified Hebrew pre-reader

מַזָל טוֹב!

____

Date

____

Teacher

____

Education Director